ROUTLEDGE LIBRARY EDITIONS:
POLITICS OF THE MIDDLE EAST

Volume 23

THE SOVIET UNION AND ARAB NATIONALISM, 1917–1966

THE SOVIET UNION AND ARAB NATIONALISM, 1917–1966

HASHIM S. H. BEHBEHANI

Routledge
Taylor & Francis Group

LONDON AND NEW YORK

First published in 1986 by KPI Limited

This edition first published in 2016
by Routledge
4 Park Square, Milton Park, Abingdon, Oxon OX14 4RN
605 Third Avenue, New York, NY 10017

Routledge is an imprint of the Taylor & Francis Group, an informa business

© 1986 Hashim S. H. Behbehani

British Library Cataloguing in Publication Data
A catalogue record for this book is available from the British Library

ISBN: 978-1-138-83939-7 (Set)
ISBN: 978-1-315-68049-1 (Set) (ebk)
ISBN: 978-1-138-92550-2 (Volume 23) (hbk)
ISBN: 978-1-138-92551-9 (Volume 23) (pbk)

Publisher's Note
The publisher has gone to great lengths to ensure the quality of this reprint but points out that some imperfections in the original copies may be apparent.

Disclaimer
The publisher has made every effort to trace copyright holders and would welcome correspondence from those they have been unable to trace.

The Soviet Union and Arab Nationalism, 1917–1966

Hashim S. H. Behbehani

KPI

London and New York

First published in 1986 by KPI Limited
14 Leicester Square, London WC2H 7PH, England

Distributed by
Routledge & Kegan Paul
11 New Fetter Lane, London
EC4P 4EE, England

Methuen Inc
Routledge & Kegan Paul
29 West 35th Street
New York, NY 10001, USA

Routledge & Kegan Paul
Methuen Law Book Company
44 Waterloo Road
North Ryde, NSW 2113
Australia

Produced by Worts-Power Associates

Set in 10 on 12 point Baskerville
by Typesetters (Birmingham) Ltd, Smethwick, West Midlands
and printed in Great Britain
by Dotesios Printers Ltd, Bradford-on-Avon, Wiltshire

ISBN 07103 0213-4

To the friendship of Mohammad Farid Mattar

Contents

Note
Many of the quotations in the text are translations; they have been reproduced as originally printed.

1 The Leninist legacy: the theoretical basis and emerging policies

Introduction

Soviet thinkers tend to regard Zionism as a manifestation of the outlook and aspirations of the world of the Jewish bourgeoisie.[1] To Soviet writers, moreover, Zionism found the ways and means to demonstrate its age-old sense of Jewishness which is reflected in Jewish ghettos. The Jewish bourgeoisie, assertion goes, 'invented' the Zionist spiritual outlook and inspired the creation of a new sense of historical destiny. Zionism, the Soviets claim, provided the Jewish bourgeoisie with 'spiritual' guidance. Soviet writers, moreover, tend to analyze Zionist activities, in which the Jews played a key part, in terms of class contradiction and antagonism. The activities of Zionists in Czarist Russia, they claim, point to this.

Zionist activities in Russia in 1873 became noticeable when a Central Committee was established as part of the Israeli United International in countries to Russia such as Germany and Austria. The work of the Israeli United International in Russia was conducted in secrecy, and its activities were aimed at encouraging politically and religiously alienated Jews in Russia. This was evident in areas like Latvia, Bolomia and the various principalities of south-west Russia. It is natural, the Soviet argument goes, that the agents of the Zionist Israeli International did not advocate and wherever possible, avoided, class struggle. On the contrary, they defended the Jewish faith and 'protected' the interests of the Jewish leaders. The activities of the Israeli United International in Russia in the 1870s and 1880s could be considered, the Soviets argue, as a pre-Zionist movement characterized by being a national bourgeoisie movement aimed at collecting capital from the Jewish masses. This 'higher' status in Jewish communities was exploiting Jewish workers.

Among prominent Russian Zionists was L. Bensker, who emphasized and propagated the idea of the existence of a 'spiritual Jewish nation'. These Russian bourgeois Jews indulged in the ownership of factories which accumulated large sums of capital. And, by the beginning of the twentieth century, the Jewish bourgeoisie attained prominent financial and social status through the exploitation of Jewish workers. This was evident in the Ukraine, Byelorussia, Poland and Latvia.[2] Many elements combined, especially the anti-Semitic policy of the ruling Czarist regime, to further Jewish bourgeois and Zionist demands.

This sectarian 'ideology' of the Zionists manifested itself in the establishment of the Bund, a Jewish association of workers from Lithuania, Bolomia and Russia, which was founded in 1897. Lenin, however, refuted the Bundist political outlook and orientation and asked its members to join the Bolsheviks – to no avail. Zionist ideas, particularly those of Theodor Herzl, were the cornerstones of the founders of the Bund. The Bund did not believe in Leninist workers' orientations, one of whose cardinal precepts was class struggle rather than the nationalist appeal of those such as Ukrainian, Georgian and Polish jews, whereas Zionist 'ideology' was propagating Jewish bourgeois aspirations as a 'pressure valve' for the Jewish masses.

Socially the Zionists, the Soviets argue, drew a line between the Jewish masses and the toiling masses in other economic strata of society. The Zionist organizations in the Soviet Union, it is claimed, used to operate and function freely, unlike the Bolsheviks who were often oppressed and jailed. Therefore, the Soviets claim,[3] there was a certain harmony between Zionism and the Czarist government. Russian Jews were active in the world Zionist movement from its inception.

Between 1897 and 1903 Zionism in Russia witnessed a noticeable expansion. The Zionists saw the Russian Empire as divided into twelve sections, and in 1901 a meeting was convened in St Petersburg which laid down the 'cultural' foundation of Zionism. From that point on, Zionist organizations spread throughout the Russian empire backed up by meticulous planning; they extended from Moscow to Tashkent and, in particular, to Siberia where the

Jewish population had reached 50,000.[4]

·In 1902 and 1903 several Zionist articles appeared in Russia which were propaganda for the Zionist cause. However, in 1903 a governmental decree was published demanding the curtailment of Zionist activities in the Empire, to which the Zionists reacted with disdain. The Soviet argument was that the Zionists were anti-socialist. Nevertheless, with the evolution of socialist ideas in Russia, a few Jews went along with this and called their association the 'socialist democrats'. Most socialist ideas in modern Israel were transmitted from socialist origins in Russia. It is worth mentioning here that these Zionist organizations, though they tended to believe, overtly at least, in socialist ideas, nevertheless did not anticipate finding in them a solution to the Jewish problem.

Gradually there evolved a belief that the Jewish question could be solved by granting Jews an autonomous region. From this period socialist ideas began to creep into Zionist organizations, and Zionist socialists began to constitute a formidable force to be reckoned with. Attempts were made on a worldwide basis to unify Zionist socialist orientations, and attention was directed toward Palestine. Zionists of all political persuasions, left or right, started to pay due attention to settling in Palestine as the Promised Land. On 16–18 July 1917, Zionist organizations met in St Petersburg and agreed to adhere to the following principles: the establishment of a national home for Russian Jews, a guarantee for the rights of the Jews, and a guarantee for the national rights of the Jews in Poland, Palestine and Rumania.[5] According to a census in Russia during this period, there were 5,200,000 resident Jews.[6] Most dwelt in ghettos, although there was also a notable Jewish bourgeoisie with a formidable financial background. Zionist ideology in Russia did not deviate from world Zionist orientation. These Russian Zionists were not intrinsically anti-Czarist neither did they take a leading part in anti-Russian Czarism.

It is claimed by Soviet writers that in 1903 Theodor Herzl arrived in St Petersburg where he conducted discussions with the Russian Interior Minister, whereby an agreement was reached which stipulated, among other things, that the Russian Minister would legalize Zionist activities in Russia and encourage Jewish emigration to Palestine; in return Herzl gave assurances that Soviet Jews would not attack the Czarist regime and would avoid carrying out socialist ideas.[7]

By the turn of the century Zionist parties had sprung up in Russia trying to implant Zionist ideas in the Russian masses, but the issue of emigration to Palestine was the salient factor. Initially Russian Zionists had pro-Czarist tendencies, but with the revolution of 1905–1907 they abandoned these attitudes and opposed, initially with reservation, the Czarist regime.

The geographical situation of the Arab world, stretching from the Arabian Gulf to North Africa, had decided the historical relations between the Czarist regime and the Middle East. This situation dictated the need for Czarist Russia to enter the Arab world scene through alliances and, at the same time, counter-offensive agreements with other major world powers. By the last year of his reign (1725), Peter the Great had accomplished much to achieve the Russian drive toward Constantinople and India and the Russian Navy advanced toward these areas. By then Czarist power had opened two sea routes to the outside world. At Russia's western extremity, on the Baltic, St Petersburg was established as an outlet to Europe, an alternative to the Pacific, which could be reached through Central Asia. The third route came into existence in 1860 when China ceded the territory between the Ussri River and the Pacific Ocean, thereby making access easier.

Relations between Czarist Russia and the Arab world were initiated by Russia's conquest of Persia in 1723 and strengthened by the occupation of Beirut, Lebanon, in 1772–1773. At this time Russia's attitude toward the Ottoman empire was governed by the role played in the Middle East by the relations and policies of the other two Western European powers, Britain and France. However, in 1768 Egypt's ruler, Muhamad 'Ali, declared his country's independence from Turkey. Czarist Russia was then engaged in a war with Turkey. This development led to the first direct contact between Czarist Russia and Egypt, which disturbed the European powers. Nevertheless, Czar Nicholas, who steered a cautious course for Russia in a manner that did not overtly antagonize the Western powers, proceeded to reach a sort of tacit agreement with Austria, Britain and Russia by signing an agreement, the London Convention, which 'defined' Muhamad 'Ali's place in the Turkish Empire. This agreement stipulated that no warships would be allowed 'to pass through the straits during peace time'. However, the Czar's ambition to seize Constantinople and the Dardanelles led to the Crimean War (1853–1856), which resulted in the defeat of Russia. The Treaty of Paris imposed certain restrictions on Russia and dictated the removal of Russian ships from the Black Sea and the dismantling of Russian fortifications around it.

Britain and France were able in this way to reduce Russian advances in these areas. From that point on, Russia paid considerable attention to European affairs and the maintenance of the status quo. Russia's political role in the Middle East was then very considerably limited. The Czarist government, however, kept a close watch on the developments that engulfed the Ottoman empire. During World War I, especially between 1915 and 1916, it was agreed that Russia would, after victory by the Allies was assured, receive Constantinople, some territory adjacent to the Dardanelles and the Bosphorus, islands in the Sea of Marmara and the islands lying on the route to the Mediterranean, parts of Armenia and northern Kurdistan. Moreover, the agreement granted the neutrality of the Hejaz.[8] Another Russo–British agreement extended the Russian presence in Persia. These agreements meant that the Caspian and Black seas would be 'Russian inland waters', whereas the 'territorial gains' in Armenia and the influence in the Hejaz would have paved the way for Russian entry into Arabia. Russia's ultimate objective, however, was to reach the Arabian Gulf, but other major developments diverted its attention; amongst them were the collapse of Czarism in Russia itself and of Caliphate rule in the Ottoman empire, as well as the success of the Bolshevik Revolution in Russia. These developments convinced the Russians to disregard and even postpone the pursuit of traditional Russian ambitions in the Middle East for the time being and to be more concerned with regaining the old borders.

Lenin's theory of revolution as applied to the Arab world

Lenin divided the world into three categories. To the first belonged the advanced capitalist-industrial countries of Western Europe and the United States. The role of the proletariat in those countries was confined to liberating the oppressed masses both in the colonies and in those Western countries. To the second belonged the developed bourgeois-democratic national movements in Russia and Eastern Europe, whose main task was to achieve the merger of the proletariat and the toiling masses with the class struggle of the workers of the oppressed countries. In the third category, of semi-colonial and colonial countries, particularly China, Persia and

5

Turkey, the socialists had to render support to the *revolutionary elements in the bourgeois-democratic movements for national liberation.* These three categories remained the cornerstone of the Soviet Union's foreign policy in the Arab world, and the Soviet Union has put its political analysis into this framework of 'national liberation' movements throughout its dealings with the Arab world. There remained the question of which socio-economic strata of the semi-colonies and colonies were to take power. At the same time, even if the 'nationalist' elements in these countries were to take power, there would be no telling which political alignment each would pursue either regionally or internationally. History was to prove the validity of this question in the Soviet Union's foreign policy in the Arab world. The main problem for the Soviet leadership, especially of Trotsky and Stalin, was the Muslim population of the Soviet Union and of the bordering Muslim countries. The logistical pre-occupation of the Soviet Union was prominent in all foreign policy considerations, which were supposed to encompass the whole of the Muslim world (of which the Arab world was part). Yet that the Soviet Union had limits, geographical, political and ideological, in the Arab world is understandable. The Soviet Union's analysis of the Arab world was totally dependent on the existing Arab Communist parties, illegal though they were. Lenin established a commission to investigate the conditions and the question of the eastern people and countries before the convening of the Baku Congress. It reached the conclusion that the Eastern people need not go through the capitalist stage of development.[9] One way in which this stage could be overcome was for the masses of the Eastern people to seek the assistance of the Soviet Union once the aid of the proletariat of the advanced countries was secured. This would lead to communism, and these countries would avoid having to pass through the capitalist stage.

In the early stages of building up their power, the Bolsheviks had to pay considerable attention to consolidating their power intern-ally. Two important factors were the need for the economic reconstruction of the Soviet Union and the need to secure its border regions, amongst which were Muslim states. If these Muslim states embarked on a course of political independence they would then be in direct collision with at least one West European power – namely Britain. After the defeat of Germany and its allies in 1918 the Western powers, especially Britain, were left on the world scene as undisputed masters of the world. Britain's position left her to deal

6

with the remnants of her colonial heritage in such a way that these colonies were left a target for division and subdivision. The rulers of these former colonies, moreover, were installed by the colonial powers in such a way that the rulers' policies reflected internally the antagonisms of their societies, and the haphazard sorting out and creation of these political entities.

The Comintern and the East

When the Comintern was founded in 1919 its basic organ, the Executive Committee International (ECI), was totally European in its composition; in it the Soviet Union played a leading role. Throughout its structural development the Comintern, with its bases, expanded in both size and function and was ever more able to express its own views against the background of the changing world political situation. It had become, by the end of the 1920s, a mass-based organization with the Soviet Union as a major leading force whether in its administrative function or in the overall policy decision-making.

To the Comintern revolution had three goals which comp-lemented each other: laying the groundwork for the Communist seizure of power; the actual and complete seizure of power; and finally, once in power, the fulfillment of Communist objectives. Thus the Comintern laid down a sort of typology for revolution which was elaborated in the following way: '(1) proletariat socialist and (2) bourgeois-democratic; and of societies (1) advanced capitalist, (2) medium capitalist, (3) colonial, semi-colonial and dependent, and (4) very backward.'[10] According to this division, the Arab world fell into one of the last two categories. This characterization of the world, especially of the East, had several implications: first, being backward and undeveloped, the East – at least according to the Comintern – had to undergo the unconventional Marxist norms of politico-economic progress, for which at its kernel the overall motive would be an all-encompassing revolutionary process. Yet it was not clear at this point of historical development who in such a social structure should carry out the anticipated revolution. Normal Marxist analysis had to be modified to fit the new element evolving in the East. Second, the major revolutionary task confronting the revolutionary process should be shouldered by local Communist parties. However, at this juncture local Arab Communist parties had not been established on mass bases; they were in a formative stage. Third, if local Communist parties were to emerge and surface in these backward countries, then political alignments within such societies had to take different forms. This last element should not be confused with the basic contradiction of class struggle in the society but should center on the reality which circles round the attainment of national independence. The whole argument revolves around the reality that conventional Marxist class contradiction, with the proletariat at its base, does not apply to the prevailing Arab conditions.

The Comintern sprang from what was then called the Workingmen's International Association,[11] whose main task was to concentrate on the European proletariat. After the end of the Association's first meeting, it became known as the First International. Karl Marx had addressed this Association when it was convened in London in September 1864. The gist of Marx's proposals at this meeting was the promotion of the international proletariat movement, but because of its uncertain path, politically, the association dissolved itself. The Second International met in 1889, on Bastille Day, where it came closer to Marxist outlook, and by 1900 it had established its headquarters in Brussels. At this meeting all the diverse trends of Marxism were represented, whether right, center or left. But these differences of opinion did not necessitate finding or establishing a new form of political gathering to replace the Second International.

The leftist flank of the Second International, under the leadership of Lenin, attained power in Russia in 1917. The divisions within the International, coupled with the events of 1914–1917, led to the creation of a new International. Lenin's writings during this period reflected the rejection of the formulas and precepts of the Second International, and 'the demand for the transformation of the "imperialist" war into a revolutionary civil war, . . . and the exhortation to form a new International'.[12] In January 1919 an invitation was sent from Moscow to various revolutionary parties to organize a new International; both Lenin and Trotsky signed this invitation. The reasons given for convening such a gathering were concerned with the following:

(1) the desire to exploit social unrest in various parts of the world, but chiefly in Europe, by organizing the world

revolution which seemed imminent; (2) the need to get support from foreign workers in order to hinder any anti-Soviet actions by the big capitalist countries; and (3) the desire to counter efforts being made by Right-wing socialists to revive the Second International.[13]

By March 1919 the Communist International had been founded; its leadership was entrusted to Lenin, Trotsky and Zinoviev. The latter played a leading role in the International until Stalin ousted him in 1926. For a decade, 1919–1928, two questions were of paramount importance: the strengthening and consolidation of the Communist role in the Soviet Union and the inability of Communist movements to seize power in other countries. In Bolshevik eyes the world was divided into capitalist, dominant in world politics although 'decaying and unprogressive', and communist; in between were the backward countries of the East. Our main concern here is with the colonies and semi-colonies of the Arab world and with the Soviet Union's view of their political and economic development. The international political map in the first two decades of the twentieth century was, to say the least, permanently unstable which in turn gave those in charge of the Comintern an optimistic sense of hopefulness centering on the 'inevitable' collapse of capitalism.

On the convening of the Second International (July–August 1920), a period when it was generally believed that the prevailing international historical climate was 'ripe' for revolutionary changes, the Soviet army moved toward Warsaw. Considerable attention was thus focused on the Communist movement worldwide. At the Second International Lenin paid particular attention to two questions of doctrine. Firstly, he developed his thesis on the potentiality of a revolutionary process in the colonies. Secondly, the national liberation movements and aspirations were considered. At the same time he warned that the Communist parties emerging in the colonies must not 'merge into the bourgeois-led movement but should "unconditionally" preserve the independence of the proletarian movement, even in its most embryonic form'.[14] Furthermore, Lenin dealt with the agrarian question in a detailed way, with an analysis of the apparatus of the peasantry in the colonies. The rich peasants constituted the main enemies of the proletariat; the middle peasants fluctuated in their alliances within the socio-economic structure of these colonial societies; the 'labouring masses' were the natural allies of the proletariat.

The Bolsheviks, and even more particularly Lenin, considered that fundamental revolutionary changes were sweeping through the world. This belief dictated the necessity of considering the world political map analytically in order to achieve an all-encompassing world revolution. This in turn imposed two realistic considerations. On one hand, the Bolshevik Revolution must be guarded against all dangers and must continue as a citadel for world revolution. On the other, the Bolshevik Revolution should be like a mirror for all other world revolutions. These two factors implied that the Soviet Union must carry out revolutionary tasks emanating from the home front which would spill over into Europe. It was believed at the time that the Soviet Union would become a haven for the world proletariat movement, which would accomplish a dual task: to combine the offensive of proletarianism in countries where the bourgeoisie remained dominant and to intensify the drive to safeguard and strengthen the home base, the Soviet Union.

In January 1919 Moscow called for the convening of the Second International, which was held that March. Delegates came from nineteen countries and set up guidelines based on three fundamental objectives: capitalist conditions, bases for reforms and, perhaps the most important, the Soviet forms that the proletarian revolution had to assume. It is important to note that the existing conditions of the international proletariat movement had been the consequence of the Bolshevik Revolution and that the task of leadership rested with it. It was as if the Bolshevik Revolution was appointed to assume such a leading role. For the following two years, the division of labor became clearer: the party devoted much of its energy to the construction of socialism within the Soviet Union, whereas the affairs and leadership of the Comintern were left to Zinoviev.

It remained one of the precepts of Marxism that the East, in its process of liberation, must rely on three basic factors: the Soviet Union's friendship and leadership; the proletariat class mainly of the industrial West; and the exploitation of internal contradictions in Eastern societies. However, the peasant's main objective should be the seizure and possession of land; the workers of these countries had to rely on the peasantry to achieve the goal of permanent revolution.

Trotsky's point of view on the permanent revolution was based upon the notion that after the revolution had been achieved, the dictatorship of the proletariat, 'leaning on the peasantry', is obliged to fulfill certain socialist tasks. This stage implied transforming 'the democratic revolution into a socialist revolution which, in peasant Russia as in other agrarian countries, suggested the elimination of the capitalist stage of development'.[15] Lenin, however, was the driving force in the first decade of the twentieth century to 'internationalize the class struggle'. He dwelt on the question of imperialism within the capitalist powers in the nineteenth century, when capitalism had been transformed from its peaceful nature to one that led to foreign capital investment which led the capitalist powers to compete for the exploitation of the colonies which possessed cheap and abundant labor and resources. At the same time, the capitalist powers were able, in their own countries, to contain materially their local proletariat 'at the expense of the masses in exploited' colonies. The nature of competition between the capitalist countries in the colonies would 'inevitably' lead to military clashes and political disagreements among the capitalist powers. These wars, if they occurred, would be of a magnitude comparable to World War I. The consequence of all this competition and war would be the final destruction of capitalism. Lenin had emphasized the role played by the peasantry in the colonies, claiming that it would bring about their demise. It was thought that class contradictions would spring up not only in factories in the industrialized societies but also in colonial countries. Thus the bourgeois-democratic revolutionary elements in these colonial countries would take a prominent role in these countries given also the two most vital elements, 'national liberation and agrarian revolution'.[16] This nationalist aspect of the colonial countries was the hope on which Lenin put so much emphasis in analyzing the revolutionary process in them. However, it was a cardinal principle for the success of the worldwide revolutionary process that the Soviet Union had both to embrace and acquire the leadership of this all-encompassing revolutionary trend.

It remained to be asked how, and more precisely, by what means, the Soviet Union could extend assistance to the revolutionary movements in the East. There were two approaches open to the Soviet Union at the time: one through the Communist International, where Arab Communist parties would have played a participatory role in the colonies; and the second an indirect way, by exploiting the various blunders into which the Western world was falling. The Soviet Union set a particular course for its handling of the former on a defined theoretical basis; and on the latter, it was left to history to judge the theoretical correctness of Marxist–Leninist precepts. These two elements combined set a definite course for Soviet foreign policy objectives in the Arab world in particular and the East in general.

But there were practical considerations to be kept in mind. The logistical strategic questions were of primary consideration: the Soviet Union had to pay considerable attention to the countries which bordered it, especially Iran and Turkey; moreover, within the Soviet Union itself in these border regions the inhabitants were of the Muslim faith. The Bolshevik Revolution had to deal with these questions. Moreover, it was evident at the time that the key point of Marxist analysis – the proletariat – was not applicable to the East. Therefore the main consideration as far as the toiling masses of the East were concerned was based on the role played by the peasantry of the region. The hope for future revolutionary upheavals was centered on the peasantry. At the same time, however, there remained the role to be played by socialist democrats; what tasks they should undertake were not yet defined.

The Bolshevik leaders concentrated upon the achievement of national independence by the countries of the East. In this effort these countries would be in direct collision with the colonial powers of the West – i.e. Britain and France. It was a period clouded by the initial political transformation of the East from colonialism to imperialism. Lenin characterized such a period as 'the highest stage of capitalist development', a meaningful description of the changes the East was undergoing. Our case studies of the Arab world show that his intellectual contributions to the Eastern question covered the most significant issues of the time.

However, it was left to his comrades, notably Stalin and Trotsky, to handle Lenin's ideas in their *practical* sense. The area of practicality posed two basic problems for the Bolshevik leaders after they attained power in the Soviet Union. Firstly, the Bolshevik Revolution had to consolidate its power in the Soviet Union, a task which posed tremendous obligations to build its bases from the inside. Secondly, the Bolshevik Revolution was a movement that was transformed into a state. Thus it follows that the pragmatic aspect was a focal point in the priorities of the Soviet Union's foreign policy.

Throughout his writings Lenin's analysis of the East had emphasized the role played by the bourgeois-democratic elements in these societies. He drew a line of demarcation between the political developments of the Western capitalistic form and the East in general. He saw two features as characteristic of Eastern countries: backwardness and foreign oppression. Lenin's analysis was implemented by Stalin as early as 1919, with its conceptual framework of the 'two camps' – that of socialism and that of imperialism. Stalin was of the opinion that the strength of imperialism lay in the 'backwardness' of the East whose toiling masses provided material necessities for the capitalist world.

The First Congress of the Communist International was held in Moscow in March 1919, two years had passed since Lenin had expounded the tasks that could be confronting the Communist international movement. At this juncture the Soviet Union emerged as both the 'symbol and the center of the world revolution', which was significant for the international Communist movement. It should be noted, however, that Lenin's conceptualization of the role played by the 'bourgeois-democrat' of the 'revolution and peasant strategy dates back to 1905–6'.[17] This meant that such a movement would have its repercussions on the revolutionary development in Europe because the latter could not survive the amputation of Eastern markets. His thesis was based on *imperialism*. Lenin's advocacy of a political program centred on the creation of a united front that would embrace within it Communist and non-Communist elements; peasants and nationalists would act in unity against the imperialists and their agents.

One of the most prominent people to have certain reservations on Lenin's viewpoint was the Indian Communist member M. N. Roy. Roy's basic concern revolved round the correctness of the 'evaluation of the nature of the revolutionary movement in the colonies and the correct Comintern relationship with them'.[18] He argued that in the colonies there existed two movements and trends, one of 'bourgeois-democratic' elements and one carried out by the majority of poor and disenchanted masses. Roy went on to argue that it would be 'unrealistic' to solve the agrarian question in the colonies by a 'pure' Communist methodology.

However, by July 1920 Lenin had drawn a careful distinction between the social forces of the bourgeois-democratic movement, and coined the phrase 'the nationalist-revolutionary' movement. He moreover dismissed as 'utopian' any analytical approach to the Eastern question based on pure Marxist terminology (that is, that the proletariat was the base). The reason for this was that the majority of the population of the colonies was composed of peasants, but this was not to negate the existence of some sort of alliance with the proletariat of these backward countries.

This analysis could be traced to both Marx and Engels. To them, what was known as the 'colonies of the East' included part of the Sahara, Arabia, Persia and Palestine. Engels, moreover, considered people of the Jewish faith in this area to be part of the oriental societies of the Middle East. He also specified in his analysis of Algeria at this point in the historical political development of the Arab world that

> The conquest of Algeria is an important and fortunate fact for the progress of civilization. . . . And after all, the modern *bourgeois* with civilization, industry, order, and at least relative enlightenment following him, is preferable to the feudal lord to the marauding robber, with the barbarian state of society to which they belong.[19] [Emphasis in the original]

It became logical, therefore, that both Marx and Engels each supported in his own analysis of anti-colonialism, colonial conquest by the Western powers in the region, for by such activity the Western powers were, in reality, generating revolutionary sentiments in the colonies. And, in the view of both Marx and Engels, it was capitalism which by its attempt to penetrate the colonies was the moving force behind the shakeup and upheavals there.

It was Engels who pointed out that the 'first phase' of the revolution would be characterized by the fact that the bourgeoisie, in carrying out its revolution, would ultimately overthrow the 'despotic' elements of these colonies. This would lead, in his opinion, to the second phase, when the local bourgeoisie would establish the groundwork for an agrarian revolution. However, between these two phases one major political development should be kept in mind: that of the triumph of the proletariat revolution in the advanced industrial societies. Marx and Engels had some reservations on the ability of the peasants to carry out the anticipated revolution. The argument centered on the 'immaturity' of the peasantry at this stage.

With the 1905 Revolution in Russia Lenin began to formulate some conceptual framework for the Asiatic and, more precisely, the Eastern revolution and how it would be dealt with. To Lenin, agrarian development was the anticipated development of the East and it was to take priority because through it would come revolution in the future. Therefore to Lenin the 'wage worker' peasantry and workers were conceived to be the 'proletariat of the backward countries'. He formulated this notion as early as 1900 when he argued that

> Precisely today, when the starvation of millions of peasants
> becomes chronic, when the government that wastes millions
> on gifts to the landlords and capitalists . . . precisely today it is
> appropriate and essential to recall what the rule of the
> autocratic government that serves the interests of the
> privileged classes has cost the people.[20]

In this revolutionary process, Lenin envisaged two aspects for these developments – one concerned with masses (who were supposed to experience a spontaneous uprising); the other concerned with the leadership of these masses which should be composed of 'professionally and politically oriented' leaders who upheld revolutionary change as a political course.

Nevertheless, Lenin had left room for the supposed alliance between peasants and workers in the sense that both elements of society should embark upon a 'temporary' alliance favorable to the proletariat. These two social forces, however, had to carry out revolutionary changes in an 'inter-related' way. Lenin, moreover, conceived Asia as being ready to erupt into revolutionary change. He thought there should be a link between the toiling masses of the East and their natural allies, the proletariat of the industrialized countries. However, Lenin's dialectical approach to the process that a revolution undergoes is that of stages. In its initial stages it should exploit nationalistic sentiments, but in its post-revolutionary phase the assumed revolutionary state should suppress this sense of nationalism. Ultimately, this process combined would lead to the weakening of the 'capitalist nations'. In 1916, he wrote on the subject, arguing that

> We shall exert every effort to foster association and merger
> with the Mongolians, Persians, Indians, Egyptians . . .
> liberation of the colonies is 'unrealisable without a series of
> revolutions'; . . . it is realisable in conjunction with a socialist
> revolution in Europe.[21]

These two approaches set out by Lenin drew a connecting line between the world revolutionary process and the triumph, ultimately, of 'socialism' in the multiphased aspects of its inherent capabilities, ranging from national and international dimensions which evolved around three concentric circles, the peasantry, national liberation movements and international class struggle. Lenin viewed these developments as conducive to the worldwide victory of socialism. In this sphere three aspects of Lenin's contribution to Marxism are noteworthy. First, while Marx gave a general view of 'oriental' societies and, more important, was not clear on the revolutionary process in these areas, Lenin laid down the 'tactics' and the course the masses should undertake to achieve revolution. Second, Lenin, in contrast to the theoretical Marx, was basically a 'pragmatic tactician' who grasped the importance of 'spontaneity' in a political movement. For the economic and social 'stages of development' to proceed, revolution was no longer necessary as a first step. The politically oriented revolutionaries in these societies, Lenin contended, should work and exploit the various uprisings and violence to reach their ultimate political objectives. Third, it was Marx who laid importance on the 'socio-economic' significance of the fact that the West colonizing the East would lead ultimately to the revolutionary process. Lenin, however, viewed this element as a 'source' of violent changes conducive to an advantageous situation for the proletariat. To Lenin, the combination of the role the peasantry played with that of national liberation movements was a 'similar' element to the revolutionary process in the world.

Marx's original conception of Jews as being 'big bourgeoisie and representatives of commercial capitalism' was elaborated upon by Lenin in finding them to occupy a different socio-economic situation in Russia and Eastern Europe. Three main phenomena were evident to Lenin:

(1) the existence of poverty-stricken Jews, the majority of whom were restricted to the isolated pale of settlement ghettos;

(2) the existence of a small group of Jews who played a prominent role in the Russian revolutionary movement in the 1880s;

(3) the rise of political Zionism at the beginning of the twentieth century, which started its development as a political movement drawing its support from the Jewish communities as a political movement.[22]

Lenin, in his ideological arguments with the Bund (the Central Jewish Workers' Union in Lithuania, Poland and Russia), rejected the notion that revolution should be based on the idea of 'national equality', stating that such Zionist ideology would 'impede' the furthering of revolution. Yet Lenin faced the reality that Jewish emigration to Palestine would create a sort of 'class struggle' in Palestine in which the Western bourgeois Jews would encounter the disenchanted Eastern European and Russian Jews. It was within this realm that a certain contradiction in Lenin's perception of Zionism lies, for Zionism, as a political movement, had a unified aspect around which all Jews might circle. Moreover, history was to prove that this element of Lenin's notion of a Zionist state was based upon an ideology that negates – in its essence and in its formative stages – the much hoped-for class struggle that, in turn, would emanate from the Jewish population's class struggle. Zionism, in reality, was a unifying political movement for *all* Jews, and therefore as an ideology it did not enter Lenin's policies. Nevertheless, at a meeting in a Paris café in April 1910 he assured Chaim Weizmann that anti-Semitism played no role in either his political analysis or any future decision-making.

It was at the Second Congress of the Comintern (July–August 1920) that Lenin drafted the twenty-one conditions for admission to the Comintern. Though the following extracts and description of the twenty-one conditions are lengthy, they are worth quoting for their relevance to this study:

> The terms of admission [to the Comintern] may be summed up as follows:
>
> Point one demanded that the party press must be edited by reliable communists, must consistently spread the idea of the dictatorship of the proletariat, and must relentlessly expose the bourgeoisie and reformists.
>
> Point two required the removal from office of all reformists and centrists – including the party organisation, editorial board, trade unions, parliamentary groups, etc.
>
> Point three called for organisation of illegal party work in all countries.
>
> Point four dealt with the need for systematic propaganda work in the army, including the need to organise communist cells in it.
>
> Point five called for systematic work in the rural districts of each country.

Point six called for an attack on social patriotism and social pacifism, and the need to argue that only the 'revolutionary overthrow of capitalism will save mankind from new imperialist wars'.

Point seven expounded on 'the need for a complete and absolute break with reformism and centrist policies.

Point eight called on communists to support the struggle of colonial peoples against imperialism.

Point nine declared it the duty of all parties to conduct systematic work in the trade unions, cooperative organisations and other mass organisations.

Point ten dealt with the need to oppose the Amsterdam (Social-Democratic) Trade Union International and to call for a break with it.

Points eleven to fourteen sought to tighten central party control over all fields of work. . . .

Point fifteen obliged each party to give every possible aid to any Soviet republic in the struggle against counter-revolution.

Point sixteen specified that the communist parties must draw up new programmes, 'in the spirit of communist internationalism', and must submit these programmes for ratification to a future congress of the Comintern or its executive.

Point seventeen dealt with the question of how far decisions should be centralised in the International and how far local conditions should be taken in account. . . .

Point eighteen required all parties to adopt the name 'Communist' and emphasized that this was not merely a formal point, but necessary to underline the radical abyss between it and social democracy.

Point nineteen called upon member parties to summon a special congress immediately to approve the work of the Second Congress.

Point twenty required that all parties must be reorganised so that two-thirds of each party's Central Committee would be people who had endorsed the Third International before the Second Congress.

Point twenty-one provided that all who voted against accepting the conditions . . . should be expelled.[23]

In the countries of the East these twenty-one points meant that local

Communists had to exist in order to qualify for acceptance by the Comintern. Locally, the task of the operation of a given Communist party was monumental, to say the least. Point four is an obvious example, and the following two points were likewise too hard to be implemented in Eastern societies. At the time the Arab world was essentially under West European tutelage. The obvious and practical step was for Arab nationalism to emerge as a notable force against imperialism. An Arab Communist party, if it ever existed, would have to embark on grassroot changes. This necessity dictated that a potential revolutionary force be in existence and that local conditions be conducive to revolutionary change. In the long run this meant that the rules dictated basically negate their realization in the Arab world.

Therefore, when the Egyptian Socialist Party made an application for membership to the Third International on 30 November 1922, an Egyptian Commission was set up to review the application. The Commission report put forward the following argument:

(1) The report presented to the Commission by delegates of the Egyptian Socialist Party is sufficient evidence that the Egyptian Socialist Party represents a significant revolutionary movement in complete agreement with the broad movement of the Communist International.

(2) Nevertheless, the Commission considers that the inclusion of the Egyptian Socialist Party in the Comintern must be postponed until:
 a certain undesirable elements are separated from the party;
 b a congress is convened, at which an attempt must be made to unite into the Egyptian Socialist Party all those Communist elements in Egypt who are at present outside the Egyptian Socialist Party but nevertheless accept the twenty-one conditions of the Communist International;
 c the Party's name is changed to the 'Egyptian Communist Party'.

(3) In view of this, the Egyptian Socialist Party is urged to convene a congress as soon as possible, and in any case not later than 15 January 1923, to resolve these problems.[24]

To Lenin the internal unity of Jewish and Arab laborers was a logical prerequisite for a unified proletariat against the 'big bourgeoisie Jews' and the Arab feudal landlords. Thus this logic conforms with Lenin's conceptualization and analysis of the 'internationalization' of class struggle. Moreover, to both Lenin and Kautsky, the expected revolution in Palestine would be 'led' by the 'Jewish proletariat of Eastern Europe and Russia, which already showed its revolutionary potential in its opposition to the Jewish bourgeoisie in Palestine'.[25] Lenin and Kautsky, moreover, though they rejected the political outlook of Zionism, believed that Jewish immigration would ignite the revolutionary process. Thus in their view these economic and social crises would ultimately lead to the achievement of the most sought-after objective, namely a political aim for the expected revolution. This, in Lenin's analysis, would necessitate the unity of the Jewish labor force with the disenchanted Arabs. However, Lenin's 'two-fold' strategy should be viewed in the context of the Balfour Declaration of 1917. In May 1917, Lenin argued (as reported in *Pravda*):

> What a pity that the masses cannot read books on the history of diplomacy, or the editorials in the capitalist newspapers. . . . 'For England takes the correct view that what you wish to acquire you must first occupy' (hear! hear!) 'and her troops are already occupying Mesopotamia and Palestine that are important to her vital interests (read: to her capitalists). . . . At all events, England will not renounce the seizure (annexation) of Palestine (for the "factual armistice" on the Russian–German front) by denying them Galicia, Constantinople, Armenia, etc.' . . . Comrades, workers and soldiers . . . do you want to fight to enable English capitalists to seize Mesopotamia and Palestine?[26]

By 7 November 1917, with the Bolsheviks coming to power, these theoretical approaches were transferred to the period of implementation. As far as Palestine was concerned, a dilemma remained to be solved. On the one hand, the Bolsheviks regarded Palestine as occupied by the British, so that it needed to be 'liberated' from foreign domination. On the other hand, the Bolsheviks advocated solving of the Jewish question and the realization of aspirations to establish a Jewish 'national home' in Palestine. This should be kept in mind when considering the Bolsheviks' overall conceptualization and analysis of the colonial questions. Perhaps because of this uncertainty in the Bolshevik mind about the course of events, it is difficult to see that at this early stage of political development the Bolsheviks did in fact contribute to the establishment of a Zionist state in Palestine, for the Bolshevik leadership was preoccupied with the consolidation of its power in the Soviet Union. Theoretically, the Soviet Union was hoping for two developments to occur: that the East would revolt against colonialism and that Western industrial societies would create their own proletarian revolution. The two elements combined would lead to an all-encompassing *international* revolutionary front in the service of the interest of the masses.

On 23 November 1917 the Bolsheviks published the full contents of the secret documents concerning the Sykes–Picot Treaty, of which the most important segment was that related to Palestine and the division of colonial spheres of influence between the two Western powers. To the Bolsheviks the 'allotment' of Palestine to Jewish settlers was a frontal step for British imperialism and, at the same time, was representative of Zionist bourgeoisie. For example, in a memorandum from the Central Committee of the Jewish Communist League, 'Komfarband', of the Ukraine to the Commissariat for Internal Affairs of the Ukraine in July 1919 it was stated that

> The aim of the Palestinian idea in the present international
> conditions, because of its very content, makes out of the
> Zionist bourgeoisie and the Zionist party one of the branches
> of the imperialist counter-revolution. The Zionist party had
> linked its fate of the Entente. . . . Only the victory of Deniken,
> Entente's ally, will give the Zionist organization the possibility
> to achieve its expectation.[27]

Almost a year later, on 16 May 1920, an anti-British-Zionist collaboration drive was proclaimed by the Bolsheviks, who argued that such trends meant that Zionist representatives were in close cooperation with the British and the French. However, up to 1917 the Bolsheviks had pondered two factors in relation to the Jews: firstly, that while the Jewish intelligentsia rejected the 'nationalistic' trends of Zionism, the Bolsheviks themselves saw revolutionary potential in Jewish ghettos, since they aspired to 'assimilate' themselves to the existing surroundings.

Thus, the argument went, since the Bolshevik Revolution embraced the Jews' political and economic problems and Russia became 'opened to all Jews', they should therefore become 'partners' in the construction of the new Russia. Lenin, however, was a pragmatic leader. In his attempt to 'neutralize' Zionist trends in Russia he offered the Jews governmental posts, and meanwhile he discouraged Soviet Jewry from emigrating to Palestine in the hope that they would participate in the construction of a new Russia. Attempts were made to establish Russian Jews in local agricultural settlements to divert them from Zionist approaches regarding settlements in Palestine. The argument for this development was taken further in a message to Jewish workers in the Soviet Union:

> The aim of the Jewish Commissariat is the construction of a
> Jewish national life on proletarian socialist principles. The
> Jewish masses have the right and the possibility to control all
> Jewish public institutions, of giving socialist orientation to our
> national schools, of presenting the Jews with the possibility of
> starting agricultural work on socialist land . . . of using all
> methods in order that the needy would receive the necessary
> governmental aid to struggle anti-semitism programs, etc.[28]

In October 1918 the Bolshevik Party, with its Jewish Communist Section, held its first conference in which it was decided to encourage Russian Jewish laborers to take agricultural work. In June 1919 a second conference was held for the same purpose. The Jewish masses were drawn into internal socialist reconstruction, and more importantly, a political line was drawn to dissuade Russian Jews from emigrating to Palestine. Furthermore, in their attempts to convince the Jewish population to get involved in the revolutionary socialist transformation, the Bolsheviks attempted to draw Jewish soldiers into deeper involvement in internal affairs, and special units were created for achieving this goal. Another important Bolshevik goal was that they hoped to create a buffer zone internally to be another form of combating counter-revolutionary elements.

For the Bolsheviks the political force and drive of Zionism was linked to British imperialism:

> The Zionists practically became English officials who turned
> out to be fully dependent upon the English government having
> no right and no possibility to do something independently.
> Moreover, by increasing their members in Palestine . . . they
> act in the service of the English secret political police or the

British . . . forces which occupy Palestine and offend the Arab population. . . . The Zionists play the role of accomplices in the English politics of colonial exploitation in the Near East.[29]

This political stand and ideological formulation on the part of the Bolsheviks had a certain relevance to Muslim and Arab masses, and it is within this realm that ideology played a significant role. But it must be stressed that in this political development, as far as the role of Marxist analysis is concerned, theory played a significant part in the Soviet Union's perception of political development in the colonial East, of which the Arab countries constituted an important segment. Bolshevik political pronouncements to the Muslim Arab countries and to Persia and Turkey had, in addition to an ideological character, a certain element of strategic considerations. For the Muslim inhabitants of these countries were under the control of European powers – Britain and France – while at the same time both Turkey and Persia had strategic needs involving the Soviet Union. By 1918, therefore, the Bolshevik Revolution established a special organizational set-up labeled the Department of International Propaganda for the Eastern People to deal with all the obstacles pertaining to these colonial, semi-colonial and dependent countries of the East. The Bolshevik leaders were of the opinion that the Jewish population of Palestine, who constituted only 16.81 per cent of the total population, was a minority which would not be able to rule the country.

By 1920 the Bolsheviks' orientation and policies toward Palestine had evolved around two interrelated facts. First, the Bolshevik Revolution had entered a new political phase as a recognized state, so that the short-run diplomatic considerations had a certain priority in Bolshevik decision-making. Second, Lenin acknowledged that the Soviet Union had entered a new political reality in that it dwelled within a 'system of states', but recognized that the Soviet Union would not be able, in the long run, to coexist with imperialist states. Palestine, under both short- and long-term approaches, had emerged as a reality in several ways. In the first place, ideology played an important role. Lenin's theory of imperialism had its effect. For he analyzed the whole situation in the context that there existed certain contradictions between France and Britain in both Syria and Palestine. Karl Radek, for example, stressed this point more emphatically by arguing that:

> The powers of the Entente will fight each other on the question
> of who should receive the largest slices. . . . England backed its
> demands for an important part of Syria, despite the fact that it
> recognised in 1916 that Syria will be possessed by France. The
> French press in the course of the past weeks conducts an
> embittered war against this play of double game of England,
> advances the accusation that the English military authorities
> arrest Syrians who are employed by France and . . . claims that
> the English offered Emir Feisal weapons in order to conquer
> Syria . . . through which must pass the railway from Egypt to
> India.[30]

In the Soviet view, Palestine was important to Britain in the sense
that it deprived France 'of its mandate over Syria', and, at the same
time, it implied that France was deprived of the means of
communication between African and Asian countries, where these
countries were under the direct control of British forces. In the
second place, the organization Narkomindel, established by the
Bolsheviks to deal with developments in the East, was reorganized
in 1918 and was made subordinate to the office of the Deputy
People's Commissar for Foreign Affairs. One section of this
organization dealt with Turkey, Egypt, Palestine, Ethiopia and
other Muslim countries. By 1919 it was subdivided into two
subsections: one dealt with the Muslim Near East, while the second
section dealt with Turkey, Egypt, Palestine and Ethiopia. In the
third place, the Soviet Union was in agreement with Turkey in its
struggle against Britain; this policy had been clear since September
1919.

In April 1920 the San Remo Conference was convened for peace
negotiations between Turkey and the Entente powers. The most
important element in these talks, as far as our study is concerned,
was the position of Palestine as a British mandate. Narkomindel's
stance on this and other related questions concerned the remnants of
the Ottoman Empire in Mesopotamia, Arabia, Palestine and Syria.
To the Soviet Union, the realization of the decisions of the San
Remo Conference was possible because Turkey had been weakened
and Britain's ascendancy to global power was a fact to be reckoned
with.

In the midst of all these political developments Turkey, under the
leadership of Mustafa Kamal Pasha, then President of the Grand
National Assembly of Turkey, received a note on 2 June 1920 from

Chicherin in support of the Turkish government. The Soviet Union, at this juncture, specifically supported the following points:

(1) Declaration of Independence of Turkey;

(2) Proclamation of Arabia and Syria independent states;

(3) Decision . . . to allow . . . all the territories of Turko-Arab population to decide their own destiny. It goes without saying that a free referendum will take place in these localities, with the participation of the refugees and emigrants.[31]

At the same time the Soviet Union did not neglect the Arab world in its pronouncements, for it viewed both Britain and Zionism as the main enemies of the Arab masses. Thus the Soviet Union's support of Turkey and the Arab population was based on a mixture of ideology and *realpolitik*.

In July 1920 the Bolsheviks concluded that relations with Britain not only in Turkey and Palestine but also in the colonies had reached a 'post-revolutionary' situation. From the Bolshevik point of view such a reversal of outlook had implications for the colonies, for if revolution were to succeed in these colonies it would dictate two diametrically opposed presumptions. On one hand, it would be in direct collision with the dominant imperialist powers, Britain and France; and on the other, such internal changes implied that local economic-political conditions would witness a new stage of revolutionary change. It had yet to be revealed by the future developments in the Arab world in particular and in the East at large whether the Soviet Union's analysis and perceptions had any relevance to current historical events. Perhaps, what was problematic at the time, as far as the theoretical approach was concerned, is the fact the the East was not 'ripe' for revolutionary changes.

At the Second Congress of the Comintern (July–August 1920) Lenin's Theses on National and Colonial Question emphasized four points through which colonial and 'backward' countries were passing. It was deemed imperative to aid the 'bourgeois-democratic liberation movement', to struggle against 'medieval elements', to support the peasantry in their fight and to 'combat Pan-Islamism and similar trends which strive to combine the liberation movement against European imperialism with an attempt to strengthen the position of the khans, landlords, mullahs, etc'.[32] Thus the Comintern encouraged the temporary alliance with bourgeois-democrats in these colonial countries.

Lenin, however, faced opposition from two notable Communists, the Indian M. N. Roy and the representative of the Poak Tayion Party, Michael Cohen. The latter raised his objections at the Congress meeting of 28 July 1920 when his speech concentrated on the definition of the Arab nationalist movement and mustered the arguments for supporting it. On Palestine he said:

> In the past, the feudal Turkish rule had sucked the blood of the Arab fellaheen [peasants], the English conquest today abandons them to capitalist exploitation. The big landlords, who previously ruled local feudal autocracies, are trying to put their property in land into the service of the big capitalist rulers, in order to continue the exploitation of the poor fellaheen by new methods. The effendis [notables] rely upon the aid provided by the British and French rulers who conquered Palestine and Syria. This is the economic essence of the Arab 'national liberation movement'.[33]

Cohen, moreover, condemned the role played by the 'Beduin sheikhs' who embarked on what these sheikhs called 'national war' of independence when in essence they were exploiting the fellaheen and the laboring masses. He went on to assert that the Arab leaders were under the influence of their religious leaders and tribal elders. Finally, he argued by implication that in Palestine, the bourgeoisie constituted a 'reactionary' force which negated the historical task which was assigned to it. Cohen's arguments were rejected, and Lenin's and Roy's reasonings were accepted instead.

Lenin's argument was based on two considerations revolving round the fact that these backward and 'feudal' societies were agrarian. On the one hand, all Communist parties must extend support to liberation movements after studying the prevailing situation in all its aspects. On the other hand, he argued that 'it is also necessary to combat Pan-Islamic and similar movements, which are endeavoring to utilize the liberation struggle against European and American imperialism for the purpose of strengthening the power of Turkish . . . imperialists, of the nobility, of the large landowners, of the clergy'.[34] Even though this analytical approach was spearheaded by Lenin himself, he nevertheless did not touch on the difficulty of achieving revolutionary changes, whether led by the proletariat and toiling masses or by any nationalist force. Politically, the world had not reached the nationalistic stage.

None the less, Lenin was a pragmatist; his pronouncements were those of a revolutionary leader who had a global outlook combined with a Marxist analytical approach, its base the proletariat class. The East posed a deviant situation for him. In this context and because of the prevailing political situation, he was convinced that the first political stage that these countries should go through was both anti-colonial and anti-imperialist. Within this conceptual framework Lenin analyzed the overall Eastern question, whereas Cohen, through his party, argued that it had supported the 'unity' of Jewish and Arab laborers against their common enemy, British imperialism. Cohen then proceeded to proclaim that his party, Poak Tayion, workers for Jewish and Arab laborers against imperialism, was the only party in Palestine which adhered to the principles of socialism. On the question of whether the 'revolutionary socialist' parties in the colonies should or should not endeavor to cooperate with the bourgeois nationalist segments of the population, both Cohen and Roy thought that they should, thus marginally disagreeing with Lenin. Cohen presented several arguments for his point of view, and in one of these instances he introduced a hopeful note; that because of the way events were evolving in the Middle East, power would shift to the hands of proletariat and a Soviet Palestine would merge into unity with other Soviet republics.

Cohen gained from Lenin the support needed to be regarded as the representative spokesman for the Socialist Workers' Party of Palestine (MPS). The Bolsheviks' decision to recognize MPS as the 'sole representative of a pro-communist movement' in Palestine was also based on the previous understanding that internal divisions existed within the ranks of the Poak Tayion Party. These divisions had come to light through the published decisions of the Third All-Russia Conference of the Jewish Section of the Russian Communist Party, held from 4 to 6 July 1920:

> The continuous process of revolt within the ranks of Zionism leads to strange combinations of counter-revolutionary nationalist ideas with the ideas of communism (Poak Tayion Social Democrats, Communist Poak Tayion) which are more dangerous than common Zionism, since they are known to secure the pressing influence of the bourgeois ideology on the awakening proletariat; and therefore those trends should be fought in a decisive way.[35]

By the end of July 1920 the Comintern recognized and admitted the MPS to its ranks. It is worth noting here the background structure of the MPS leadership. British intelligence reports at the time referred to its leaders as 'young immigrants from Eastern Europe who introduced Bolshevism to the country'.[36] The names of these young Russian and East European Jews were noted – Yehiel Sokolovsky, Avraham Lomonossof, Mordechai Haldey, Aryed and Yasha among others, who arrived in Palestine in 1919 and 1920. The MPS held its Second Congress from 2 to 4 October 1920, when the basic principles and political guidelines were formulated; they ranged from the advocacy of 'socialism as a final goal' to revolutionary class struggle as its base and finally the dictatorship of the proletariat. This political orientation had an effect on future political developments between the Soviet Union and the newly independent State of Israel. Such attachments, both politically and in terms of human capabilities, created a 'natural link' between the Soviet Union and future State of Israel. It is, moreover, worth mentioning that in the absence of any indigenous and recognized proletariat movement in Palestine, Jews of the Soviet Union and Eastern Europe, who were most used to dwelling in these countries' ghettos, were to constitute a formidable working-class force in Palestine. In his last years Lenin viewed this development as a step toward the revolutionary change which would engulf the backward East. It was with this last situation and with predictions for the future that Lenin was then concerned.

When World War I ended Lenin was of the opinion that 'international world revolution' was all-encompassing and that imperialism would not be able to stop its progress. The evolving world political situation was a signal to him that the social structure of the East seemed fertile ground for Communist seed. Europe was in the midst of tumultuous changes, of which the most important political development was the overthrow of the monarchy in Germany and the collapse of the Austro-Hungarian ruling house. By the end of 1918 the British Labor Party issued a statement calling for a conference of international Socialist and Labor parties to be held in either Paris or Berne. To Lenin, this signaled the revival of the Second (Socialist) International. He opposed this socialist attempt, and in January 1919 addressed an open letter to the workers of Europe and America 'urging them to found the Third International'. Soviet Foreign Minister Chicherin sent out invitations in March for an international conference to meet in Moscow, and a boycott of the British Labor Party's call was urged. On 2 March 1919 the First Congress of the Communist International (Comintern) met in Moscow. The First International (1864–1872) had been an international meeting to lay down the theoretical basis for international revolutionary movement. The Second International (1899–1914) had laid the institutional foundations for an international organization, and its growth was noticeable. The Third International was better defined in the form of the working-class potential of an international workers' movement, and followed the ideal of proletarian dictatorship.

In the Arab world, however, major developments were occurring at this period. On 2 November 1917 the Balfour Declaration was made public; the British Foreign Secretary sent the Declaration to Lord Rothschild, promising that his government viewed the Jewish question favorably and was not opposed to the establishment of a national Jewish home in Palestine. The American, French and Italian governments declared their acceptance of the British stand. It was the British announcement that prompted Weizmann and others to proceed to Palestine in 1917, and from then until 1921, they and world Zionist organizations laid down the future basis of Israel. Weizmann's Jewish committee acted as a liaison between world Jewry and Britain, and it was from this point onward that the Zionist movement could be recognized both as a viable movement and as a government in the process of formation. For the purpose of our study, it is worth mentioning here that the San Remo Conference (of the victors of World War I, 16-26 April 1920) reached the decision that France would have Mandatory powers over Syria and Lebanon, while Britain would exercise Mandatory powers over Palestine and Iraq. By the end of 1920, when the Zionist London Conference was convened, the Zionist movement had attained its political goal as far as Palestine was concerned. It was from this moment that world Jewish emigration began steadily to build its foundations in Palestine. The leading forces behind the Zionist movement were East European and Soviet Jews who regarded the solution of the Jewish question as centering on the establishment of a Jewish state in Palestine. The Jewish-Zionist leadership played a leading role in facilitating Jewish emigration from the Soviet Union and Eastern Europe to Palestine. This element, which can be called the natural link between the future state of Israel and these countries, was to play an important role in these countries' recognition of the State of Israel. It was this 'natural link' that laid the basis for recognition by the Soviet Union and East European states. These Soviet and East European Jewish emigrants to Palestine were instrumental in the establishment of the first Zionist paramilitary organizations in Palestine, the most notable of which was the Zion Mule Corps, established in 1915.

2 From the Bolshevik Revolution to the Baku Congress, September 1921

After World War I Communism had some appeal in the Middle East, especially in Turkey, Egypt and Palestine.[1] This early period of development was characterized by deliberate opposition to religion, political institutions, traditional norms and government. The obstacles which the Communist movement faced were thus immense and, in addition, any attempt to create a mass-based party was doomed to failure largely because of the lack of an industrial proletariat. Thus the Communist parties of Turkey and Egypt began to disintegrate almost before they could begin to be successful. The Soviet Union, however, considered that the Middle East was going through the stage of the 'non-capitalist path'.[2]

From the Leninist period the political development of the Arab world was seen as supporting the 'oppressed' countries of the East and their national liberation, these countries being regarded as the natural allies of the world proletariat. Lenin's fundamental principles for the *new* type of international relations were formulated at both the second All-Russia Congress of Soviets and in the Decree on Peace, November 1917. In this he advocated a policy of peaceful coexistence among nations with different social systems, together with precepts of respect for territorial integrity and national sovereignty, equality among different states regardless of size, non-interference in the internal affairs of states, peaceful means of cooperation and repudiation of aggression.

Such principles were assumed to be directed not only at 'bourgeois governments' but also at their working classes, upon whom was laid the task of ending the war and of achieving liberation from foreign exploitation. Such a policy, moreover, was viewed as the 'true road to liberty'. To this end Lenin's precepts were adopted in December 1917 with a special appeal 'to the working Muslims of Russia and the East'. Lenin contended in 1919 that the working classes of those countries who were implementing the 'socialist revolution' had not only carried out the task of a struggle against the national bourgeoisie but had also carried out the further task of combating imperialism. He had declared that because millions of the masses belonged to 'under-privileged' states who had been the objects of international imperialist exploitation, the struggle against imperialism must continue, and went on to argue that a bond had been created between the struggle of the world proletariat for social emancipation and the struggle of the oppressed peoples for national liberation. Hence the dialectical connection between the two rested on the collaboration of the oppressed peoples of the colonies who had accomplished the first task of combating imperialist exploitation, with the world proletariat setting the stage for a victorious liberation struggle of all oppressed people.

The next step should logically be an alliance of these independent states with the socialist camp whose duty was to foster and encourage this relationship. Thus, it was argued, the merger of the forces of socialism and the national liberation movements would lead to the 'victory of the proletariat on a worldwide scale'. So the scene was set to accomplish the different stages of development. Progressive forces within the countries of the East would be allied with the proletariat. Once independence had been achieved, these new states would find alliance with the socialist camp a natural outcome; that is, an international proletariat would be a natural consequence of the development of events.

The new stage of 'contradictions' would therefore then be elevated to a worldwide scale, the result of which, as Ivan Kovalenko predicted, would be the fall of world imperialism.[3] The October Revolution had led to a merger between the socialists and the national liberation movements, which in turn had resulted in the emergence of national liberation revolutions in these countries. He contended, moreover, that the revolutionary experience had indicated that the national liberation movements of colonial countries was part and parcel of a worldwide socialist revolution.

Lenin argued in 1920 that the proletariat of the advanced industrial states could render assistance to the backward countries passing the capitalist stage of development in their countries. In

Lenin's precepts, the Soviets argued,[4] a transitional stage existed which had a worldwide application and it would be borne out by the development of these countries from the pre-capitalist stage to socialism. His argument embraced the effect of the combination of the twin policies of the principles of proletarian internationalism and of peaceful coexistence of states with different social systems. These two precepts were dialectically interconnected, as attested by recent developments worldwide.

It was argued that the main tasks of the USSR were to combat imperialism, lend support to revolutionary liberation movements and direct its foreign policy toward cooperation with countries with different social systems. At the time, the tasks of these newly independent states lay in getting rid of foreign domination over their countries by following the course of national liberation, and it was Lenin who first advanced the notion that it was necessary to furnish material assistance to these countries and establish broad economic cooperation with them. To that effect the Soviet Union was basically concerned with its closest eastern neighbors, Iran, Afghanistan and Turkey. In this context, it envisaged establishing relations with these countries and then later engulfing Afro-Asian states in order to further the steps that would lead to national liberation in those states, thereby progressing one more stage in the achievement of socialism.

Whenever it was claimed that the imperialists tried to infringe the interests of these emerging states, the Soviet Union, it was claimed, did not hesitate to lend support in areas where it was needed. This was a new development on the international scene in the resolution of international problems and the withering away of obstacles in the way of 'backward' states. Given the early emergence of Lenin's precepts, the 'backward' states and their proletariat had a tremendous task to reach the first stage, disadvantaged as they were by this very backwardness. Having reached a further stage, the necessity for furthering national independence – at the core of which was the struggle against imperialism at the developmental stage – dictated an alliance with the socialist camp, headed by the Soviet Union.

When capitalism entered its last stage, that of imperialism, the question arose of how the 'national colonial' topic fitted into the 'context of the general struggle of the working class and all the working people against the capitalist and imperialist oppression [which] is a major ingredient of that doctrine'.[5] Lenin, moreover, had contributed to Marxist theory, taking as a point of departure the proposition that freedom would be negated when one nation oppressed another nation. He argued that the national question at the highest stage of imperialism should be viewed on an international basis because the world had been divided into two forces, imperialist oppressor countries and the oppressed. In this way the national question emerges as a worldwide phenomenon. He reached the conclusion that imperialism would collapse because of two interconnected factors: firstly, because of the working class in the advanced industrial countries; and secondly, because the national liberation struggles of what would later be known as the Third World would seek self-determination. During the imperialist period and at the turn of the nineteenth century, two historial tendencies emerged to impinge on the national question. In the first place, the capitalist developmental approach had engendered a feeling of nationhood, which in turn gave rise to national movements against colonialism. In the second place, relations between various states had witnessed strong interconnections between the various fields which gave rise to awareness.

When the surge of anti-colonialism began to emerge in a united call for national self-determination, the emerging states began to form their own broad unit against imperialism, which had two basic demands: general programs for democracy and support for national movements.

The national bourgeoisie, according to Soviet precepts, played an awakening role in the backward countries in the sense that they spearheaded the struggle against imperialism for the sake of national independence. However, the alliance between the international working class and national liberation movements, Lenin thought, could possibly inspire the masses in the backward countries to demand national independence even when a proletariat did not exist. Therefore, this stage of political development in backward countries should be achieved in order to attain the goal of political independence.

Lenin had also pointed out that tactical and strategic principles had to take two forms of revolutionary struggle. First, the 'revolutionary class' must have the ability to master each and every form of social activity. Secondly, the revolutionary class must be able and prepared to form new conditions for the struggle in the most masterful way and be able to replace one form with another; that is, they must be ready to employ covert and overt tactics, in which both peaceful and armed struggle should be intermingled.

The point was made that once national and political independence was achieved, the situation would evolve into the wider spectrum of the struggle against the colonial aftermath. Thus the era of change had been developed in a form where new contradictions evolved, generating a new development stage. One of the features of the new stage was the struggle against capitalism and for social emancipation.

Nevertheless, the countries of the East had produced and evolved four types of political development. First, there were countries which, even though they were in the stage of a national liberation movement, had chosen the 'people's democratic' path; second, those who had embarked on a course with socialistic prospects for the achievement of political independence; third, those countries who had opted for the capitalist road; and finally, those countries which had taken a middle road in which the question of development was being decided in the course of acute struggle.

Although the idea of nationalism was considered a bourgeois ideology, it played an important role in the struggle for national independence. In many cases power had fallen into the hands of the leading bourgeoisie who, when faced with crisis within the bourgeois nationalist ideology, showed that the bourgeoisie in the developing countries could not carry through the vital tasks of liberation and revolution to the very end. When faced with mounting crisis and also with 'contradictions' between the objectives it laid down for the completion of the twin tasks of carrying out national revolution and embarking on radical socio-economic transformations, bourgeois nationalism failed to complete this stage.

Acccording to Lenin, what later was known as the Third World, its salient feature backwardness, was supposed to have witnessed a new stage of development called the non-capitalist road of development, which was supposedly achieved by two routes. The first was that a socialist revolution must take place in the developed countries of Western Europe, whereby the proletariat of these countries would take power and supply all the necessary forms of political, economic and social assistance to the backward countries. The other was that the backward countries should carry out their own revolution, ridding themselves of all kinds of backwardness and 'corrupt influences', and then receive assistance from the developed countries where revolution had succeeded. in this fashion the backward countries could bypass the capitalist stage. None the less, there remained two interconnected reservations concerning such a program. Firstly, that the developed countries of Western Europe were embarking on a course that was not necessarily one that guaranteed the success of proletarian revolution in the foreseeable future. Secondly, a successful revolution in the backward countries did not necessarily lead to a socialist revolution, let alone to an alliance with the countries that had chosen the socialist path.

Between the two stages of development, some backward countries would have a leadership which would opt for allying their countries with the capitalist world in order to develop. Lenin perceived that the attainment and course of world revolution engaging all world forces against imperialism would be a long and arduous path. Although the historical mission of the working class was one of organizing, consolidating and enlightening the other strata of society in their struggle against imperialism, history testified that almost the entire leadership of the Communist movements, either in the Arab world or the other backward countries, was rooted basically in the intelligentsia, far removed from proletarian leadership.

Lenin thought that the 'proletariat' of the Soviet Union could establish links with various national liberation movements. Then they would become 'allies'. Thus this issue of the non-capitalist path of development would be part of the broader spectrum of combating imperialism. At the same time, it was the duty of a socialist country to render assistance to those countries which were engaged in opposing imperialism and to assist them in bypassing the capitalist stage of development.

Such a non-capitalist path in essence meant that the 'pre-capitalist structures' were to be rapidly transformed on socialist lines through different 'transitional' stages, combined with various methods of struggle for the attainment of the stage of national independence, the central task. This transformation would lead to the direct development of socialism, thus bypassing the stage of capitalism, provided that assistance was rendered to them by countries where a socialist stage of proletariat dictatorship had been established. The non-capitalist path, Lenin argued, had a two-fold purpose: on the one hand, the 'reshaping' of the different pre-capitalist structures, and on the other, a new socialist prospect for the development of the emergent countries of the colonial world. It was the duty of a Marxist, Lenin argued, to demand the freedom of self-determination for all oppressed countries; for relations between all countries to become closer and, with their eventual union, for the people of the world to reach a transitional period when classes could be abolished. However, the proletariat of the oppressing nations had to struggle to promote the rights of those nations seeking self-determination, which is in itself an expression of 'internationlism'. And at the same time the proletariat of a particular oppressed nation should be clear that the idea of self-determination was only one step toward socialism. Whenever the proletariat of the oppressed nations successfully accomplished the stage of self-determination, . the leadership of that nation should advocate the unity of two proletarian nations and close cooperation between them, which was viewed as an expression of internationalism. In this manner the Marxist-Leninist parties of both nations would be able to advance toward the fulfillment of their international duty in their struggle against imperialism and 'colonial oppression'.

Later, Soviet writers point out that there were historical precedents for countries taking the non-capitalist path of development, of which the Soviet Republics were only one example; others lay in the Third World countries that had achieved socialism and a socialist stage.[6] In the example of the Soviet Union, the argument goes, the proletariat of the advanced sector of society had allied itself with the peasantry and other strata. Thus for it to succeed on an international basis, an alliance between the world proletariat and the peasantry of the developing countries was but one way to reach the goal successfully.

The 'international' proletariat had a duty to render all means of assistance to the developing countries, be it in the realm of organization, materials or ideology. In return, the larger scale, anti-imperialist tendencies of the Third World would manifest themselves in a desire to lead a joint alliance between the two forces of the international proletariat and the socialist states. But it was later realized that the Third World, which had undergone tumultuous changes, had its own idiosyncrasies, for most of its countries lacked the organized proletariat and base, most had no Communist party, their economic structure was still primitive and imperialist influence still constituted a heavy burden.

However, in their struggle to achieve true independence, the 'people' of those countries were to reach beyond the stage of development and bypass the capitalist path by installing a system of socialism and socialist development; an alliance was to be created with the world proletariat to ensure that the non-capitalist path was successfully taken. Such theoretical formulations did not state that such means were the only genuine path, for when we accept such precepts, then the stage has been set for true socialism, and the question of bypassing the capitalist stage negates itself. More important, perhaps, political changes that occurred subsequently in the Third World were largely responsible for the military aspect of their societies. In the Arab world, only two exceptions to the rule have occurred in recent history: the People's Democratic Republic of Yemen (South Yemen) and Algeria.

For geographical reasons Arab knowledge about the early revolutionary period filtered mainly through Iraq and to a lesser extent through Egypt; according to Soviet writers[7] Algeria alone at this early stage had some 'socialist' organizations affiliated to the Second International. But from 1917–1918 the spread of Communism and socialist parties in the Arab world, small in numbers but still significant for such developing countries, was noticeable earlier in Egypt in the form of the Socialist Party. In 1921, the Palestinian Communist Party was established, and in 1922 a Communist Party was established in Syria, Lebanon, Algeria, Morocco and Tunisia.

The precepts of foreign policy were of an open-ended debatable nature which included peaceful coexistence of nations with different social backgrounds, the right of every nation to decide its own future freely and the right of every nation to independent statehood. Such precepts and demands meant that the states of the East, especially the Arab World, should embark on a course that was basically against Western imperialism and would most certainly lead to a confrontation between the Arab states and the West.

This struggle, if it ensued, was most likely to lead to an alliance between these emerging Arab states and the socialist camp headed by the Soviet Union; the Western camp would be weakened not only politically but also strategically. The 'transitional' societies of the developing countries, the Soviet argument went, were going through a process of acute social stratification; because of this, it made it difficult to draw a clear distinction between the different social classes and social groups. This social structure of a transitional society, since it was partitioned and lacked an ideological and organizational base, would lead to none of the social classes being able to provide a nationwide movement for social purposes. Thus, a need arose for a Marxist analysis to distinguish the features of social class-stratification in the Third World; in most of these countries, because of a blurred picture of social classes and distinction between them, the stage of politico-economic development had to be analyzed within a coherent Marxist analysis.

While analyzing such special features of development in the Third World, one should also look at the increasing number of new developments in the struggle of the 'masses' against exploitation in most of the liberated countries. Here, the national liberation movement had been a new feature developing within the struggle, a phenomenon where the regrouping of social classes had historical significance. In the first place came the emergence and growth of local bourgeois elements and the merging of their interests with the traditional pre-capitalist 'categories of exploiters', followed by a new type of exploiter who extracted the 'surplus value' through the use of modern capitalist methods and pre-capitalist, mainly traditional, means to produce primary and secondary means of exploitation. In the second place, there was the steady growth of the wage labor force, the proletariat, with its industrial core in both quantity and quality reforming peasant labor owners and the ideological maturity of the working class, which all led to the developing force of the national liberation movement.

Finally, a growing division emerging in the middle social strata of the country – the intelligentsia, the students, office employees, small producers, property holders and others – would lead to the establishment of conservative pro-bourgeois and 'national progressive stands of the socio-political movement'.[8]

The balance of social forces would thus determine the type of 'socio-economic' transformation to be achieved in the course of a national liberation revolution, and this would classify the developing countries under various forms. One group could be classified, according to Soviet thinking, as the 'theoretic monarchist' regime under which feudalism prevailed; any progressive elements and trends would encounter weighty social and political forces. Another group would be one where revolution from above occurs, when the monarchist or the bourgeois landowning elite attempts to break the 'archaic' structure and set a course for rapid capitalist development; Saudi Arabia is given as an example. But the socio-political structure and situation were characterized by a dual nature. If, on the one hand, these countries were to embark on a rapid modernization of their social and political structures they might, on the other hand, well be the scene of dramatic changes which would result in influencing the social orientation.

A third group might include those states with relatively developed capitalism and a clearly defined proletariat; the socio-political changes would not exceed the 'framework of capitalist relations', but progressive changes would be introduced into their socio-political structures. As the class struggle in those countries intensified, the situation would become conducive to a 'balance' of political forces which would lead toward conditions of a transitional period in the structural socio-economic transformation which was a sign of 'transition' from a national liberation revolution to social revolution. This group would encompass socialist-oriented states where the revolutionary-democratic forces had achieved power in the course of the class struggle. In these countries, in spite of the fact that some 'inconsistencies' had occurred, a way had been opened up for the creation of the necessary prerequisites for the eventual transitional period of socialist relations of production.

Under such circumstances, the national liberation movement could develop into revolutionary socialism through the national democratic revolution. But, so far as the practicality was concerned, it would take the non-capitalist path and would orient itself toward socialist forms. To achieve the highest stage of socialist development, the 'national democratic revolution' should pave the way for a subsequent stage of socialism and thus proceed to a stage of socialist development; however, in view of the backwardness of Third World countries, the process would take a long time.

The most significant requirement for the development of the socio-economic and political processes that had engulfed the Third World and the growth of national and class 'self-consciousness'. was concerned with striking a balance between the politics of 'internationalist unity' of all those countries which followed a policy of anti-imperialism. This required the strengthening of national independence and state sovereignty, which at the same time involved a fight against reactionary forces and imperialism at large which might use the growing national self-consciousness to spread the ideals of religion and 'national exclusiveness' for anti-communist and nationalist purposes.

None the less, Soviet perceptions of socio-economic and political development in the Third World tended to postulate that the prevailing ideological climate there was conducive to the development of progressive social orientation on the lines of scientific socialism and a gradually diminishing orientation of anti-communism. The Third World, as the Soviets put it, had to achieve one of two alternatives: either to follow the capitalist road and face up to the consequences of backwardness and retardation, or to take the road which would lead to social 'justice' – namely, communism. That would mean national liberation, and it was within these confines that the struggle should be viewed. The Arab world, however, with its backwardness, could and would bring about a tremendous achievement if it followed the precepts that had been laid down for the orientation of the Soviet Union and the latter's analysis of its socio-economic development.

The historical relevance of the Baku Conference, September 1921

When the Baku Conference met (1–8 September 1921) to discuss the events the peoples of the East were experiencing at the period, there were four Jews and three Arabs amongst the delegates; three others were declared to be of the Muslim faith.[9] The chairman of the Conference, Zinoviev, dwelt on the progress of the important trends prevailing in the world which he claimed was divided into different categories: nations that enjoy sovereignty, nations that are followers of others, the exploiting and the exploited nations. Before World War I, he claimed, the international situation had been divided between the six great powers, who had a population of over one billion people.[10] In the world, he went on, there are two movements. The first is personified by the strong, sweeping movement which was to be seen in Russia, Germany, France and Italy. The second was a weaker one emanating from the progressing nations, which some-times takes an indirect approach to its realization and is not always clear what it aspires to in reality. Both this second movement and the nations in which it occurs suffer from British and French capitalism; 'We want these two movements to get closer to each other and for the second to get rid of the complications and nationalistic sentiments; we want these two directions to merge into one and dispel all the handicaps and purify the land from its chronic diseases.'[11] After World War I, he argued, which was a fight between the Anglo-French alliance and Germany with its allies to dominate the world, the victorious powers aimed at enslaving the masses of the world. Even at the level of states, for example, Britain 'occupied' the Arab East and Iraq while France 'occupied' Syria. These powers aimed not only at crushing the Turkish sultan but at the division of Turkey; thus they granted Syria and Iraq nominal independence. He then posed a rhetorical question: 'What are the prominent feature of this independence? . . . France promised to establish a free Syria and find a stooge for it in the person of Prince Faisal. . . . And the English were also talking of the independence of Iraq. The English capitalists owned every oil well in Iraq, which is all the Iraqi people possessed.'[12] He came to the conclusion that the process which Soviet Russia had undergone was a worthwhile example for the East to follow, if the workers and peasants of the East persisted in seeking to liberate themselves from exploitation, since victory was attainable just because the enemy was constantly being weakened by the prospect of total economic collapse. Finally, he drew the attention of his audience to the fact that the struggle against the British capitalist would be a long one because the masses of the East were 'not liable to progress speedily'.

This sort of pronouncement deserves certain comment. First the international, political and strategic map of the Arab world after World War I reflected the prevailing circumstances of the victorious Western allies in which the British and the French had become the supreme powers in the world. Thus, slicing the world into pieces and spheres of influence was the natural outcome when it became the domain of these two powers. The Arab world was then ruled mostly by monarchical forms of governments; notable among these were Egypt, Transjordan, Iraq and the whole of the Gulf and the Arabian Peninsula. The Arab world's entire political and economic map was a prey to French and British desires and plans for its division. The West, at this point in history, was enjoying its moment in the Arab world as the undisputed power with the task of drawing up its final and practical approaches.

When Bavlutch addressed the Conference, he stressed that 'the major task which lies before the Third International and before every true communist in the world is to spread the following simple truth: for as long as the black and yellow races suffer from oppression and the lackey Europeans slaughter the Turks, Iranians, Arabs, Egyptians and others, so the European worker will remain a slave to the capitalist who will be unable to free himself. Therefore, and for this reason in particular, the Third International calls upon the European workers to struggle for the liberation of the East'.[13] From this point, he went on to argue that the peoples of the East would not be able to gain their freedom unless they united with world proletariats. For this path, he argued, would be realizable only when the toiling masses of East and West united to carry out the struggle on two fronts: against foreign capitalism and national bourgeoisie. Ryskolov on the other hand argued *inter alia* that 'if the socialist movement in the West had taken a communist orientation, we must expect that it will take in the East a communist outlook. For the revolutionary movement there [the East] will be oriented towards the small bourgeoisie outlook and will reinforce the nationalistic aspect. But this movement will change, out of necessity, to a social and an agricultural movement.'[14] Blakun, however, argued that 'the bourgeoisie in the colonialized and semi-colonialized countries normally distinguishes between the inhabitants and the ruling class, and uses the former at the least expense and least bloody means. The Sultans, Emirs and all the ruling parties in the East are always welcome to play the role of tax collectors for the imperialist oppressors.'[15] He gave two examples; the Shah of Iran who had suffered Russian and British imperialistic periods, and Prince Faisal of Transjordan who accepted bribes from Persian bankers to divide the Turkish nation while, at the same time, he kept the 'peasant class' in his country as a flock of sheep, imposing taxes on them without mercy. He went on to draw a comparison between Soviet power in the West and dictatorship over poor peasantry.

Shatshko, however, presented the most succinct argument in the conference, outlining the political and economic steps that should be taken to ensure the final triumph of the revolutionary process. He began by laying down the historical process which the countries of the East were undergoing by arguing that 'all the countries are agricultural countries' and because of the various and oppressive conditions imposed by the European imperialists on the people, the latter had been unable to establish their own industrial base and confined themselves to an agricultural base. The peasants therefore constituted the oppressed majority in these societies of the East. Thus, he concluded, the liberation of the peoples of the East meant at the very least the liberation of the peasantry. He then volunteered a value judgement by arguing that the Islamic Qur'an adheres to the fact that the land should be owned only by the one who tills it. The religious Islamic mullahs who owned the land, as they did in Iran, were the first to violate the fundamental principles of Islam and were not the protectors of this religion but exploiters of it. These mullahs were parasites and oppressors at the same level as the landlords. Then he advised that for the peasantry to transform itself into a 'practical force' it must merge into a unified force as the revolutionary proletariat was doing in the industrialized West. He cited examples from the East – Turkey, Iran and India – where the mass of the peasantry were collaborating with the bourgeoisie to gain national independence. This, he concluded was 'the correct path'. Nevertheless, he inserted the reservation that political independence and the simultaneous preservation of a capitalist society was not necessarily the ultimate liberation. He would not exclude political independence from the process of industrial capital development. Finally he dwelt on the agricultural question at length. The argument he put forward[16] dealt with detailed points as to how the peasantry should operate and what 'objective' conditions they were experiencing. Several of his points were based on the thesis that the peasant class in the East was the 'only producing class' but its labor went to feed the big landowners, bourgeoisie and bureaucrats. Then he proceeded to list the reasons 'for the oppression and exploitation' that the peasantry faces: the continuation of traditional landlords who enslave the peasantry; the landlords' possession of the available land which allows them, because of its scarcity, to transform the laborers to mere workers and enslaves them though written law guarantees them freedom; the authorities' ownership of the land granted only to capitalists and the classes who enjoy privileges, leaving the rest only as peasants; the heavy burdens imposed upon the peasants in the form of taxes and the way these are collected through a handicapped bureaucracy form forms an oppressive tunnel; the absence of individual freedom and the prevalence of organized theft by savage travelling tribes who, in turn, use different means of oppression against the peasantry with the collaboration of the state. All these elements bear down on the peasantry in such a way as to increase their misery, which leads them to resort to borrowing, which in turn leads them to problems in repaying the interest. The peasantry's lack of tools, capital and seeds constitutes a handicap between the peasants and the organization of their agricultural economy even if they owned plots.

He went on to argue that for the Eastern peasantry to liberate themselves from this intolerable exploitation and destruction and achieve the conditions necessary for organizing their own economy and its progress they must take the following steps. First, the destruction of the power of local oppressors (sultans, shahs, princes, bureaucrats and the like) and 'parasites', taking control of all administrative, economic and financial infrastructures. Second, the establishment of peasant soviets, local or central, and the Eastern peasant soviets would unite with Soviet republics of the West. Third, the complete rejection of the execution of the principles of feudalism, undermining their status, and the confiscation of extensive estates in private ownership. Fourth, codification of all existing agricultural laws and the transfer of all available land to state ownership; for the future the principle would be that he who tills the land owns it. Fifth, the organization of local committees administered by local peasant soviets. Sixth, cancellation of all taxes, and for which nominal country produce to assist city workers and the army would be substituted; the right of land ownership would be reserved for the local soviets, and in return peasants must receive all the industrial produce. Seventh, the cancellation of all peasant debts demanded by the state, scientific and religious institutions and by merchants. Finally, when peasant and soviet republics were instituted, they must seek the assistance of soviet republics in Europe to help facilitate means of agricultural equipment and development. He concluded by stating that 'the mere declaration of political independence for the countries of the East – Turkey, Iran, Afghanistan, etc. – is not sufficient to liberate the peasants of the East from exploitation and destruction'.[17] He concluded by claiming that the ultimate victory for the 'social revolution' and the building of communism on the international level was the only means by which the 'peasant class' in the East would get free of destruction and misery. Thus, he concluded, that it remained the duty of Eastern peasantry, in their struggle, to collaborate with 'revolutionary workers' in Europe and the soviet republics, to stand against 'capitalist conquerors and local oppressors' and continue their struggle until the final victory against 'international bourgeoisie' was achieved.

At the conclusion of the Conference, a declaration was issued to the peoples of the East detailing recent historical events. Posing a rhetorical question the declaration asked, 'What has England given the Arabian Peninsula and Iraq?' It declared that 'there the Muslim states had gained independence but, in fact, these states had become its colonies. It kicked the Arab owners off their land, withheld from them the most fertile rivers of Dejlah and Furat, and confiscated the most precious of all sources in Musal and Basra. . . . What does England offer Palestine? To satisfy a small group of Jewish and English capitalists, it kicked the Arabs from their land and granted it to Jewish settlers; and to ensure at the same time an outlet for Arab discontent it gave power to the Jewish colonies which it [England] constructed, thereby implanting discontent and hatred among all the tribes and weakening both parties so that it became the gainer. What had England offered Egypt where its people were suffering for eight decades from English capitalists' might which is worse than the Pharoahs?'[18]

Officially the convening of the Baku Congress of Eastern peoples had been prompted by an official invitation from the Executive Committee of the Communist International, in July 1920, whereby it appealed in the name of European and American workers to the 'enslaved peoples of Persia, Armenia and Turkey', inviting them to a congress in Baku to be held in September in order to discuss 'together . . . the question of how the forces of the European proletariat can be united with your forces [the East] for the struggle against the common enemy'. The appeal went on to justify the convening of the Congress mentioning, *inter alia*, to the peoples of Persia, Armenia and Turkey that 'your joining the workers and peasants in Europe and America will accelerate the end of world capitalism and will guarantee the liberation of all workers and peasants throughout the world'.[19] From its inception, the Congress was dominated by the Russian Communists who were its main speakers, whereas the non-Russian representatives were, to say the least, bewildered as to their role and what was required of them. But 'the geographic position of Baku, Tashkent and Irkutsk made them convenient starting points for three-directional communist activities in Persia and Turkey; Tashkent in Turkestan housed institutions assigned to work in India; Irkutsk became the center for propaganda and organizational work in the Far East'.[20] Special training schools, following the example of Moscow, were established in Turkestan, Baskiria, the Caucasus and elsewhere.

Between January and April 1921 a cadre school was established, based in Moscow, to deal with the issues and problems of nationalists and the East. Stalin, on the fourth anniversary of the established university, put the task before the students that they must concentrate on questions concerning Soviet eastern nationalities and 'provide guidance to students from colonial countries'.[21] All the same, even as the Soviet Union was proceeding with this program, it paid equal attention to its normal diplomatic relations with the governments of Turkey, Persia and Afghanistan. Treaties which the Soviet Union concluded with these countries were intended on the one hand to proceed through normal diplomatic channels to consolidate its position in these countries through peaceful means and the other hand to widen the gap and create tensions between the colonies of the East and the imperialist powers.

This twin approach by the Soviets was imposed upon the new Bolshevik regime by the realities of the international situation and, in particular, by what was termed the 'people's organizations' which manifested themselves at the time in local Communist parties.

Nevertheless, the Soviet Union, as G. V. Chicherin, then the People's Commissar for Foreign Affairs, noted in December 1920, regarded the obstacle which were at issue in the following light:

> The movements which are taking place in the East are national. The liberation movement in the East is directed against imperialism but essentially it differs from communism. As Communists, we favor the liberation movement of the peoples of the East, a compromise between us and the national states which are struggling for their own independence against the imperialism of the West.[22]

Thus by February and March 1921 treaties of friendship and alliance were signed between the Soviet Union and Persia, Afghanistan, Turkey and the Yemen. Strategic considerations were paramount in Soviet perceptions at this early stage of development. Simultaneously Communist parties sprang up in parts of the East; prominent among these was the Persian Communist Party, founded in June, and the Turkish Party, established in the same year.

Thus at this early period of Bolshevik history the emerging Soviet Union had to give due consideration to its borders and, at the same time, assist the promotion of local communist parties. This double-edged policy served the Soviet Union at this stage in ways that were not otherwise feasible. The strategic element had an importance which overrode the theoretical Marxist-Leninist approach; theoretical justifications were left to the level of the masses and Arab Communist parties.

For two reasons it would be misleading to analyze the Soviet Union's foreign policy in the Arab world in Lenin's time only theoretically or to confine Soviet approaches to the question to pure national interest. In the first place, the Soviet Union had just witnessed a new revolutionary trend, manifested by the October Revolution of 1917, so that Lenin and the Communist Party were basically concerned with nation-building. This task was Lenin's overriding priority. On the other side of the coin the question, however, was concerned with the Arab world itself. At this time the Arab world was under the direct domination of the West European powers (Britain and France), and these two powers had a free hand in these Arab domains thus determining their destiny. At the same time the Arab Communist parties, which were under Soviet tutelage, were operating illegally, causing these parties to cling to theoretical Marxist analysis in regard to Arab class structure. This analysis had no real and applicable substance to Arab society and structure – quite simply because if the Arab world were interpreted on a Marxist basis, it had no industrial or workers' proletariat. The official Soviet approach to the Arab world could only have a nationalistic appeal. Such an approach, were it ever to bear fruit, would eventually mean that any Arab domain aspiring to independence would ultimately have to encounter either France or Britain; the latter was considered by the Soviet Union to be a former colonial and present imperialist world power. At this stage of political development, however, the Soviet Union was in the formative stage internally, and its foreign policy beyond the neighbouring states was confined to a theoretical Marxist-Leninist analysis of only minimal application. In practical terms, there was little action that could be undertaken.

3 The Interlude Period, 1921–1945

Throughout its analyses the Comintern laid stress on the procedure for attaining power, before which two necessary prerequisites for the final stage of revolution in the East would have to be accomplished: the emergence or availability of a critical condition whereby the existence of the ruling elite was threatened: and the emergence and availability of a Communist party and the collaboration of other potential revolutionary elements in the society. The Comintern further divided the social conditions produced in these societies into 'objective and subjective' prerequisites. The former meant the existence of a 'severe crisis' in the social fabric, and the latter the presence and leadership of a Communist party in this evolving crisis.

From this originated the Marxist term, the 'bourgeois-democratic revolution', which employed Marx's terminology and description of a feudal society to replace the capitalist stage in society. The Comintern also adopted Marx's phrase 'the proletarian-socialist revolution', derived from the original meaning of the 'proletarian revolution', which meant, in turn, that the capitalist social stage was replaced by the socialist stage. Such terminology meant that in the 'bourgeois-democratic revolution' the feudal system terminated the 'rule of nobility', while in its economic sense, the 'bourgeois-democratic revolution' would mean a revolution against 'feudalism and mercantilism' and the limiting of government interference in the sphere of the local economy. Furthermore, in its social context, it meant that the 'bourgeois-democratic revolution' negated all the 'existing privileges' granted by a regime.

Thus the ultimate aim politically, economically and socially was the transformation of the society in a way that corresponds to the coming to power of the Communist party, which has its base in the proletarian class. In a successful proletarian revolution, the Soviet Union, as the spearhead of Communism, would have a primary role in the political direction of that society. The 'bourgeois-democratic revolution' was terminology coined basically to fit the East; its leadership had to be spearheaded by the local Communist party. In the Comintern's approaches to the Eastern question the whole argument and analysis centered on political developments in China and India. For the Comintern the East possessed three character-istics: the lack of a well-founded industrial basis, the prominence of the 'Asiatic' mode of production whereby feudalism flourishes and, finally, imperialist control which decides all means of production available in these countries. For these realities, it became appro-priate for the Comintern to designate the 'bourgeois–democratic revolution' as the convenient type of revolution, but this was to be under the leadership of the Communist party. In what became labeled the colonial, semi-colonial and dependent countries, the Comintern, however, thought that the appropriate form of rev-olution was that which it labeled the 'bourgeois-democratic rev-olution'. This in turn meant that the 'peasant revolutionary movement', which was aimed against the feudal system and the 'pre-capitalist' means of exploitation, 'class struggle' would develop, would be stratified and would entail overall changes in these societies.

Nevertheless, the Comintern was of the opinion that the East in general was not yet capable of or ready for a 'proletariat-socialist revolution', even though it was undergoing changes. The Comintern did, however, pay, briefly and in passing, some attention to what it labeled the 'more backward' countries (those where tribal insti-tutions prevailed; Africa fitted this categorization). But the Com-intern pointed out that in these countries, the proletariat and the national bourgeoisie did not exist in the political processes. As a result of the above analysis, the Comintern therefore concluded that 'national uprisings' in these societies would lead these societies to 'bypass' the capitalist stage in general, and aid would be forth-coming from the proletariat-based countries. However, even here the presence of a Communist party was a necessity for the achievement of revolution; this in turn implied that allegiance to the directions and outlook of the Comintern necessitated the leadership of the Soviet Union.

The Comintern had set up three pre-conditions for the acceptance of any Communist party applying for admission: (1) adherence to the 21 points in its 'definition of orthodox theory, (2) the problem of erroneous beliefs and ideologies, and (3) the attitude of a Communist party toward the Soviet Union'.[1] It became common knowledge that orthodox Marxism was embodied later in Leninism and Stalinism. The contributions of the two latter were to be a guiding force behind the Comintern outlook and guidelines. The influence of Stalin in particular ultimately manifested itself in the final conclusions and decisions of the Comintern. The protection of the Bolshevik Revolution and strengthening of its status and existence became a prime consideration. A resolution adopted by the Seventh World Congress of the Comintern in 1935 explicitly stated:

> Both under peace conditions and in the conditions of war
> directed against the USSR, the strengthening of the USSR, the
> increasing of its power, and the assuring of its victory in all
> spheres and in every sector of the struggle coincide fully and
> inseparably with the interests of the working people of the
> whole world, . . . they are the conditions for, and they
> contribute to, the triumph of the world proletarian revolution,
> the victory of socialism throughout the world.[2]

Our concern here, as stated earlier, is confined to the Comintern's analysis and political assessment of the East in general, which was lumped together with the characterization into divisions of colonial, semi-colonial and dependent societies. Within these countries the Comintern laid down further distinctions in terms of what the East was going through. The East possessed three notable features. First, the imperialist 'subjugation' of these countries and, concomitant with it, the absence of local nationalistic forces. Second, the overwhelming presence of the feudal system, although an 'elementary' pre-capitalist form was, at the same time, in existence. Third, the availability of the mass of a peasant population with a lesser admixture of bourgeoisie and proletariat. For the above reasons, the Comintern contended that a 'bourgeois-democratic' revolution under the control of the local Communist party was the most appropriate for these countries. An important question remained the components of the leadership of the revolutionary movement in these countries. The Comintern disputed the assumed reality that the bourgeoisie had increasingly nationalist sentiments, especially among educated intellectuals, the urban middle-classes, merchants and in a few cases military officers. However, 'by 1928, the Comintern had concluded (1) that the native bourgeoisie must inevitably go over sooner or later to the counter-revolutionary camp without the task of the "bourgeois-democratic" revolution (including particularly the partition of large holdings among the peasants), and (2) that the Communist party supported by the proletariat must come forth as the leader of the revolution and must exercise hegemony over a group of allies which should include as its most vital component the peasant masses to whom the Communist party would promise a land partition'.[3]

The dialectical approach laid down by the Comintern on the Eastern question was that the 'bourgeois-democratic' segments of the society would pass two further stages before the Communist seizure of power. The first stage would be when political conditions yielded to the promoting of Communist power, leading to a second stage which would bring about a Communist and proletarian hegemony; this in turn would produce an alliance of the bourgeoisie with counter-revolutionary elements. However, in these countries, the comprador class, who are engaged in trade, would be 'dependent upon the imperialists' because of the nature of their vocation. Moreover, it was believed that in the initial stages of the 'struggle of the peasantry' against the landlords, the proletariat could go along with the peasantry.[4] But it was stipulated that in the process of seizing power in these countries, the revolutionary forces should rely on the proletariat in the advanced industrial capitalist countries.

During the period preceding the world economic catastrophe of the late 1920s and early 1930s, the Comintern believed that both the United States and Europe, spearheading world capitalism, had been weakened overall to a large degree. From 1928 to 1934 this Western weakness was manifested in the failure of the League of Nations either to sustain peace or to achieve an effective program for international disarmament. Meanwhile, Stalin was consolidating his power in the Soviet Union; in October 1927 he had removed Trotsky from power and from the Comintern's ECI. By 1920 Stalin ruled the Soviet Union alone. In November 1933 diplomatic relations were established with the USA, and by 1934 the Soviet Union was able to create a 'security system' encircling Eastern Europe. Within the Comintern the Soviet Union reached two conclusions about the task of world revolution; that world capitalism was becoming less stable and that multi-faceted revolutionary movements were occurring in the world.

It laid down general guidelines on tactical and strategic ways and means to deal with the Comintern's policies for colonial, semi-colonial and dependent societies. On the Eastern question the developments engulfing the Chinese political scene were stressed. Within what the Comintern considered to be an important political factor in these non-proletarian societies, an attempt was made to 'work within' peasant associations. Nevertheless, this 'two policies' orientation of what was considered to be the masses' leadership of the proletarian class cannot have taken second priority. By 1928 the Comintern categorically laid down the principle of the 'hegemony of the proletariat' as a rule and guideline for future political development.

However, between 1928 and 1934 the policy of 'go-it-alone' was formulated; it was combined with the expectation that revolutionary fervor was sweeping through colonies, semi-colonies and dependent societies and, with the effects of the Depression, in the West. But by 1934 this policy was abandoned for the basic reason that no notable revolutionary movement other than the Bolshevik Revolution had made its appearance. Indeed, the anticipated revolutionary movement had basically failed in Western Europe, particularly in Germany.

From 1934 to 1939 two salient features were apparent in the Soviet Union: its speedy economic recovery and the growth of Stalin's personal power at the expense of that of other party members, illustrated by the Great Purges of 1936–1938. Three notable leaders of the Comintern went out of power – Zinoviev and Bukharin as well as Trotsky.

In the 1930s the Arab political map was overshadowed by both French and English domination. Syria and Lebanon were French mandates. In 1939 France suspended the Syrian and Lebanese constitutions and exercised direct administration over the two countries. Several countries were bound to Britain: Egypt, by a treaty signed in 1936, whereby the former pledged to put at British disposal all its logistical apparatus if a threat of war occurred; Iraq, by a treaty of alliance of February 1928: Yemen, by a forty-year treaty of friendship and mutual cooperation signed in February 1934; Saudi Arabia by the terms of the 1927 Treaty of Jidda, which was renewed in 1936 for seven more years. The Arabian Gulf sheikhdoms were also under British control. This division of the Arab world into French and British domains presented the Soviet Union with a tremendous task in terms of penetrating the region.

At the end of the 1930s the Soviet Union's relations with the Arab world showed certain signs of improvement. Rashid Ali's regime was recognized by the Soviet Union in May 1941, although relations lapsed after a change of power in Egypt. Between October 1943 and September 1944, diplomatic relations were resumed between both Egypt and Iraq and the Soviet Union. In the fall of 1944 both Lebanon and Syria received their formal independence from France, but the latter retained its military forces in these countries. By the end of 1945, after the surrender of Germany, nationalistic fervor began to take a new turn in the Arab world. Both West European powers promised the gradual military evacuation of their troops from the Levant. None the less, this Western promise was not satisfactory to Arab nationalists, who brought the subject to the attention of United Nations' Security Council. At this point the Soviet Union sympathized with Syrian and Lebanese demands, and it consequently vetoed a resolution in the Security Council in accordance with the wishes of Syria and Lebanon. At this time the Soviet Union sought to fulfill Arab aspirations for complete independence.

It remains to analyze the stand taken by the Soviet Union on Palestine prior to the recognition of the State of Israel in May 1948. To Stalin, for example, Zionism represented a reactionary force that was upheld by the Jewish bourgeoisie, and it aimed at the separation of Jewish proletarian masses from the 'general struggle of the proletariat'. As early as the last years of Lenin, Zionist activities had been banned in the Soviet Union. To Stalin, moreover, backing the Jewish and Arab masses was more significant than the recognition of the surrounding reactionary regimes under which the masses had dwelt. A line was drawn by Soviet thinkers between the Jewish question in Europe and the Palestinian Jews; for the former had to witness a new phase of 'democracy' in European countries of which the real aim would be economic reconstrucion.

By 1946 a twin Soviet policy was operative: opposition to largescale Soviet emigration to Palestine and persecution of 'bourgeois nationalism' among the national minorities of the Soviet Union, including the Jewish. Meanwhile, the Soviet Union's foreign policy objectives coincided with Arab aspirations in the sense that these were opposed to the British mandate over Palestine. The Soviet Union considered that both Jewish and Arab inhabitants of Palestine were opposing and struggling against a common enemy manifested in British domination. Their 'struggle' was considered 'justified'. The Soviet Union's stand on Palestine at the United Nations demonstrated a new outlook on the Palestinian question. After the failure of the London Conference attended by the Arabs and Britain the question was referred by Britain to the United Nations. The Arab stand at the UN was for a speedy termination of the British mandate over Palestine and the proclamation of an independent and united Palestine. This Arab demand was in agreement with the Soviet Union's desire that Britain end the situation in Palestine.

By May 1947 the Soviet Union favored the Arab position of discussing the matter at the UN in the hope that Britain would evacuate Palestine. This position was maintained until May 1948, when a Jewish, but no Arab, state was established in Palestine. A year earlier in the course of the debate at the UN the Soviet Union had recognized the fact that peaceful coexistence between Arabs and Jews was an impossibility under the prevailing conditions. It was forced to support the Partition Plan of the UN which, in so far as it recognized the rights of both antagonists, meant that it also satisfied their demands. It does not however imply that the Arab side was content with the Soviet Union's attitude. Looking at the Arab–Israeli conflict through Soviet eyes, this stand launched it upon what it saw as an even-handed approach where it could benefit the most. The subsequent political history of the Arab–Israeli conflict developed along very different lines.

The Soviet Union had hoped to achieve at least three objectives in transferring the question to the UN. It aspired, firstly, to terminate the British role in the area. Second, by dealing with the matter at the UN's Security Council and various UN agencies, the Soviet Union had an opportunity to become involved in decision-making on a vital area of the Arab world. Third, in the event that a decision should be reached by the UN for the future involvement of the Security Council, the Soviet Union, by implication, would be included. Gromyko, the Soviet Union's representative at the UN, advocated the partition of Palestine, but defended the Jewish right to Palestine on both 'historical and humanitarian' grounds. He left open an argument that led him to claim that 'peoples of the Arab East' were undergoing a stage of liberating themselves from the yoke of colonialism. When the vote on the partition of Palestine was cast on 29 November 1947, the Soviet Union, with the US, voted in favor.

4 From observation to involvement, 1945–1948

The Soviet Union and the Palestinian Partition Plan

In the Middle East, and in the Arab world in particular, two major developments bedevilled the Palestinian question. The first involved the whole scope of East–West relations as they developed during the Cold War era, and encompassed the fear of Communist infiltration of the area through either the official channels of state-to-state relations or through the Arab and Israeli Communist parties. This produced an attack on the Arab Communist Parties of Palestine, Syria and Egypt. The second was the repercussions of the United Nations' proposal for the partition of Palestine into two different states. The Soviet Union hoped that such a proposal would be an appropriate solution of the Palestinian question because it would be an outlet for fulfilling the aspirations of both the Jewish and Arab populations, an approach in accord with the Soviet Union's long-term strategy to combat the remnants of colonialism, clearly manifested by the British role in the Arab world. In following the concepts and precepts of a *two-state* policy in Palestine, the Soviet Union could, at this early stage, remain silent both on the theory and progress of the Zionist movement in the area and, more particularly, on Jewish emigration to Palestine.

The Palestinian question was not and did not constitute an urgent issue in the Soviet Union's foreign policy immediately after World War II. The question centered rather on the issue of the 'displaced' Jewish people, the remnant of the Nazi policies, throughout the world, mostly Eastern European Jewry. The 'practical' aspect of Jewish emigration was basically one for the Eastern European countries rather than the Soviet Union. None the less, the Soviet Union's knowledge of, and tacit consent to, the Jewish emigration question effectively gave it the go-ahead. However, for both the Soviet Union and Eastern European countries, agreeing to and allowing Jewish emigration to Palestine was basically a contradiction of foreign policy as far as the Palestinian question was concerned. The Zionist movement, with its ideological background, was not an issue at the time; Zionism held a rather low place, if indeed it had any place at all, in the Soviet Union's foreign policy.

Three basic issues confronted the Soviet Union at this relatively early period. First, there was the question of Jewish emigration to Palestine; the influx of Jewish emigrants from the Soviet Union and Eastern Europe had a profound impact on the establishment of the emerging Jewish state. The contradiction lay in the remarkable 'coincidence' of solving the Jewish question which was also a central element in the fulfillment of Zionist ideology. Second, the Soviet Union was concerned with the whole question simply by being one of the Big Five at the United Nations. When the Partition Plan was voiced at the UN, the Soviet Union had two seemingly contradictory objectives: the recognition of the right to exist of two diametrically opposite forces; that is, the Jewish right to a state and the Palestine Arabs' right to a separate entity in the same geographical area. The Soviets thought that both Jews and Arabs should live as two separate entities in one geographically defined area, and it hoped that they could so dwell. The combination of Jewish emigration and the military training of Jews, encouraged within Eastern bloc states, played an important role in Soviet support for the idea of the establishment of the State of Israel. Thirdly, the overriding issue in Soviet Union foreign policy was opposition to the British Mandatory role in the area.

There was, nevertheless, an element of contradiction in Soviet foreign policy. Opposition to British policy and presence in the Mandate, and support for both antagonists for the right of 'self-determination' in Palestine constituted a dilemma. The Soviet Union's active involvement, even though it was marginal, was a hindrance to the formulation of an overall and coherent independent policy for the whole issue. The Soviet Union was still a power emerging on the international scene, still searching for a role. The internal developments of the Soviet Union after World War II and external constraints constituted an obstacle to finding, or even seeking to find, a defined and clear-cut foreign policy.

The Palestinian question was thus considered by the Soviet Union after World War II in its regional context rather than as a Jewish–Palestinian issue. The conflict was seen as one to be solved within an international arena, for the conflict had engulfed the whole region and the Soviet Union would have a role to play therein.[1] Nevertheless, the Soviets had no clear-cut policy on the Palestinian issue except to advocate 'cooperation between the Arab and Jewish masses against imperialism'.[2]

Soviet reporting and analysis of the situation approached it from a different point of view and was basically centered on the British role. Writing in *Pravda*, the Soviet commentator Boris Izakov stated:

> In the British White Paper published in 1939 Palestine was promised independence by 1949, on condition that the Jewish–Arab dispute was settled. . . . On the other hand, neighboring Transjordan has received a half-backed independence for which she exchanged her position as a mandate policy. . . . In fact, Transjordan remains a British military base in the Middle East, and the granting of independence appears an unsavory trick.'[3]

As early as the beginning of 1946, the Soviets had an interest on the question of Palestine and Jewish emigration to Palestine. All Soviet discussion was founded on a single approach. The question was an internal problem – that is, the direct participation of the feuding parties concerned.[4] At the same time, there was no role for the Soviet Union to play except to condemn British policy in the area concerned and especially the Working Paper of the United Nations Commission on the question of Palestine. The decision to partition Palestine was considered the appropriate solution and a 'just' one for both Arabs and Jews.[5] Gromyko, chief Soviet delegate to the UN, speaking at a gathering of the American Committee of Jewish Writers, Artists and Scientists, stated the Soviet Union's hope of cooperation with the Americans to solve the Palestinian problem, and added:

> We cannot agree with the assertion which implies that the decision on the Partition of Palestine is aimed against the Arabs and Arab countries. It is our deep conviction that this decision corresponds to fundamental national interests of both Jews and the Arabs . . . The Soviet Union supports and cannot

but support the aspirations of any state and any people, no matter how small its weight in international affairs, in the struggle against foreign dependence and remnants of colonial oppression.[6]

Gromyko's speech had set out three main Soviet foreign policy objectives. While he acknowledged the right of 'Displaced Persons' – the term coined at the time for Jews – to both a homeland and a state, at the same time he acknowledged the right of the Arab inhabitants of Palestine to an independent state of their own. Furthermore, and perhaps more important, the two future states, in the Soviet Union's view, would be able to get rid of 'British colonialism'; thus the Soviet Union would be able to penetrate the area through the political aspirations of the countries concerned. The establishment of two states would, therefore, most certainly serve Soviet designs in the area. The pursuit of a non-discriminatory approach to both Jews and Arabs would most certainly mean that the Soviet Union was far more advanced than any other power – in particular, the other members of the Big Five at the United Nations. Lastly, the Arab inhabitants of Palestine, if given an independent state, would be or would become an 'anti-colonial' state and so serve two purposes. Firstly, it would be rid of the 'colonial' power of Britain and their 'agents', the national bourgeoisie of traditional leaders of both Palestine and what was then known as Transjordan (for example, the grand Mufti of Palestine, who allegedly had a record of collaboration with Nazi Germany). Secondly, Palestine would reach the stage of establishing 'democracy' with a multi-party system of institutions because of the very nature of the emergent, progressive states. None the less, Arab fears that the Soviet Union would interfere in the area, particularly Palestine, were voiced by King Abdullah of Transjordan in an interview after the Partition Plan had been accepted at the United Nations. He spoke in the strongest terms, saying that he 'had reason to believe . . . that many Russian officers and officials were working with the Haganah and that Russian arms and ammunition were being supplied to the Jewish forces'.[7]

When the Palestine Committee was set up in November 1945 by the USA and Britain, K. Sorezhin argued in *New Times*[8] that the Committee's recommendation did not put forward proposals to 'ameliorate' the conditions of European Jews who had suffered Nazi persecution, but was aimed at strengthening the position of the

Committee members in the Middle East, and the only 'constructive' recommendation that was made was to allow 'displaced persons' to emigrate to Palestine. He went on to argue that Britain's infamous Balfour Declaration of November 1917, which promised a 'national home' for Jews in Palestine, had led to the purchase of Arab land by 'reactionary' Zionists which added to the fomenting crisis within the Arab community. Because of Britain's stand, armed struggle ensued between the Arab and Jewish communities. The question of British involvement in Palestine and the far-Right reactionary movement of Zionism, which were to be blamed in the whole Palestine question, led to antagonism between the two communities. The proclamation of a *Jewish state* was not attacked or even condemned by the Soviet Union and so the policy of *two* states emerged. At the end of the deal, it was to this policy that it adhered.

In a later article Sorezhin made almost the first mention of Tel Aviv by Soviet commentators, called it a 'product of Jewish capitalist immigration', and a 'symbol of Zionist paradise'.[9] No other Palestinian town matched it in modernity, and he cited the Balfour Declaration which showed that the British were behind these designs. Palestine 'was occupied by British troops', and Jewish immigration into Palestine through the medium of the Zionist movement meant the strengthening of British rule in Palestine, which was conducive to the resulting Arab revolt. He argued that because of American capital in Palestine and the Middle East, Britain had embarked on a deal with Zionism and, at the same time, strengthened already deep resentment of Arab leaders in Jewish quarters. Throughout twenty-five years of Mandatory British rule over Palestine, 'normal' conditions of existence for the Jews had not been created.

L. Sedin,[10] however, argued that by the end of World War II a new form of Arab demand had emerged that had asked for independence from Western powers to end the old era of 'oppression'; but with the arrival of the USA, a new scene had overtaken the Arab world, for the former slowly supplanted the British in the area and replaced their role with their own exploitation of oil, taking over the strategic situation of the Arab world. His argument was to the effect that the question of Palestine, with its concomitant problems, had diverted Arab attention from their own impending problems of foreign domination and exploitation, and the British claimed that if the Palestine problem had not existed, 'it would have been worth inventing'. Since the situation in Palestine had deteriorated, it enabled the British to justify their physical presence in Palestine. Even though they were inciting Jews against the Arabs and vice versa, the British tried to convey a message that they were the 'guardians of order and security' in the Arab world. Another accusation was that the British had regarded the 'Palestinian problem not only as a means of furthering the antagonism between the Jewish and Arab inhabitants of Palestine, but were also inciting the Arabs against the Soviet Union'. The latter's position at the UN had been portrayed as anti-Arab. He went on to argue that the Soviet Union, in voting on the Palestinian question at the UN, had followed the majority of the delegates supporting the resolution, because 'under existing conditions that [was] the only possible *practical* solution' and that it was a 'minority' of delegates who proposed the resolution that the establishment of a feudal state in Palestine of Arab and Jewish states was conceivable, given the prevailing circumstances there (emphasis added). He then noted that the policy of the Soviet Union and its delegation at the UN was 'aimed at one sole objective', which was that the future and destiny of Palestine should be 'entrusted to the peoples that inhabit her as early as possible'.[11] Nevertheless, the whole argument was intended to be a critique of the role Britain played in the area in general and in Palestine in particular. For the Soviet Union, Britain had reached its zenith so far as world power was concerned; it was at a stage where it was declining and was no longer a world power. On the other hand, the US was becoming entangled in the area.

To two rhetorical questions on the subject of the Partition Plan – 'what will be the boundaries of the interdependent Arab and Jewish states into which Palestine is to be divided in accordance with this decision and what will be the geographical, economic and political character of the two states?' – A. Dannuniboir volunteered the following answer:

> Dividing the land of Palestine between Jews and Arabs,
> though sometimes unevenly, of which the most important of
> the whole answer was the industrialization of the City of
> Jerusalem whereby authority on it will be exercised in the
> name of the UN by a Trusteeship Council. Moreover, the two
> anticipated states will share the irrigation and power resources
> of the River Jordan and would have equal rights to exploit the
> natural resources of the Dead Sea.[12]

61

Throughout his narrative the author neglected two points: *how* to implement such a division of Palestine into two states with regional and international obligations; whether the local inhabitants, Jews or Arabs (and if Arabs, *which* Arabs), would accept such a division.

Needless to say, even had there been a likelihood of success, the dual-state policy would have encountered resistance from both Arabs and Jews, for it went counter to both Zionist designs and Arab aspirations to thwart the Zionist movement in Palestine. Even if the Partition Plan had been accepted, its implementation by the UN would have entailed the Soviet Union having a role to play in solving the problem, for the whole problem would have had to be discussed and enforced through a unanimous consensus of the members of the Security Council, which meant that the Soviet Union would have to deal with the problem in view of the diminishing role of Britain.

By the end of the 1940s, the Soviet perception as to how and to what extent the Arab-Jewish Palestinian problem should be resolved had different facets but one general approach. It was argued, at the time, that both Jewish and Arab inhabitants of Palestine should, or should have the right to, establish *two* separate states. But it meant that both sides would have to set aside several existing conditions. The first was that the area should cease to be under the control of 'imperialism', notably British but also that of the United States, which was now entering the picture. The Soviet standpoint was that *both* the Arabs and Jews should have a right to self-determination; independence would be granted by the middle of the decade, but an interim government must exist and be entrusted to a special agency or commission under the supervision, if need be, of the UN Security Council, in which the Soviet Union would have a role to play.[13]

Certain points remain for consideration, the first being that of how and to what extent the Arabs would be able to establish an independent state given the 'imperialistic' nature of the area's existing rule. Because this question remained without a satisfactory answer the Soviet Union's knowledge of Zionist aspirations and its political program, which sought to further its dream of a state in the area, seems to have been misunderstood immediately after World War II. It is important to note here that the Arab inhabitants of Palestine were in such a state of disarray that the success of their whole movement for independence, even without taking into consideration the impending struggle against Zionism, was rendered almost impossible. The only way in which the Soviet Union could play a role was through the medium of a UN consensus on the idea of supervising the establishment of *two* states in the area. Between the announcement of the UN Partition of Palestine on 29 November 1947 and the declaration of the State of Israel on 15 May 1948 the Soviet Union gained enough time to play a role both as one of the Big Five at the UN and outside, notably among Arab states.[14]

The Soviet Union's attitude to the Arab League

Soviet commentary on Arab development was wide-ranging and versatile. In 1948, on the third anniversary of the formation of the Arab League, L. Sedin wrote an argumentative article in *New Times*[15] in which he argued that after World War II the Arab League had come into being at a time when 'national liberation movements' in the world had markedly advanced, and that the League had been established to achieve Arab unity and the fulfillment of Arab aspirations. Nevertheless, Britain's role in the whole affair, as a patron of the League, demonstrated a desire to link the League to its own orbital and global designs and to use it for its own objectives. Though the League, Sedin argued, was the product of 'intricate' play and of conflicting interests, it would have to achieve several objectives, the basic demands being those of the Arab national liberation movement – that is, the withdrawal of foreign forces, basically the British, from the Arab world, the ending of the Mandate system, the abolition of unequal treaties and the establishment of 'genuine' independence.

The League, Sedin went on, had not fulfilled these demands and had failed to exploit the existing conditions in order to further Arab aspirations. The League's policy with regard to the Palestinian dispute not only consumed all its energies but because of its opposition to the UN decision to set up 'two' independent states in Palestine could only serve the interests of Britain.

From its inception, he argued, the Arab League had been unable to sustain itself and resist pressure, notably from the Western world. Moreover, it had become an instrument in the 'hands of the invaders of the Arab peoples', and its leaders had a tendency to be pro-American and British. Finally, the League had not pursued the ideal of seeking the unification of the Arab people, but merely constituted a 'combination' of Arab rulers who guarded their own interests.

Perhaps the argument had some justification, for at the time of the formation of the Arab League both Syria and Lebanon were still under French Mandate, Egypt and Iraq were still bound by treaties with Britain and Transjordan was still under British Mandate. The formation of the League was probably the most the Arab states could achieve at the time. It provided a forum within which disputes and grievances could be aired and direct, perhaps useful, contacts could be made between the leaders of the Arab world. None the less, it was not seen as a force to finalize all pending disputes but it was hoped that it would be a first step toward the achievement of the cherished idea of Arab unity.

The idea of establishing the Arab League resulted from several factors that emerged during and after World War II. One of these was to achieve the solution of Palestinian problems, through the offices of the British, by creating a sort of Arab federation whereby the issues could be jointly debated. There existed in the minds of many, however, a mistaken idea that by creating a federation of the Arabs, the fear of Jewish domination might be diminished and opposition to British suzerainty might be reduced. Finally, the British hoped that the French stand over Syria and Lebanon would be weakened, for at the time the rivalry between the two powers for domination of the area could not be ignored.

The Soviet Union had some reservations about the founding of the Arab League. In the first place, the League originated from Western initiative for regional aims – namely, to safeguard Western interests in the Arab world, amongst which the question of security was prominent. Secondly, to the Soviet Union such regional collaboration would mean the establishment of some sort of military pact which in the end would be basically anti-Communist. In the third place, it may be thought that such regional designs, if successful, would constitute a hindrance to progress toward the attainment of genuine political independence for Arab member states. Finally, such close Arab cooperation, tied to the West, would mean that given prevailing Arab conservatism, the suppression of any progressive elements in the Arab world would be vital to Western interests.

The Arab League, nevertheless, was seen as a forum for espousing grievances and, it was hoped, one where Arab political aims would somehow converge with Western objectives. The Soviet Union considered the Arab region as a domain of Western influence and any move to group the Arab world into some sort of regional unity would ultimately mean a significant development that, in the final analysis, would be directed against the Eastern bloc at the head of which was the Soviet Union. The strategic position of the Arab world and the richness of its oil deposits ranked high in Soviet considerations and the Palestinian question was a factor of major importance. The League was preoccupied with this latter question in one form, whereas the Soviet Union's attitude had changed drastically to that of fulfilling the aspirations of the two communities, Arab and Jewish, which the League members had rejected in totality.

The Soviet Union's reaction to the creation of Israel

From its inception the State of Israel faced Arab hostility. When on 13 May 1948 Britain announced the termination of its Mandatory power in Palestine hostilities broke out between Arabs and Jews. A. Kanukinov argued that they were the result of the UN decision to partition Palestine.[16] An article in *Pravda* in May 1948 argued that

> By means of armed force, the Arab states seek to prevent the realization by the Jewish people of their rights to national self-determination and creation of their independent state. The actions taken by the Arab states cannot be qualified as other than an act of unprovoked aggression infringing on the lawful rights of the Jewish people in violating the basic principles of the [UN] Charter.[17]

The Soviet press put part of the blame on the British, who were said to be behind all the turmoil and upheaval, and part on what it termed 'Arab aggression', behind which the Arab governments internally were 'suppressing' all the democratic forces in the Arab world.

On 15 May 1948 the troops of Transjordan, Egypt, Lebanon, Syria, Iraq and Saudi Arabia crossed the Palestinian borders and attacked the newly born State of Israel. Giving a detailed military account of the situation, Kanukinov argued that the Arab forces which 'invaded' Palestine (as he put it) were composed of various groupings and that 'volunteers' were composed of 'reactionary and semi-fascist' organizations such as the Muslim Brotherhood, the Lebanese Phalange, the Brothers of Freedom etc. while amongst

Arab ranks and army units were a number of German Nazis and Turkish officers; as for the Iraqi army, this was composed 90 per cent of Shi'ite Arabs, the rest being Kurds. He continued that although the Arab armies were sent under a unified command directed by the Arab League, 'serious rivalry' was revealed among them from the beginning of the 'invasion'. Moreover, the kings of Egypt and Saudi Arabia hastened to dispatch their main forces to join the army which had advanced furthest, that of King Abdullah of Transjordan, and they were aiding Abdullah 'not only with armed forces but also with the Hitler ex-mufti of Jerusalem, Amin El-Hussani, who aspired to be president of a united and indivisible Palestine'.[18] The British, he argued, were behind the events that engulfed Palestine and British intelligence coordinated the staff actions of the Arab armies. To his argument he added that both British and American weaponry had been furnished for the use of the Arab armies just as the Iraqi army could not have moved without the permission of the British. Furthermore, the armies of Saudi Arabia could not have acted without the direction and permission of the Americans, and the policy of the Western powers was to inflame national passions in the Arab East, resulting in armed intervention by the Arab countries in Palestine. Finally he stated:

> Throughout every stage of discussion of Palestine's future, the Soviet Union had pursued a clear and consistent policy in defense of the interest of *both the peoples* of Palestine international security. The recognition of the Soviet Union of the State of Israel and its provisional government will facilitate the fulfillment of the decision of the United Nations and the establishment of peace in Palestine.[19] [emphasis added]

This argumentative analysis needs comment. In the first place, it portrays the Arabs as the aggressors, though by implication, against the newly declared State of Israel. In the second place, the analysis given of the composition of Arab armies was that they were riddled with 'reactionary' forces, and it attacks the motives and designs of the Western powers. In the third place, and concomitant with the previous argument, the ranks of the Arab army were composed of reactionary elements and alleged former associates of the Nazis, an allegation that must be treated with some reservation. The two final points deserve some further consideration in the light of future developments, for, in the first place, the argument presented seems to justify the defensive measures undertaken by the newly established State and, by implication, that it had the right to exist. It sees the Soviet Union's old solution to the problem, that of two states in Palestine, as the best option. Finally, the commentary is markedly silent on the development that engulfed the new State of Israel, for no question was posed as to *how* and to *what extent* Israel was able to counter the 'invading' Arab armies; and what, above all, would be the designs of Zionism in the Arab world and Palestine in particular? What is important in this Soviet narration is the fact that Zionism, as a movement, implied the negation of the existence of any Palestinian state whether in Palestine proper or in any other Arab country.

On the subject of the United Nations and the Palestinian question Soviet commentators were emphatic on how to deal with the problem. Following six discussions in the General Assembly the majority had voted for the Partition of Palestine in the resolution adopted in November 1947; subsequently, in the Security Council, both the Soviet and Ukranian delegations were of the opinion that the UN decision on the division of Palestine should be implemented; the Soviet stand was unchanged, and the best solution remained the establishment of a 'democratic' state in Palestine where both the Arabs and Jews would have states of their own.

It can be seen, in retrospect, that the existence of Israel as an entity was *not* in question as far as the Soviet Union was concerned. The solution advocated by them was considered to be the best under the prevailing circumstances because it conformed 'to the national interests of both people, each of which has a right to independent statehood, and would promote tranquility in the Middle East, and hence international security'.[20] The Soviet position not only meant, intrinsically, that the existence of the State of Israel should be guaranteed but it also showed a certain misunderstanding of the outlook and aspirations of both communities in Palestine; above all, it overlooked the position of the Arab governments on the Palestinian question.

It was argued that the Soviet Union had made two proposals in UN debates; the first was for the 'withdrawal' of the armed groups that had 'invaded' Palestine – that is, the Arab forces – whose aim had been to stop the implementation of the UN decision; the second, concomitant with the first, was for the termination of the 'invasion' by armed forces. From the point of view of the Soviet Union, the

Arab armies were 'financed' by the British taxpayer, the oil interests of the West in the Arab world being behind Western maneuvers. Arab troops, it was alleged, were trained by British officers to take part in the 'hostilities' being fomented in the area. Finally, according to the commentator, 'the Soviet Union is consistent in its policy. Considering the Partition of Palestine into two states the most just and correct solution in the given circumstances it recognized the State of Israel proclaimed in accordance with the decision of the United Nations.'[21] Two main ideas emerge from this discussion; the first is that the central element in the whole affair is the fomenting of disturbances in the area by the British and other Western powers in their scramble for oil; the second is that Arab forces had designed and carried out a plot of 'aggression' against the newly established State of Israel, due, it is presumed, to the entanglement of Britain, which took the side of the Arabs.

To the Arabs, the first Arab–Israeli war was fundamentally a just war against the incursion of Zionism into the heart of the Arab world; the creation of a foreign state on its soil meant, by its nature, that the Palestinians would have to carry the burden and consequences of such an act. To the Soviet Union, however, the whole issue centered on the plight of the Jews after World War II and their hope for the creation of an entity that would fulfill their aspirations and their longing for a state of their own. The Palestinians, however, were also entitled to a state of their own. This dual Soviet program not only illuminates its misunderstanding of the situation but also the reality that, for their own different reasons, neither the Jewish nor the Arab communities would accept two states.

5 The Soviet Union's recognition of Israel: the natural link

Almost all governments welcomed the establishment of the State of Israel, for various reasons. The question of 'Jewish guilt' was one of the most important factors. The horror of the Jews' experience of Nazism was of such magnitude that it became the justification for the Jewish people to establish their own independent state. Such a step was universally welcome, for this development relieved the world's conscience in a *practical* way. There was thus little difficulty in achieving the recognition of the newly established State of Israel since both East and West were of the opinion that the Jewish people deserved and had the right to exist as an independent entity in virtue of their sufferings under the Nazis. The Soviet Union was the first state to recognize Israel *de jure*. To a certain extent Soviet recognition sprang from its own harsh experience of the Nazi invasion of the Soviet Union, for in a sense this created a common enemy, so Soviet *de jure* recognition was almost unthinking. In addition, the Soviet Union undoubtedly had a definite conception of why the Jews aspired to an identity of their own and thought that such a development would definitely solve the Jewish question and rid them of suffering. Needless to say, the Soviet Union, if indeed it had any idea of the ideology of Zionism, regarded it as incomprehensible, for Zionism had the long-term strategic objective of extending Palestine to the Euphrates. Moreover, the magnitude and far-reaching aspirations of the exponents of Zionism at the time were realized and fulfilled only in a small and relatively insignificant geographical area of the Arab world and the Middle East. But in a practical sense there remained the fact that a state with all its various apparatus, essentially military, had been established, had become a reality in the midst of an ocean of backwardness and in an arena dominated by Arab entities basically divided in every aspect that the imagination can conjure up.

Concomitant with this, the Soviet Union was bewildered as to how a unified Arab nation ever could, or was likely to, exist. To a major foreign power such as the Soviet Union even the concept of Arab nationalism must have appeared as an idea void of all practical reality. The map of the Arab world showed the scattered domains of a multitude of tribal entities and monarchical thrones lumped together and divided between the spheres of influence of the Western camp, notably Britain and France. This division of the spheres of influence left the Soviet Union with no other choice than to find an outlet through Israel to penetrate the region, for the Soviet Union had no close relations of any sort with the Arab world, save those with Arab Communist parties which, in turn, had no meaningful political role to play in the Arab world. It is significant here that the domination of the Arab world in all aspects was totally under the influence, direct or nominal, of the Western European powers. It was their powerful presence that warranted the struggle to acquire influence in the Arab world for a power like the Soviet Union. It demanded slow and progressive steps, notably through diplomatic means, towards finding an opening in the region. Israel granted an opportunity that could not be neglected. The benefits of recognition were thus reciprocal. Israel benefited from the fact that the leader of the Communist international movement had accepted the idea of recognition, which in a practical sense meant that other Communist states, with the exception of the People's Republic of China which had not yet declared itself as an independent state, followed suit. Soviet recognition was a forceful backing for the existence of the new state as an independent entity in its own right. Recognition by both East and West introduced a new dimension to the balance of power in the region because Israel would be able to defeat all Arab armies combined and establish a newly built entity with all the infrastructures of a state. That was the reality generated from pragmatism. Soviet recognition attested to the degree to which Israel was able, and in a position, to maneuver both the Eastern and Western camps to fulfill its own ultimate objectives.

In so far as Israel had been created by the emigration of Soviet and Eastern European Jews it is natural that a natural link between the two countries should exist. Since the Soviet Union wished to penetrate the Arab world but was hindered by the division of the world into different political spheres of influence, it was not unnatural for it to make use of the several opportunities Israel offered it. The first was a unique chance to observe the political developments in the area at close range. Changing circumstances rendered insufficient, and indeed unsatisfactory, the gathering of information from either the Palestinian or Iraqi Communist Parties, for these two channels of information presented a basic and overwhelmingly theoretical analysis rooted in the role and unity of the toiling masses. The second was that by legalizing its Communist Party, Israel afforded the Soviet Union an opportunity to become involved in the region. Thus when Soviet scholars count amongst the reasons for recognition the statement that Israel was the only 'democratic' state in the region,[1] they mean only that there existed in Israel a certain norm of freedom which permitted the Israeli Communist Party to function legally. All Arab Communist parties were illegal, with the exception, perhaps, of the relatively insignificant Lebanese Communist Party. The Israeli Communist Party was able to maneuver freely and have an Arabic ear for its more wide-ranging political platform. When the Soviet Union acknowledged the existence of the State of Israel it gained the luxury of maneuvering the Israeli Communist Party so that it would fall in with its own overall political objectives. The Soviet Union had only to evaluate its approaches to the Arab world in the light of the existing conditions and assess to what extent the Israeli Communist Party was able effectively to maneuver within Israel.

Another strong reason for the Soviet Union's recognition of Israel can fairly be explained by the political conditions pertaining in the Arab world at the time. To the Soviet Union, the dominant power of Britain in the area constituted a threat that had to be opposed by all possible means. Palestine offered a political opportunity. Arabs and Zionists were engulfed in a struggle so violent for most of the time that Britain, as a Mandatory power, was left in an unenviable situation. The Soviet Union blamed all the discontent on Britain, although it viewed the whole situation as part and parcel of eliminating Britain from Palestine. At the same time, the Soviet Union was of the opinion that Palestine should be partitioned by Arabs and Jews into two states. However, the Soviet Union's ambivalent foreign policy at this period was clouded by uncertainties. For example, if the British withdrew from Palestine, what assurances were there that an independent Arab state would be created? It appears that the Soviet Union did not have a clear explanation of this question. This element in Soviet objectives in the

Arab world, particularly in Palestine, produced another which was important to the Arab side. It evolved from the notion that the Soviet Union's recognition meant that not only had a major world power extended recognition to Israel, but also that Communist states all over the world would follow suit. The Palestinians had to counter all the burdens that the establishment of a Jewish state laid on them. The magnitude of the implications of the Soviet act of recognition had to be faced. The Soviet Union's stand should not be confused or thought to mean the same as recognition by Western powers, for the simple reason that the Soviet Union differed from the rest by being the citadel of Communism which believed, among other things, in upholding the rights of the disinherited Palestinian people.

Obviously, once the Soviet Union established formal diplomatic relations with Israel, it became involved directly in the Arab–Israeli conflict which resulted from Israel's creation and sooner or later it would have to decide how far it was willing to proceed in its relations with Israel. Israel had been created by Soviet and Eastern European Jewish emigration to Palestine. Because of this the Soviet Union hoped that perhaps Israel would provide a route for the achievement of socialism. The argument put forward by most Arab intellectuals about the reasons for Soviet recognition of Israel tends to run that under Stalin notable Soviet Jews functioned in the power base and apparatus of the Soviet Union. The available evidence suggests otherwise. During Stalin's purges, high-ranking Party and military personalities were executed on different pretexts, especially in 1935; two of the leading Jewish Bolsheviks, Kamanev and Zinoviev, and earlier Leon Trotsky, each a well-documented case all lost their lives. At the same time, quite a few Jews followed Stalin's policies, amongst them Lazar M. Kazanovitch who was in charge of the forcible collectivization in the Ukraine. How far these Jewish followers of Stalin's policies had an effect on the recognition question is uncertain, for Soviet Jewish lobbyists amongst Stalin's high-ranking decision-makers cannot have seemed of major importance given the circumstances in the Soviet Union at the time. Even though in Stalin's time three of the Soviet Union's deputy foreign ministers, Maksin Libvinov, Nan Maiski and Solomon Iozovskii, were Jews, they lost their positions during the purges of 1946. The argument that the presence of Soviet lobbyists within the Soviet leadership influenced Stalin's decision to recognize Israel does not therefore hold good. The available evidence suggests rather that most Soviet Jews suffered in Stalin's purges. At the outbreak of World War II six million Jews had resided in the Soviet Union, making it the largest single Jewish community in the world.

During Stalin's rule prior to World War II, an attempt was made to resettle Soviet Jews in agricultural communes in the Ukraine and the Crimea; a Jewish commission known as the Kamzet was formed which designated the Biro-Bidzhan area as an agricultural Jewish settlement. None the less, the Jewish settlers were told that Zionism was a 'tool of British imperialism', whereas the Biro-Bidzhan area had a purpose not unlike areas inhabited by other nationalities within the Soviet Union. However, Biro-Bidzhan came to be viewed by the Soviet leadership as a Jewish settlement, not as an independent entity in its own right but as similar to other nationalities in the Soviet Union. In its initial phase, 1928, the Biro-Bidzhan area witnessed the settlement of a few thousand Jews, but they were not able to endure the hardships of life and many abandoned the project. When the Japanese invaded Manchuria in 1931 Stalin gave primary importance to settlements along the Soviet Union's common border with China. Three years later the idea of a Jewish settlement in Biro-Bidzhan received new impetus, and the Supreme Soviet officially declared it an autonomous Jewish region in 1934. But in 1935 Stalin announced his purges and the leaders of Biro-Bidzhan fell victim; Stalin abandoned his idea of resettling Soviet Jews.

But while like the rest of the population many had to endure the hardships of existence under Stalin, those with Zionist visions emigrated to Palestine to lay the foundations of the new State of Israel. These Soviet and Eastern European Jews took socialist ideas with them. Thus a natural bond between Soviet and Eastern European Jews and their original homeland existed in both practical and theoretical senses. It must nevertheless be emphasized that the idea of socialism emerged within the Zionist movement in Palestine out of necessity. External circumstances dictated in tenets on Zionism.

It is worthwhile to trace the background to the period of Stalin's rule, in particular the Balfour Declaration and the earlier Sykes-Picot agreement of 1916. The latter contained a plan for Britain and France to divide the Arab world between themselves after the collapse of the Ottoman Empire. The most backward entities in the Arab world (Saudi Arabia and Yemen) were to be allowed to obtain independent statehood. France was to take over Lebanon and Syria, while Britain would get Iraq and Transjordan; Palestine would be administered internationally. The Balfour Declaration grew out of the Sykes–Picot agreement, but its political repercussions outweighed the latter's impact on the Arab world as a whole. The two agreements were concluded at a time when the Soviet Union had power. Nevertheless the Bolsheviks were basically concerned with internal questions, and matters of foreign policy beyond its immediate border regions took second place. The Sykes–Picot consultations brought them to Petrograd to consult with the Russian government on the future domains of the Ottoman Empire.[2] Britain's share was extended from southern Syria across to Iraq and the area then known as the Persian Gulf, whereas France had a slice of North Africa and the Musel District of Iraq. Finally, Russia concentrated on what was then called Eastern Anatolia which adjoined a large section of the Turco-Russian frontier. However, the area which became known as Palestine was reserved for a 'special international regime', which at the same time became an area of dispute between the three powers. Whereas France was pressing to have all Syria, including Palestine, Britain opposed this plan for two reasons. Firstly, it wanted to have a port in the Acre–Haifa area for use as an outlet from Iraq to the Mediterranean; and secondly it did not welcome the idea of having either France or any other major power establishing itself on a route that came close to the Suez Canal.

This plan for the division of the remnant of the Ottoman Empire had a profound impact on the future political development of the Arab world, especially in relation to Palestine. It is interesting in this connection that Palestine was given international status, although apparently the area was designated for the use of the Jewish people. Thus even at this early stage of development the Jewish question was an issue that was thought of, planned for and above all connected with a piece of territory that suited the justification for a Jewish existence. At this early period when both Jewish statehood and the Jewish right to exist in Palestine were under consideration the Soviet Union was aware that the question of the Palestinian people was widely debated. It was agreed that the Jewish question had to be 'solved' in the manner that served the best interests of the Jewish people as a final solution. This solution, determined by all powers, both East and West, tallied with Zionist aspirations and plans for Palestine. It was certainly a political move with major consequences. But the choice of Palestine simply because it was a tract of land under direct British rule as the land which would fulfill the Zionist dream implied for the Soviet Union the need for its own encroachment on the Arab world.

By 1948 the sheer weight of numbers of Jews assembled in Palestine, many of them from the Soviet Union and Eastern Europe, brought into being 'natural links' between the new state and the original homelands of its settlers. Immigration had started at the end of the nineteenth century and it occurred in waves, each new wave of settlers bringing political ideas of different hues and shades to color the existing pattern. The theoretical aspect of the socialist thought and orientation of Zionism was made up of two elements which, it should be emphasized, complemented each other. One of these elements at least, the socialist orientation of Zionism, had its fundamental origins in Russia and Eastern Europe and thus almost inevitably influenced the Soviet decision to recognize the newly created State of Israel. But to explain the existence of this 'natural link' we must examine the historical background of the Jews in Czarist Russia.

In 1818, the Jewish members of Eastern European societies were divided according to the following figures: 68 per cent were merchants, 11·6 per cent were professionals and 1·9 per cent were peasants.[3] The transformation of Jews to a proletarian class produced two contradictory elements; as part of the proletariat they came to believe in socialist thought, but in their struggle for an economic amelioration of their conditions, non-Jewish elements came into competition with other economic strata of the societies in which they existed. This second element led the Jews to a period of isolation, which in turn caused non-Jewish members of society to be anti-Semitic. By the end of the nineteenth century, a Jewish socialist movement was initiated which manifested itself in the creation of a Socialist-Marxist movement called the Bund, an association of socialist Jews drawn from Poland and Russia. The association's basic concern was the furthering of Jewish socialism. From its inception the Bund, as a socialist association of Jews, rejected Zionism. But at the same time the Bund recognized that the plight of the Jews could be solved in two ways: by socialism and by the par- ticularly Jewish nature of the movement. The Marxists in the Bund, though they too rejected Zionism, were not able to tackle the issue of Jewish isolationism in the societies in which they dwelt. The Bund, however, at its conference in Russia in 1901, recognized the reality of the existence of a Jewish nationalist question, an issue that it had not previously accepted. The conference further demanded that the Russian authorities should designate an area in Russia as an autonomous Jewish domain.[4] This demand was put forward by the Russian Jews at the Bund Conference in 1905 in Russia. But the Bund was defeated in its objectives because of the contradictions existing between socialism and the idea of an independent community for the Jews.

Another important Jewish-socialist movement that originated in Russia was that called Poali Zion, which was established in 1897, from which sprang other Jewish socialist organizations. Poali Zion was led by Buroshov from the Ukraine. He was able to combine Marxism with Zionism, though he realized the existing contradictions between the two. He pointed out that a mental gap existed between the workers and the middle classes, which manifested itself in Zionism. He attempted to acknowledge also that there existed a link between Marxism and Zionism. The contradictory elements in Zionist and Marxist thought were the basic problems facing theoreticians on both sides. Marxism, which was based, among other things, on the betterment of workers' livelihood and the solving of class contradictions, could not be reconciled with Zionism simply because the latter's central thought was the plight of Jews in the world. It is worth mentioning here that although the World Zionist Workers applied for membership to the Second International, they were refused in 1907.[5]

Jewish emigration to Palestine began at the end of the nineteenth century, though the rate of immigration was not then regulated. Once the Eastern European Jews were in Palestine they rejected on socialist grounds the agricultural aristocracy they faced in the country. In the spring of 1907 the Zionist Workers' Party was organized under the leadership of Ben Gurion. Its general program consisted of the following principles; first, the nationalization of the means of production on a socialist basis, the only way to achieve this class struggle; second, on the national Jewish question, the Party aspired to the fulfillment of self-sovereignty for the Jewish people in Palestine; third, taking into consideration that the progress of the Jewish proletariat depended on the immigration of those who upheld the means of production, the Party thus undertook to struggle against all other forces that might constitute an obstacle to Jewish emigration to Palestine; fourth, for the sake of Palestine and for the freedom of working within it, the Party would send representatives to attend the Zionist International Conference.[6]

Zionist organizations in Palestine were responsible for the introduction of the economic unit which became known as the kibbutz, an agricultural collective unit that rejected free ownership. The institution developed out of the socialist background from which the immigrants originated – ie the Soviet Union and Eastern Europe, and as a weapon to face the exigencies of existing conditions. The kibbutz was basically an agricultural-economic cooperative unit around which all other aspects of daily existence were built. It centered on the struggle against the conditions that Soviet and Eastern European Jews had to face both immediately on arrival and thereafter. At the time the fact that the new economic units were to constitute the nucleus for building a Zionist state was not recognized, but they were in reality one further bond in the 'natural link' between the newly established State of Israel and the Soviet Union and Eastern European states.

Zionism as a political movement to establish a Jewish national homeland in Palestine existed in Russia long before Theodor Herzl wrote his famous book, *The Jewish State*, in 1896. The theoretical origin of socialism dates back to Czarist Russia in the 1870s and 1880s when the majority of Jews lived in southern and western Russia, Poland, Lithuania and Galicia. Soviet Jews were at the time influenced by the revolutionary upheavals taking place amongst Russian intellectuals. One of the Russian Jewish gatherings, known as the Vilna Circle, was established in 1872, and from it came the 'fathers' of Jewish socialism. It was from this time onward that the Soviet Jewish proletariat came into being, although Czarist oppression led to mass Jewish emigration to England and the United States.

This Jewish-socialist-oriented outlook was responsible for the foundation of the General League of Jewish Workers in Lithuania, Russia and Poland in 1897 in Vilna, popularly called the Bund. Its basic aim became the creation of an 'inclusive association' that would embody all Jewish workers within the borders of Czarist Russia. Its Founding Congress decided that the movement should embrace all 'militant Jewish workers' and that it should pave the way for Jewish workers to join the general proletarian struggle. However, the idea and concept of explicit communism was not mentioned by the Bund, a fact which Lenin later criticized for the absence of Marxism in its program. The founders of the Bund, who originated from the Jewish intelligentsia, considered themselves to be Russian socialists who were supposed to execute the task of carrying out agitation and organization within the ranks of the Jewish population. The Bund's national program rejected the ideas of assimilation and Russification and began to unfold the idea of 'national striving' of Jewish workers. However, the general political platform was not amenable to reaching a definite conclusion on a Zionist territorial solution of the overall Jewish problem, for such aspirations were alien to the Bund. They were, moreover, beyond the outlook of Russia's Jewish proletariat and outside their personal experience. One of the major contradictions in the Bund centered on the denial of the international character of the Jewish proletariat movement, for it saw its main tasks as confined to Czarist Russia alone.

Ber Borochov, the pioneering theoretician of the Diaspora, criticized the Bund's attempt to define the cultural elements of Jewish history as 'reactionary'. He argued that

> The Bund has very much to its credit in its activity for the
> Jewish proletariat and the Bund's name is inscribed in letters
> of gold in the history of the Jewish labor movement; future
> generations of the Jewish proletariat will erect it a splendid
> monument in Palestine. It cultivated the Jewish workers'
> consciousness of themselves as a class, educated them to
> organized struggle for their interest, developed their spirit of
> discipline and cultivated their democratic concepts.[7]

However, a segment of the Jewish socialist intelligentsia rejected the National Program of the Bund, their basic reason for disenchantment being the lack of concentration of Jewish people in the territory of Palestine. They sought to correct this by concentrating Jewish workers in Palestine. Their leader was Chaim Zhitlowsky, one of the noted figures of the populist wing of Russian socialism. In his writings at the end of the nineteenth century he emphasized the notion that Russian Jews did not hold assimilationist ideas, and in a series of articles portrayed what he perceived to be the core of the Jewish revolutionary struggle to further the sense of Jewish nationalism and culture. It was at this same time that the tenets of socialism began to penetrate the Zionist movement. One of the advocates of the idea of socialist Zionism at the end of the nineteenth century was Nahman Syrkin, who maintained that Zionism and socialism were compatible. In 1901 he wrote:

Zionism is not possible without Soviet Zionism. That is what
broadens the concept of Palestine and makes it possible to
begin immediately in materializing the Jewish State. It brings
Zionism and the material and spiritual interests of the masses
of the People into agreement and transforms Zionism into a
great ideal for which it will fight and live. It arouses the
healthy, enlightened and ambitious elements in Judaism and
makes them the pioneers leading the camp. We socialist
Zionists now raise the flag of true freedom for the Jewish
people: we rejuvenate Judaism by bringing to every one of its
cells the great idea of Socialism.[8]

The compatibility of Zionism and socialism effected a combination
of those in the Jewish labor movement and those who upheld
socialism within the Zionist movement, which called itself Paoli
Zion, the Workers of Zion. There were other socialist Jews who
rejected the idea of class struggle and the struggle for socialism until
after emigration to Palestine; they abhorred indulgence in political
underground activities in the countries they dwelt in. Political
divisions among the Jewish population were a natural outcome of
these debates, one of which was between declarative Zionism, which
devoted much time to debating the final political goal of the
movement, and practical Zionism, which laid stress on putting
Zionist theory into practice. The majority of those supporting the
latter were from Eastern Europe. It was in Kiev in 1906 that these
debates culminated in the creation of the Socialist Jewish Workers'
Party.

In the unfolding of events in Russia where populism prevailed and
with the approach of World War I, most Russian Zionists identified
themselves as Zionist socialists. Consequently, 'when the second
countryside Congress of the Russian Ziere Zion [Youth of Zion] met
in St Petersburg in May 1917, most of the members considered
themselves *personally* to be socialists of one shade or another'[9]
(emphasis in original). However, the differing political coloring of
the movement emerged later at a meeting in Kharkov in May 1920
when socialism was formally accepted and a socialist party was
created. At the same time the movement started to gain momentum
in Eastern European countries with headquarters in Prague and
Poland. However, Ziere Zion set about establishing its political
organization on a worldwide basis, with its center in Palestine. Its
centers in the Soviet Union and Eastern Europe formed a new

organization named the Alliance of Socialist-Zionist Workers in 1921. The leadership of this Alliance was drawn from the Soviet Union, Poland, Lithuania, Palestine, the United States and Germany. An attempt was made to create a parliament encompassing all these Jewish traditions in the form of political autonomy.

Chronologically, Jewish waves of emigration to Palestine divided into the First Aliya, 1882–1900; Second Aliya, 1901–1918; Third Aliya, 1919–1923; Fourth Aliya, 1924–1927; and Fifth Aliya, 1929–1944. The Second Aliya coincided with revolutionary upheavals in Russia between 1905 and 1907. Events at this time demonstrated the longing for social justice and the sense of national liberation imbued in the Jewish masses at this period when especially they were facing different kinds of prejudices. This led Jews to plan seriously to emigrate to Palestine in the hope of finding a solution to their problems in the homeland. The Palestinian Poali Zion made a major contribution in instilling Marxism and the idea of class struggle into Palestinian Jewish workers and masses, and creating certainties between the average Jewish worker 'and the international Jewish workers' movement, in laying the foundations of urban trade unions and the beginnings of trade union and educational activity among the Oriental communities, etc., in addition to their activities in Hashomer and Hahoresh'.[10] Internationally, however, the Poali Zion organization was not a coherent unified movement. One wing adopted Marxism while also maintaining a territorial claim to Palestine. In Czarist Russia its members leaders leaned fervently toward revolutionary underground activities, adhered to orthodox Marxism and were exponents of military socialism. In the first decade of the twentieth century, the Palestinian Poali Zion was connected to, and influenced by, the socialist appeal of Russia. However, in 1909 the American Poali Zion rejected Marxism by abandoning the principle of class struggle.

Another political party called Ahdut Haavod (Unity of Labor) was founded in 1919, most of whose participants were Jewish citizens from the Soviet Union and Eastern Europe. One notable figure among these was David Ben-Gurion, who represented Poali Zion. In Palestine itself the labour movement had sprung from, and had had as its backbone, the Zionist element of the Jewish labor movement in the Diaspora on the one hand and on the other the fathers and pioneering figures of the socialist wing of the Zionist movement. During the Third Aliya (1919–1923) appeals were made to unify the Jewish labor movement in Palestine, resulting almost immediately in the creation in December 1920 in Haifa of the General Federation of Jewish workers (Histadrut). The period of the Third Aliya brought with it a utopian idealism, which emigrants aspired to practise in Palestine. At this period Nahman Syrkin began to advocate certain 'constructive activities' which might suffice for the success of Zionism and socialism together. After World War I he went to Palestine with a Poali Zion delegation and reached some conclusions about building the country on 'cooperative' basis. In 1919 he wrote:

> Zionism faces two possibilities; one is that capital, both large and small, will flow in, in confusion, for fear of bolshevism, and start business, speculation, land competition, and bring in cheap labour from Egypt and Syria. Zionism will become a mockery for the Jewish worker and the Jewish nation; Palestine will become a refuge for frightened capitalists. The doctrine will be falsified and our land will belong to foreigners. The second is that the Jewish nation will make a great national effort, national capital will come and Zion will be built on a socialist cooperative basis. Jewish labor will prosper the spirit of Judaism living in the Bible, in Prophets, in the Midrash, in Hebrew philosophy and Hassidism, will its historical answer. If Zionism is imbued with this spirit, there will be a Jewish National Fund with an annual income of tens of millions, a national loan of hundreds of millions. Zionism will be able to turn to the entire progressive world for aid.[11]

The Jewish socialist orientation emanated from Russia, both under the Czars and later under the Bolshevik Revolution and also from Eastern Europe. It is worthwhile noting that socialism was adopted by certain influential Zionist leaders out of necessity, as a practical means of facing the prevailing conditions in Palestine; even if Zionist socialism did not adhere to the Marxist precept of class struggle, Soviet sympathies lay with this Zionist-Socialist trend. Undoubtedly, the origins of socialism in Israel of May 1948 date back to the nineteenth century in Russia and Eastern Europe.

Eventually the various parties, in particular Poali Zion and Hapoel Hatsair, merged in what became known later on as the Mapai Party. The success of the Bolshevik Revolution in 1917 led to the split of the world Jewish movement into 'right' and 'left' wings.

This split was based on the choice between joining the Communist International or participating in the Zionist Congresses. The left Jewish movement applied to join the Communist International in the hope of gaining support for Zionist territorial claims in Palestine, but the application was turned down in 1922. Nevertheless, the left wing Poali Zion continued to encourage Jewish emigration to Palestine and sought to achieve common ground with the Labor Zionist parties. Its argument ran as follows:

> The construction of a Jewish socialist Palestine can only come about in agreement with the main principles of revolutionary class struggle, and its development will take on strength with the development and victory of the social revolution. . . . Bourgeois Jewish settlement, conducted up to now on the basis of private property and exploitation, had gone completely bankrupt, both socially and nationally. The growth and success of the Jewish settlement in Palestine have proven that Palestine can only be built by the immigration and settlement of large masses of Jewish workers, supported by their own labor and organizing their activity according to the aims of constructive and creative socialism. . . . Together with class struggle we must even today – in the period of capitalism's transition to socialism – take all the practical and socio-economic measures both in the Diaspora and in Palestine for socialist settlement in Palestine and future dictatorship of the Jewish proletariat over Jewish life in Palestine.[12]

Ironically, the destruction of Jewish labor movements in Poland and other Eastern European countries negated the possibility of the existence of a Jewish labor movement in the Diaspora, the labor movement in present-day Israel being its only heir.

The last steps were taken when in May 1942 a Zionist conference was convened in Palestine under the leadership of Kaplanski, who held socialist beliefs and convictions. From this conference stemmed an organization called the Victory League. In August 1942 this organization convened its first meeting attended by, among others, two members of the Soviet Union's embassy in Ankara, Turkey.[13] These two Soviet envoys were 'impressed' by the idea and function of the kibbutz and the Israeli Labor Organization, the Histadrut – scarcely surprisingly in view of the prevailing backwardness of the Arab world. A similar reaction was experienced by the Soviet

Union's Deputy Foreign Minister, Ivan Mayski, when he paid a visit to Palestine[14] on 2 October 1943; both David Ben-Gurion and Golda Meir accompanied him when he visited and inspected the kibbutz. Nevertheless, in November 1942, the Mapai Party held a conference in which the delegates were divided between several opinions. Among these was that advocated and represented by Ben-Gurion, Secretary of the party, which argued that the United States was the main power able to defend Zionism in the building and founding of the future Jewish state.[15] Within the Zionist movement itself there emerged three political groupings: the first concentrated on relations with the United States, the second was under the leadership of Weizmann and devoted much attention to the role played by Britain, while finally, Jabotinsky's wing took upon itself to normalize and establish solid relations with the Soviet Union. This latter faction provided nominal aid to the Soviet Union's Red Army in April 1943 through the Soviet representative in Tehran. To the Soviet Union, the Zionist planners, with their socialist orientation, represented a politically 'progressive' trend, especially in contrast to the surrounding 'reactionary' Arab conditions, internal and external. The Zionist-socialist orientation was a major contributory factor to the Soviet Union's recognition of Israel in May 1948, largely because the upholders of Zionist-socialism originated from the Soviet Union and Eastern Europe.

Tables 1 and 2 indicate the background of Israeli Ministers from May 1948 to December 1972. Their relevance to our study is to indicate that the 'natural link' theory has its foundation in the number of immigrants who originated from the Soviet Union and Eastern Europe. These Zionist leaders in Israel must have played a role in influencing the Soviet decision to recognize Israel. Moreover, the Zionist leader were influenced by the socialist approach to building the newly established State of Israel that played a determining influence in Soviet decision-making in May 1948. The entire Arab world was then under the tutelage and domination of the two major Western European countries, France and Britain. The sea of Arab backwardness and political stagnation led the Soviet Union to believe that it was not possible to penetrate this Arab area politically under the prevailing circumstances, for internal conditions were not encouraging and there was no flicker of socialist orientation. It is thus perfectly possible, even if ironic, to argue that the first Soviet political foothold in the Arab world came through Israel in May 1948, even if temporarily Israel was to gain more politically and strategically from recognition than the Soviet Union.

Table 1: *Country background of Israeli Cabinet members,*
May 1948 – December 1972

Country of origin	Members	Percentage of Cabinet
Russia	18	28.1250
Poland	23	35.9375
Palestine	7	10.9375
Austria	1	1.5625
Romania	2	3.1250
Germany	6	9.3750
South Africa	1	1.5625
Iraq	1	1.5625
Canada	1	1.5625
Hungary	1	1.5625
Syria	1	1.5625
Bulgaria	1	1.5625
Yemen	1	1.5625
TOTAL	64	100

Table 2: *Geographical and national origins of Israeli Cabinet*
members, May 1948 – December 1972

Country/Geographic area	Members	Percentage of Cabinet
East Europe and U.S.S.R.	45	70.3125
West Europe	8	12.5000
Arab Countries	2	3.1250
Palestine	7	10.9375
Others	2	12.5000
TOTAL	64	100

Table 3: *Origins and ministerial posts of Israeli Cabinet members,*
May 1948 – May 1972

no.	Name	Place and date of birth	Party	Ministerial position	Period
1	Almogi, Yoseph Aaron	Poland, 1910–	Mapai-Rafi-ILP	Without Portfolio	Nov. 1961 – Sept. 1962
2	Aranne, Zalman	Russia, 1899–1970	Mapai-ILP	Without Portfolio	Jan. 1954 – June 1954
3	Bar Yehuda, Yisrael	Russia, 1895–1965	Ahudt Ha'avoda	Interior	Nov. 1955 – Nov. 1961
4	Barsilai, Yisrael	Poland, 1913–1970	Mapam	Health [Also Posts Without Portfolio]	Nov. 1955 – Nov. 1961; Nov. 1958 – Dec. 1959; Dec. 1969 – June 1970]
5	Begin, Menahem	Poland, 1913–	Herut-Gahal	Without Portfolio	June 1967 – Aug. 1970
6	Ben Aharon, Yitzhak	Romania, 1906–	Ahdut-Ha'avoda	Transport	Dec. 1959 – May 1962
7	Ben Gurion, David	Poland, 1886–1973	Mapai-Rafi-State List	Prime Minister and Defense Minister	May 1948 – June 1963
8	Mordekhai, Bentov	Poland, 1900–	Mapam	Labor and Construction	May 1948 – March 1949
9	Carmel, Moshe	Poland, 1911–	Ahdut-Ha'avoda	Transport	Nov. 1955 – Dec. 1959; May 1965 – Dec. 1969
10	Dinur, Ben Zion	Russia, 1884–1973	Mapai	Education and Culture	Oct. 1951 – Nov. 1955
11	Dultzin, Arye	Russia, 1913–	General Zionist Gahal	Without Portfolio	Dec. 1969 – Aug. 1970
12	Eshkol, Levi	Russia, 1895–1969	Mapai-ILP	Agricultural and Development, Finance, Prime Minister, Defense	Oct. 1951 – June 1967
13	Golili, Yisrael	Poland	Ahdut-Ha'avoda-ILP	Without Portfolio	Jan. 1966 – Jan. 1973
14	Geri, Jack Myer	Lithuania, 1901	Non-party	Commerce & Industry	Nov. 1950 – Oct. 1951
15	Govrin, Akiva	Russia, 1902–	Mapai	Without Portfolio	Dec. 1963 – Dec. 1964
16	Gruenbaum, Yitzhak	Poland, 1879–1970	General Zionist	Interior	May 1948 – March 1949
17	Gvati, Haim	Poland, 1901–	Mapai-ILP	Agriculture and Health	Nov. 1964 and Dec. 1969 – July 1970
18	Hazani, Michael	Poland, 1913–	Ha-po'el-Hamizrahi-NRP	Welfare	Sept. 1970 – Sept. 1973
19	Kaplan, Eliezer	Poland, 1891–1952	Mapai	Finance, Commerce & Industry; Deputy Prime Minister	May 1948 – July 1952

	Name	Origin	Party	Portfolio	Dates
20	Kol, Moshe	Poland, 1911–	Progressive (Independent-Liberal)	Development and Tourism	Jan. 1966 – Dec. 1969
21	Landau, Haim	Poland, 1916–	Herut-Gahal	Development	Dec. 1969 – Aug. 1970
22	Lavon, Pinhas	Poland, 1904–	Mapai	Agriculture	Nov. 1950 – Oct. 1951
23	Levin, Robbi Yitzhak Meir	Poland, 1894–1971	Agudat Yisrael	Welfare	May 1948 – Sept. 1952
24	Luz, Kadish	Russia, 1895–1972	Mapai	Agriculture	Nov. 1955 – Dec. 1959
25	Maimon, Rabbi Yehuda Leibb	Russia, 1875–1962	Mixrahi-NRP	Religious Affairs; War Veterans	May 1948 – Oct. 1951
26	Meir, Golda	Russia, 1898–	Mapai-ILP	Labor; National Insurance; Foreign Affairs; Prime Minister; Justice	March 1949 – Sept. 1972
27	Mintz, Benyamin	Poland, 1903–1961	Po'abi-Agudat	Posts	July 1960 – May 1961
28	Namir, Mordekhai	Russia, 1897–	Mapai	Labor	June 1956 – Dec. 1959
29	Murock, Rabbi Mordekhai	Latvia, 1884–1963	Misrahi-NRP	Posts	Nov. – Dec. 1952
30	Peled, Natan	Russia, 1913–	Mapam	Immigration and Absorption	1970–1973
31	Peres, Shimon	Poland, 1923–	Mapai-Rafi-ILP	Without Portfolio; Transport	Dec. 1969 – July 1970; Oct. 1951–Aug. 1952
32	Pinhas, David Zvi	Hungary, 1894–1952	Mixrahi	Transport; Communications	May 1948 – Nov. 1950
33	Remez, David	Russia, 1886–1951	Mapai		Dec. 1969 – Aug. 1970
34	Rimalt, Elimeleh	Poland, 1907–	Gen. Zionist-Gahal	Posts	Nov. 1955 – Aug. 1970
35	Sapir, Pinhas	Poland, 1909–	Mapai-ILP	Commerce & Industry; Finance; Without Port.	Sept. 1953 – June 1965
36	Serlin, Youseph	Poland, 1906–1974	Gen. Zionist	Health	May 1948 – Oct. 1951
37	Shapira, Haim Moshe	Poland, 1902–1970	Ha-po'el Hamigrahi, NRP	Immigration; Health	
38	Shapiro, Ya'accov Shimshon	Russia, 1902–	Mapai-ILP	Justice	Jan. 1966 – July 1972; Sept. 1972 –
39	Sharef, Ze'ev	Romania, 1906–	Mapai-ILP	Commerce & Industry; Finance	Nov. 1966 – Dec. 1969
40	Sharett, Moshe	Russia, 1894–1965	Mapai	Foreign Affairs and Prime Minister and Foreign Affairs	May 1948 – June 1956
41	Shazar, Zalman	Russia, 1889–	Mapai	Education; Culture	March 1949 – Nov. 1950
42	Shemetov, Victor	Bulgaria, 1915–	Mapam	Without Portfolio	Dec. 1969 – July 1970
43	Warhaftic, Zerha	Poland, 1906–	Ha-po'el Hamizrahi	Religious Affairs	Nov. 1961 –
44	Zadok, Haim Yoseph	Poland, 1913–	Mapai	Commerce & Industry; Development	May 1965 – Jan. 1966
45	Zisling, Aaron	Russia, 1901–1965	Ahdut Ha'avoda	Agriculture	May 1948 – March 1949

Source: M. Brecher, *Decisions in Israel's Foreign Policy*, Oxford, 1974, pp. 582–9.

6 The Soviet Union and Arab political development, 1948–1953

World War II and its aftermath introduced the Soviet Union to political and strategic opportunities that all preceding attempts of the previous two decades had failed to secure. This period saw the triumph of communist-led revolution in Eastern Europe and also in North Korea. At the same time, the East as such was not totally neglected; for the long-term strategic aim of the Soviet Union was to deny the backward colonies to Western powers, thus altering the balance of international power. Tremendous and significant changes took place in the 1940s, perhaps the most important being that major Western powers went through a phase when they gradually granted national independence to some of their colonies. This political reality presented the Soviet Union with opportunities that could not be neglected. They were made more attainable because of the emergence of the Soviet Union itself as a world power to be reckoned with, and because the upsurge of nationalist trends in the colonies brought about a train of upheavals. Where these upheavals occurred their political significance was to undercut the foundations of the old colonial powers. Secondly, where the question of national independence had arisen then implicitly a direct collision with the Western powers would occur. Thirdly, once national independence acquired the character of an international phenomenon, then the polarized international political spectrum would naturally imply the upgrading of the Soviet Union's stature if it sided with one of these former colonies. Fourthly, this meant that the Soviet Union had become equal to the most influential Western power – the United States – in shouldering world political responsibilities. Finally, the change of status in former colonies and semi-colonies meant that they were seeking an alternative political alignment and that further political developments could be expected. The Soviet Union could provide this alternative. Since the Soviet Union had become, for all practical purposes, a super power in its own right, it had thus entered a new political phase which implied that the bi-polar system was operative in the balance of power in the world.

The Soviet Union was basically concerned with two developments; the internal and basically economic reconstruction of its own polity, and the post-war divisions of the world into spheres of influence where the main Soviet considerations revolved round the consolidation of power within Eastern Europe. Outside this sphere concern with national liberation movements had to be shelved for the time being; outside Eastern Europe, such movements had to be dependent on their own capabilities.

The implications here are an open-ended argument in the sense that after the world political situation became more or less defined between the two major powers, the United States and the USSR, national liberation movements took two forms. The first was that of people's armed struggles, the most important examples of which were the Chinese and the Vietnamese; in both the Soviet Union played a leading part in their suppoort. The second form crystallized round the invited support of the Soviet Union which was characterized by an upheaval of nationalist sentiments. This latter form, as far as this study is concerned, had to wait until the end of the 1950s. However, in both cases, the role played by the Soviet Union was confined to three aspects: arms supplies, military advisers (a consequence of the first) and finally assistance rendered in the field of economic reconstruction. Thus World War II granted the Soviet Union political and military opportunities to enter the world political scene with the widest available means. The bi-polar system of world politics dictated, according to Soviet writers,[1] the political reality of two choices 'only' available to former colonies, socialism and imperialism. These former colonies, the assertion went, had no other alternatives. These colonies, moreover, had two objectives which needed to be carried out: the first task was to combat 'imperialism' and terminate its existence in the colonies, the second was confined to local revolutionary agrarian changes. On the first point, the end of the 1940s witnessed new nationalist sentiments in Egypt, Iran and North Africa; in each the upsurge was directed against the British and the French.

Under Khrushchev the first half of the 1950s was a period of uncertainty. A new and extended theoretical Marxist-Leninist approach, forced on the Soviet Union by the political situation after the Stalin era, was introduced to deal with the emerging Arab states. The most prominent change was the introduction of the policy of peaceful coexistence. The Marxist notion of class struggle remained unaltered, since class struggle is surrounded by economic and ideological formulations which produce the violent changes in societies. Furthermore, political analysis cannot ignore the passing of the colonial era, a noticeable political change. The era that had witnessed two world wars and their aftermath rendered the former colonial powers unable to implement their military might to enforce their power over former colonial countries.

These new developments introduced Soviet theoreticians to two related problems. First, 'an explanation for the voluntary withdrawal of Western colonial powers had to be given. And, second, the question of the possibility of a third force in the world had to be considered.'[2] To the Soviet Union, the 'voluntary' abandonment of colonies by former colonial powers had to do with the economic and political support that was extended to these colonies by itself, and so the Soviets argued that the imperialists were 'compelled' to grant political independence to the colonies. The Soviet theoretician V. Semyonov maintained that the former colonies and underdeveloped states in general were divided into three categories. In the first category were states that won 'complete liberation', countries like China, Korea and Vietnam. The second included states that had attained national independence, but that dissociated themselves from entering military blocs with former colonial powers. Within this category were India, Indonesia, Egypt, Syria, Burma and others. Thirdly, there were countries which had attained formal political independence, but were linked with the imperialist powers in 'unequal treaties', countries like Iran, South Korea and the Philippines. This 'disintegration' of the old colonial powers had led Semyonov to observe two forms of nationalism, one prevalent in the West, whose basic manifestation was national chauvinism, and the other that of the peoples of former colonies, which had other dimensions. Amongst other things this form of nationalism is characterized by struggles against Western imperialism, and the peoples of these countries aspire to 'pursue progressive aims'. The political objectives of former colonial countries would ultimately weaken the imperialist powers with the abolition of their military bases and by reducing their 'economic advantages', which they had hitherto enjoyed unabatedly. The Soviet Union considered that this second form of nationalism would lead these former colonies to collaborate with it in the process of attaining political and economic independence.

Under the leadership of Khrushchev, Marxist-Leninist tenets were slightly modified, and included the peaceful transition to socialism, alongside peaceful coexistence in economic, military and ideological spheres. In each of these three spheres Khrushchev aimed at upgrading the Soviet Union's power until it was parallel with that of the Western powers. Molotov, who assumed power after Stalin's death, had also agreed with the idea that war could be averted, and that contradictions existed among the capitalist countries so that war would eventually erupt within this camp. At this point of development the basic tasks of the Soviet Union's Communist Party in foreign policy were:

(1) to continue to struggle against a new war;
(2) to continue to pursue a policy of international cooperation;
(3) to strengthen and develop relations with the other states of the communist camp; and
(4) to tirelessly strengthen the defense power of the Soviet state.[3]

Stalin's death left certain legacies with which Soviet leaders had to contend; including a 'fixed' mode of Communist thought, which dictated a certain line in strategical thinking. Both elements entailed a worldwide organization whose central aim was to influence strategic thought in relation to the Soviet Union. The Soviet Union, furthermore, had inherited an 'empire' to rule, along with all its theoretical and strategic importance. In view of all this the Soviet Union embarked on a massive industrialization scheme, with plans to accomplish the following aims:

a The 'world outlook' which sees the world and history as a process of class struggle, and extends the class struggle to international affairs by dividing the world into socialist (i.e. Communist), capitalist-imperialist and oppressed colonies.

b The Communist concept of morality which provides a moral imperative and justifies any method to achieve Communism on the ground that Communism represents the highest good for mankind. Stalin contributed little to Communist Moral

Philosophy; he simply carried it to its logical conclusion in practice, and thus set the tone of Communist strategy and conduct in international and national affairs.

c The view of the historic meritability of Communist victory worldwide.

d The concept that a 'series of frightful collisions' must inevitably occur between the Communist and capitalist states before the final triumph of Communism. Such a view makes any effort to arrive at peaceful solutions to international problems a deliberate fraud or a temporary expedient for the Communist, and eliminates the possibility of a policy aimed at a lasting peace with the non-Communist states . . .

e Accompanying the above principle, and closely associated with it in its effect on strategy, is the doctrine of continuing hostility as long as two classes exist and the denial of any right of capitalism to survive . . .

f The concept of imperialism as the logical outcome of advanced capitalism, the view that capitalism has survived only because of the 'looting' of the colonies, and the incorporation of this view into a general strategy of weakening the capitalist states by depriving them of the colonies.

g The continued acceptance, from 1920, of the need for centralized control of Communist world strategy and policy and the need for a class of professional revolutionaries to formulate, direct, and execute strategic decisions. The corollary policy was, of course, iron party discipline . . . In terms of strategy formulation, the fact that effective centralized control existed was an important element in determining what strategies were feasible.[4]

Certain pre-conditions were necessary for the accomplishment of the second element. Prominent among these was the strengthening of the Communist international base – namely, the Soviet Union. Concomitant with this was the political reality of avoiding a direct confrontation with the capitalist system. In addition, attention had to be given to Soviet war preparations. Former colonies had to be liberated from the yoke of the colonial powers, and in this process of liberation local Communists were to take the leadership. All this would lead to the furtherance of Communist objectives in the world. Finally, the socialist states were to unite in one solid alliance to further and advance Communist objectives and aims. This last element remained one of the most important in future Soviet Union foreign policy, and it had its effect on the future development of the Soviet Union's relations with the Arab world.

Even before the Soviet Union entered the Arab world it had a comprehensive knowledge of the events in that area, derived partly as a by-product of the Cold War and emigration to Palestine from Eastern Europe and the Soviet Union, and partly stemming from the need to formulate an attitude toward handling and finding a solution to a crisis which witnessed armed uprising within Palestine itself.

When the State of Israel had come into being, V. Molotov, the Soviet Foreign Minister, sent a telegram to his Israeli counterpart; he said that the establishment by the Jewish people of their sovereign state would serve the cause of strengthening peace and security in Palestine and the Near East, and he expressed confidence that friendly relations between the Soviet Union and the State of Israel would develop successfully. Soviet commentary was basically favorable to Israel and accepted the plan of partition into two states in accordance with the general principles of the United Nations.

By June 1948 diplomatic envoys had been exchanged with the Soviet Union and the newly established State of Israel, with Mrs Golda Meir representing the latter. Pavel I. Yershov represented the former[5] and, arriving in August, was the first representative of a great power to reach Israel.[6] The Soviet Union, by the mere fact of being one of the first great powers to establish diplomatic relations with Israel, had taken the leadership much more quickly than the United States, and the way was open for the exchange of trade between the two states.

When war broke out in May 1948 between the Arab states – Egypt, Syria, Transjordan, Saudi Arabia, Iraq and Lebanon – and Israel *Pravda* argued that

> Undoubtedly, one of the reasons for the military conflict in
> Palestine is the attitude adopted by Britain and the USA to the
> Palestine question. The second reason, inseparably linked with
> the first, is that the rulers of certain Arab countries are
> pursuing a policy which is by no means in accordance with the

interests of the Arab peoples but is subordinated to foreign interests and influence. . . . The Soviet Union defended and will continue to defend the independence of Arab States and peoples. However, it should be clear that in waging war against the young Jewish State, the Arabs are by no means fighting for their own national interest nor for their own independence, but against the right of the Jews to create their own independent state. . . . With all its sympathy for the national liberation of the Arab Peoples, the *Soviet public cannot but condemn the aggression of the Arab States against the State of Israel and against the right of the Jewish people to create their own state in accordance with the decision of the UN General Assembly.*[7] [emphasis added]

The violence was consistently attributed by the Soviets to Britain's instigation because of Britain's policy of hegemony in the area. J. Vilstorov added two more points to the argument:

First it [Britain] put forward a plan for the partition of the country into four provinces, which would have meant these provinces being given to the neighbouring Arab states. Then it put forward a plan to join Palestine to Transjordan. All these plans, however, failed. The United Nations Organization took a different view. On November 29 1947 a decision was adopted for the Partition of Palestine and the establishment there of two independent states, Jewish and Arab. The Partition Plan, which suited the interest of both the Jewish and Arab peoples, was supported by the Soviet delegation.[8]

Once the Soviet Union had entered the Arab world through Israel, fears began to grow in the West, particularly in the United States and Britain, that communism was penetrating the whole of the Middle East; the Soviet Union's Mission to Israel, opened in Stalin's time, had already sparked off these fears.

Soviet reporting on Israeli political development in the early part of 1950 concentrated on its internal development as far as the labor movement was concerned. For example, when on 11 May 1950 the Executive Committee of Histadrut, the General Federation of Jewish Workers, introduced and passed a resolution for the withdrawal of the Histadrut from the World Federation of Trade Unions, this was viewed as an attempt to split the unity of workers internationally. It was seen as an offense against the Soviet Union.[9] It was thought that the move came about because of American influence on Israel in order to bind the latter to the policies of the Western bloc, and it gave prominence to the stand taken by the Israeli Communist Party. The Soviet Union opposed the attempt by the United States, France and Britain to arm the Arab countries and Israel, and saw this as a step toward disturbing peace in the region with, as regards Israel, two objectives: first, the 'reorganization' of the Israeli army and second, the establishment of military bases, on Israeli territory, both acts demonstrating that the designs of the 'Triple' nations in the area were aimed at the militarization of both antagonists.

Israel's internal economic crisis was one of the outcomes of American 'imperialistic' designs launched in the hope that Anglo-American influence on the Israeli government would manifest itself through such crises, and of furthering and enhancing the rightist tendencies within Israel. *Pravda* further accused the retiring government's leadership and the Mapai Party of embarking on a policy to cut Israel off from the camp of peace, headed by the Soviet Union, and of being prodded into the camp of the Anglo-American warmongers.[10]

Soviet reporting of the development of events in Israel had presented the governmental crisis of 1948, which resulted in the appointment of Ben-Gurion to head the new government, according to the Israeli Communist Party's analysis of events. This stated that Ben-Gurion's government was, in the first place, dependent more and more on the Americans because of pressure from the latter, and that such pressure had resulted in anti-Soviet and anti-Communist sentiment in the Israeli government; that this policy had prompted the Israeli delegation to the United Nations to support the stand of the United States which threatened to harm the bargaining powers of that organization; and that Mikunis, the General Secretary of the Israeli Communist Party, had stressed and demanded in the debates of the Israeli Knesset that new elections should be held to 'ensure the formation of a people's government of the working people of the middle strata of the population on the basis of community of interests in defense of peace, independence, democracy, equal rights for Arabs, and the everyday interest of the masses'.[11]

Izvestia also carried an editorial on conditions in Lebanon in which it argued that Lebanon had rejected unification with Iraq on the basis that it would be transformed into a 'British colony', that the cause of governmental crisis in that country was a result of Anglo-American rivalry, and the 'subjugation' of the country by the Americans was only one step further towards its domination of the whole of the Near East. Finally, the United States' attempt to increase its influence was aimed at the creation of military bases in the Mediterranean.

The theme of Anglo-American 'rivalry' in the Middle East was expounded further by Orkho in *Pravda*[12], where he elaborated certain points of interest. In the first place, there existed an observable contradiction between the interests of the United States and those of Britain, which had manifested itself in the scramble for oil resources by these two powers in the Middle East resulting in their establishing oil monopolies in the region. However, in this regard, the British position was weakening. Second, the importance of the region should not be neglected, since the United States was attempting to involve these countries in military pacts in order to establish military bases there in a fashion comparable to the NATO alliance, and possibly to supplement that alliance. Third, in this battle, the USA, in its attempt to counter the British presence and objectives, had become stronger mainly because British 'colonialism' was going through a period of weakness.

This analysis upgrades 'contradictions' in the world balance of power and the Middle East in particular to being a factor in augmenting American national interests. For if the Arab countries wished to attain *political* independence, then their struggle should be directed against the new force of imperialism, an imperialism that was encountering the old guard of the now defunct colonialism. Once the economic offensive of the new force of imperialism had been concluded, the Arab world and the entire Middle East would be directed toward military alliances of one kind or another to ensure the global interests of imperialism.

Once the two stages of development had been completed, then the primary objectives would be directed toward the 'oppression' of the peoples of these countries and the creation of a bloc, basically military, against the Soviet Union and the socialist camp. The analysis also contained an inherited contradiction which neglected the fact that due to the nature of the disunity that prevailed in the Arab world the designs of the imperialists – however logical and intelligible at certain stages – would be thwarted in their efforts to produce military pacts on the large scale conceived by the Soviet Union. Some prominent Arab states did indeed achieve political independence, but this did not mean that they indulged in military pacts aimed solely against the Soviet Union and the socialist camp. None the less, in the conditions prevailing in the late 1940s and the early part of the following decade, military alliances among some Arab countries were a conceivable or likely development on a smaller scale, but again this did not mean that they could be put to work in either the long or the short term against Soviet interests.

The question of oil 'monopoly' in the region belonging to the Western countries ignores the fact that the scramble for oil was carried out by the oil companies themselves, with little consideration for the military balance or pacts; the two issues are of a complementary nature and did not, as it happens, follow each other in the scramble for power in the Arab world and the Middle East at large. However, one of the remarkable changes in Soviet policy was in its attitude to Western exploitation of oil resources in the Arab world.

Writing in *Pravda*,[13] Marinin pointed out that the United States did not act alone but in conformity with Israel's requirements, the former being dependent on the latter for shaping its foreign policy in the Arab world. He claimed that the Israeli economy was totally dependent on the Zionist lobby and its influence in the USA; that there existed a close 'connection' in the military sphere between the two countries to carry out American designs in the Arab world and the Middle East; and finally, that this close alliance had been followed by a 'secret' agreement with Turkey on military bases.

Israel, from its creation and even more from the early part of the 1950s, was regarded with reserve by the Soviet Union and viewed, because of its alliance with the West and the United States in particular, as a country demonstrating the *military* extension of the West in the area, which put it on a level with most Arab states.

What is remarkable about these commentaries is the lack of any remarks which would ameliorate the plight of the Palestinian people; action was confined to pronouncements by the Israeli Communist Party, while the Soviet Union's main concern at the time was the maneuverings of Arab countries in their relations with the West.

N. Ilyin, writing in *Izvestia*,[14] and Y. Zvagin discussing events in the Middle East and the Arab world in particular in *Trud*[15] in September 1950, noted five ideas on the current developments in the area. First, the Arab world, rich in oil and other natural resources, was essential to the designs and conspiracies of British–American imperialism which had set these Middle East countries on the way to prepare for a 'new war' by drawing them into military pacts. Second, the national industries of Syria and Lebanon were in the grip of the Americans and the British, which resulted in severe competition that, in turn, resulted in worsening conditions of unemployment in these countries. Third, the colonial and 'imperialist' policies of the Americans and the British with the collaboration of the present rulers of these countries had resulted in severe disatisfaction among the working people, leading to large demonstrations and strikes. All this had increased the 'fears' of the authorities. Fourth, in the sharp competition between the Americans and the British, the former had been able to out-maneuver the latter, almost replacing them in the oil industries. Lastly, both powers were opposing the anti-imperialist movement on a united front: the people were demanding the nationalization of the oil industry, most vociferously in Iran, and the two powers were awaiting with concern the development of this crisis hoping that it would not extend to other Arab oil-producing countries.

The oil crisis in the Middle East was given much attention by the Soviet Union, which claimed that the Arab states were at a stage of ridding themselves of Western influence by a variety of means. But the objective of the Western powers was to 'enslave'[16] the Arab world by means of a political approach and by drawing these countries into various military pacts that one way or another were connected with the NATO alliance. The establishment, for example, of a Middle East Command as a 'defensive' alliance between the United States, France and Turkey pointed to the true nature of the West's designs in that it was remarkably similar to the NATO alliance. This Command had been established primarily against the eventuality of the United States taking military action whether or not a war was in progress, but also because of the increasing rise of the 'national liberation movement' in the Arab world. This was considered to be a threat to the interests of the Western powers, especially the United States, which, in response, would provide not only military assistance against the people of the Arab world but would also reward Arab governments by arms deliveries.

The American approach was one that aimed through 'propaganda' to foster the idea of the 'threat of Communism' and, at the same time, play 'a handful of venal reactionary rulers, fearful for their power, against the masses'.[17] The Middle East Command had been established more specifically to ensure the defense of the

Middle East in the event of military aggression emanating from the Soviet Union. Once arms deliveries had been accomplished, 'economic aid' in a variety of ways would follow; refusal by Egypt to get involved in such military pacts was highly commendable.

The Soviet Union had kept a close watch on developments in the Middle East and the Arab world in particular; when the idea of the Middle East Command was introduced the Soviet Union viewed it as having two main objectives. On the one hand, it was seen as a move to foment 'aggression' against the Soviet Union and the Eastern bloc and, on the other, the whole alliance was designed to 'strangle' the Arab national liberation movement. This plan hoped to station foreign armed forces in the Middle East under an Allied Middle East Command with its headquarters in Egypt. By November 1951, the organizers of the military alliance had issued a joint declaration about the principles that would be governing the formation of the Middle East Command.[18]

This supposed military alliance, the Soviets argued, was aimed at linking the area with NATO forces to achieve the two objectives mentioned above. They claimed that with the exception of Turkey, none of the Middle Eastern countries had signified consent to the project. The Soviet Union had indeed expressed its objection by delivering notes, on 21 and 22 November 1951, to the governments of Egypt, Syria, Lebanon, Iraq, Saudi Arabia, Yemen and Israel, pointing out the intention of the projected alliance. The Soviet move could perhaps have been instigated for several reasons, amongst them the creation of a military bloc which would engulf the Middle East and the Arab world in a new Cold War between the East and the West. Finally, the Soviet Union alleged that the projected military alliance was directed against the Arab peoples rather than to the assistance of those governments which had linked their interests with the Western powers.

Shortly before the 1952 Egyptian Revolution, Soviet commentators volunteered their opinions on various facets of internal conditions in Israel. This came about for several reasons. First, it was a period when the Soviet Union had established diplomatic relations with Israel but not with the majority of Arab states. Second, the Arab world was viewed as the preserve of Western influence, and everything that happened there was regarded as yet another example of the West's objectionable political aims. Lastly, if any disturbance did occur, the Soviet Union could not act for logistical reasons, and thus the time had not been reached where clear-cut policy objectives could be set out for the Arab world.

D. Davydov, writing in *Trud*,[19] considered the ills that had overtaken the structure of Israeli society. He argued that the Histadrut was closely allied with American policies and trade unions, which resulted in withdrawal of the Histadrut from the World Federation of Trade Unions, although its labor force had objected to this move. The argument was to the effect that the new economic policy measures introduced by the Israeli government had contributed to the worsening of the conditions of the labor force. This policy was intended to pay for military expenditure, made necessary basically by American intrigue, which was simultaneously following a policy of imposing conditions on the peoples of other countries. Even American foreign aid constituted a burden to the Israeli working class, and the reactionary leadership of the Histadrut dictated unfavorable conditions for the workers by imposing measures which did not allow participation, through the channels furnished by Moscow, in the amelioration of working class conditions in Israel.

At the Soviet Communist Party Nineteenth Congress which was held in October 1952 in Moscow, most of the Arab Communist parties attended, along with the Israeli Communist Party; the two jointly and vehemently attacked their 'common enemy', manifested in 'Western Imperialism'. The Israeli Communist Party delegate, Mikunis, put weight on the unity of Jewish and Arab workers and unleashed an attack on Ben-Gurion's governmental policies. Amongst his accusations were the following:

> The Israeli Premier's pro-US policy worsens the workers'
> conditions, violates democratic rights, discriminates against
> the Arab community, permits US control of Israel's support of
> the Middle East anti-Soviet bloc and collaborates with
> Western neo-Nazis. The Israeli people oppose Israel's
> conversion to a US base.[20]

It was noticeable, in relation to the Soviet Union, that Israel had a political structure that provided a political breathing space called democracy. Within this conception of democracy there were several gains that the Soviet Union hoped to achieve. In the first place, the mere fact that the Soviet Union was able to gather Israelis and Arabs on the same political platform was a testimony to its power. Concomitant with this, secondly, the Arab and Israeli Communist parties had assembled under one banner, of anti-Western imperialist designs. In the third place, the fact that the Soviet Union was able to operate in an independent way in the Arab world, through both the Israeli and Arab Communist parties, opened up a wide range of political options within which to maneuver. The 'unity' of the Jewish and Arab masses spearheaded by their respective Communist parties meant that the Soviet Union as the moving force behind international Communism carried certain political weight. One salient point remains, that the political entity of Israel was sufficiently impressive to attract the recognition of the Soviet Union and its Eastern bloc.

On the occasion of the October Revolution 1952 Ben Gurion, the Israeli Premier, sent a message to Stalin stating *inter alia* that

> In this period of development of our homeland, . . . we think of the part played by the USSR in defeating the Nazi enemy and we feel gratitude for the USSR's support of Israel since the establishment of the state.[21]

Ben Gurion's message to Stalin underlined two facts. On the one hand it harked back to the time of World War II when the common enemy was the Nazi from which both Jewish and Soviet people had suffered dearly. On the other hand, for the State of Israel to express gratitude to the Soviet Union for extending recognition upon its establishment was a pioneering and important statement. Relations had reached an acme.

When the military *coup d'état* occurred on 23 July 1952 in Egypt, the Soviet Union's reaction was one of caution and bewilderment. *Tass*, for example, reported the incident without any direct comment, while *Izvestia* gathered its information from an Israeli publication and stated:

> The military coup d'état in Egypt has received wide comment in the Israeli press. The newspaper *Kol Ha'am* believes that the coup in Egypt is a consequence of the struggle taking place between the American and British imperialists for strategic positions in this part of the world, *and that this struggle will lead to formation of a regime of military dictatorship.* The supremacy of the military clique in Egypt, the paper says, *is to facilitate it joining the notorious Middle East Command, which as is known, was set up by the Americans as a supplement to the North Atlantic bloc.*[22] [emphasis added]

Y. Zvyagin, writing in *Trud*,[23] argued that the whole situation in the Middle East and the Arab world was evolving into a succession of events which warranted certain observations. He said that the Middle East had been an area of an 'imperialistic' struggle for influence, especially as regards oil. Because of its strategic situation, the British design had been to 'protect' the area from penetration by the Americans whose success had been more evident in Saudi Arabia.

The murder of King Abdullah of Jordan in July 1951 constituted a setback for the British because Abdullah was the supporter of the plan to create British tutelage to the detriment of American influence. Such Anglo-American rivalry for influence in Syria, he asserted, had been intensified because oil pipelines ran through the heart of Arabia to the Mediterranean across Syria, and the latter had an important role to play in the establishment of a Greater Syria. None the less, this contradiction of policies between the two Western powers did not prevent them from acting jointly in the suppression of the 'national liberation' struggle of the peoples of this area. The events in Egypt were basically connected with the American approach to include it in the Middle East Command.

Commenting on Lenin's article 'The Socialist Revolution and the Right of Nationalities to Self-Determination', Akopyan[24] summarized Lenin's ideas of the 'national struggle' in the Near and Middle East. The world, according to Lenin, was divided into three categories. To the first group belong the capitalist countries of the West, including the United States. This group has two characteristics: the local progressive bourgeoisie is exhausted and these states oppress foreign nationalities within the country itself. In the second category are the Eastern European countries such as the Soviet Union, Austria and those in the Balkans, which have witnessed the rise of the national democratic movement of the bourgeoisie and the intensification of the national struggle. In the third category Lenin classed the semi-colonial countries such as China, Iran, Turkey and other colonies which are characterized by the fact that the democratic role played by the bourgeoisie is negligible, even non-existent.

In this last category, the role of a socialist is to offer the firmest support to the 'more revolutionary elements in the bourgeois-democratic national liberation movements in these countries' using a variety of means to revolt against the oppressive imperialist powers. Stalin, according to the author, had elaborated further on the natural struggle of the third category and added three conditions without which it would be impossible to direct the revolution correctly: that each country obtain a distinct feature of nationalism; that the Communist parties must provide the proletariat of those countries with support and rally the masses even though this support is temporary; and that propaganda and agitation by itself is inadequate for the political agitation of the millions of the masses.

One of the main features of colonial and dependent countries, as seen by Stalin in the 1920s, was their diversity and differing conditions at any given moment. It was thus difficult to analyze completely the prevailing directions of the colonial countries to reach a unified concept. Within the category of the colonial states, three further subdivisions emerge: countries such as Morocco, with no proletariat of their own and underdeveloped industrially; countries such as Egypt, characterized by a small proletariat due to the existence of small-scale industry; and finally countries such as India, which 'have a certain degree of capitalist development and a more-or-less numerous national proletariat'. Thus, it would be difficult, according to Stalin, to lump these countries together, and it is the duty of the proletariat to exert every effort to liberate the oppressed people of these countries from imperialism and local reactionaries.

In combating the forces that are against them, the proletariat faces two stages and types of oppression: those emanating from within (basically landlords and capitalists) and those from without (the imperialist bourgeoisie). None the less, the working classes in these countries are not alone in this struggle, for the other stratum which should ally itself with it is the peasantry, who constitute the majority of the population in colonial and dependent countries. The role of the working class is to win over this segment of the population and break them away from the capitalist class, although, second to this, the role of the 'revolutionary intelligentsia' and youth should not be neglected.

At certain stages and times the national bourgeoisie and dependent countries 'can support' the revolutionary movement of their countries against imperialism. Yet, in the imperialist countries themselves, the bourgeoisie oppresses both its own working class and the other stata of society, and it plays a counter-revolutionary role in all stages of the revolutionary process. In colonial countries, foreign monopoly both oppresses the working class and 'impinges' upon the interests of the national bourgeoisie. A further stage develops in the course of the struggle against imperialism. Concomitant with the growth of the revolutionary movement, the national bourgeoisie 'splits' into two parts: the revolutionary petty bourgeoisie and the conciliatory large bourgeoisie. The former carries on the revolutionary struggle and the other allies itself with imperialism. Akopyan cited two examples in the Arab world to which Stalin had already pointed in 1925: Morocco and Egypt. In the former, its national bourgeoisie did not yet have 'the basis' to split up into revolutionary and conciliatory parties; in the latter case, the national bourgeoisie had accomplished this task, but the conciliatory parties had not had the opportunity to ally themselves with imperialism. Thus, as Stalin had diagnosed, the revolutionary process in colonial countries passes through different stages.

One of the salient features of the Middle Eastern countries is their agrarian nature combined with very weakly developed industry; with the exception of Egypt, Turkey, Israel and Iran, where a few industrial enterprises belonging mainly to foreign companies exist, these countries have a system of feudal land ownership with a large agricultural population comprising an agricultural proletariat. The system of land ownership is also divided into three main categories: the agricultural proletariat which works for hire, semi-proletarians who rent land, and party peasants, who own small plots of land. However, countries like Egypt, Iraq and Jordan 'have been occupied to date by British forces and are colonies or semi-colonies of Britain, which has imposed unequal treaties and predatory concessions on them'.[25] Countries such as Kuwait, Bahrain, Qatar, Oman, Hadhramaut in the Arabian Peninsula and the Arabian Gulf region, which are under 'merciless exploitation' by the British monopolies and local feudal lords, belong to the category of 'oppressed colonial possession' of Britain. A new element has emerged on the scene, Akopyan argued, in that American penetration has increased, thereby weakening the positions of France and Britain which had been relegated to the status of 'united partners'.

The United States had 'seized' an important advantage in the economies of Egypt, Syria, Lebanon and Yemen following Truman's Four Point program and the program of military and economic planning. This had created a sharp contradiction within the imperialist camp. The national liberation movements in the Middle East had widespread responsibility for four main tasks they had to undertake: the removal of foreign bases from their land; the 'struggle for freedom and national sovereignty'; the abrogation of 'enslaving treaties'; and the ensuring of democratic reforms. Such tasks lay upon the working class and their allies, the 'peasantry', who had a minor but not negligible role to play as one of the 'revolutionary intelligentsia' to be taken into the national liberation movement.

The national bourgeoisie of the Middle East had split into two parts: one, because of its inherent interests, had come to terms with the imperialists and were prone to compromise; the other, whose interests were 'affected by foreign capital', was carryng on the struggle for the independence of their countries. The most obvious feature of this latter segment was its 'inconsistency'.

The distinctive feature of the national liberation movement in the Middle East was that it was passing through its *first stage* of development which was mainly directed against imperialism; it had not yet become a powerful 'agrarian revolution', of which the prime example was the political development of Iran, Egypt and Iraq.

Events in Egypt, according to Akopyan, had taken a step towards the realization of the first stage. One the night of 22–23 July 1952 a military coup was staged by army officers headed by Brigadier General Najib Pasha, which forced the King to make certain concessions. By instituting certain changes in the form of the new government, General Najib came to power, dissolved all political parties and confiscated their property. The situation

> which has arisen in Egypt shows that while the working class,
> in alliance with the peasantry and the revolutionary element of
> the national bourgeoisie, is intensifying the struggle against
> imperialism to achieve the realization of national aspirations,
> the reactionary element of the national bourgeoisie, feudal
> lords and compradors are trying to suppress the liberation
> movement of their own people and to come to terms with
> imperialism.[26]

Finally, the colonial world, of which the Middle East and the Arab world in particular was a part, could rely on the 'sympathy and constant support of peace and democracy, headed by the Soviet Union, which invariably stands as a consistent champion of the interests of people in colonial and dependent countries'.[27]

Thus, the stages of political development that a Middle Eastern, or basically Arab country, should undergo for the attainment of national independence was a cycle that should encompass the entire development of the region. In the first place, not necessarily conforming to Soviet precepts, the national bourgeoisie had in most cases been in the forefront in combating imperialism. Perhaps more important, the Soviet authors had neglected the role of the army in these countries. The army, in many cases, had been an instrument of change as its anti-imperialist actions attest – notably, in the case of the Arab world with Egypt – and thereby fulfills the first stage of the precepts set out by Soviet authors.

The role played by the intelligentsia was not appreciated by Soviet authors nor was it given due consideration; because of their intellectual status the intelligentsia does in fact play a major role in the struggle for national independence. In any given country in the Arab world, the working class *per se* hardly exists at all, for these are basically peasant societies with little industrial activity; due to Soviet preconceptions, unfortunately, the degree of attention given to the workers exceeds that granted to the other strata of society in these countries.

Prior to the Egyptian Revolution of 1952 the Soviet Union viewed the progress of Egyptian internal policy alliances, especially Anglo-Egyptian relationships, as being influenced by Britain because of British internal representation in Egypt by 'feudal landowners and collaborationist elements of the national bourgeoisie'.[28] Through these agents Egyptian history had been maneuvered in a variety of ways. In 1914 the British declared Egypt to be their protectorate; in 1922 it was declared an 'independent kingdom'; and finally in 1936 they had 'imposed' upon it a secret military treaty by which Britain was granted the right to maintain military bases in the Suez Canal Zone and elsewhere. The British, moreover, under the sham 'independence' granted to Egypt, reserved the right to many privileges, such as the establishment of military bases in different parts of the country, thereby ensuring British 'overlordship'; the organization and training of the Egyptian army had to be carried out by the British. Britain, through Egypt, had not altered the 'colonial' status of the Sudan, which was administered by a British governor-general.

After World War II the question of Egypt's independence became critical and due to this 'a powerful national liberation movement, headed by the working class, developed in Egypt in 1946',[29] one of whose demands was the abrogation of the secret military treaty. These upheavals had resulted in a succession of unstable governments; one of the reasons for this was the obstinacy of the British over collaboration with American 'imperialists' in military matters.

The Wafd Party, once in power, had acted to impose martial law and prosecute 'democratic individuals'. It had also embarked on the creation of an alliance of Mediterranean countries, allied in turn to the Western powers to obtain security in the area through the American 'Marshallization' of the Arab countries under the pretext of 'concealed' programs of assistance.

The Soviet Union kept close watch on and analyzed the development of events in Egypt.[30] When the government of al-Nahas resigned, a new 'non-party' government was formed by Ali Mahir; its basic tasks were to eradicate military resistance to the struggle of the Egyptian people and create an atmosphere conducive to negotiations with the imperialists. For this purpose, a national emergency was declared and activist and nationalist elements were suppressed. In the vanguard of those pursued and prosecuted in the first days of the *coup d'état* were the leaders of various *fedayin* elements and democratic organizations; the syndicates and the nationalist groupings were crushed, and the military courts were active in the processes of prosecution.

Between 27 January and 22 July 1952, there were six changes of government, none of which was based on party lines and organization. The constant changes demonstrated an inability to alter the internal political situation and showed that the higher echelon of the Egyptian hierarchy was in a state of constant crisis, unable to rule under normal conditions. Even the National Assembly had been dissolved, ample proof that these successive governments lacked a basis and support within the country.

At an early stage the reactionary governments were faced with postponing the elections which were supposed to take place in May 1951; later, they were canceled indefinitely. The armed struggle which took place in the Suez Canal Zone clearly showed that the feudal lords and small bourgeoisie in Egypt were unable to lead the struggle to attain independence. It is worth mentioning that the existence of a large number of political parties and the disputes among them during the monarchical era were sources of weakness in the people's struggle for independence. Against such turmoil and uncertainty, the army seized the leadership; and on the night of 23 July 1952 the 'Free Officers', with their secret organizations, took power in a *coup d'état*. The new leadership arrested all the former military leaders, most of whom came from the higher feudal and bourgeoisie elements.

The coup was carried out meticulously to the plan put forward by

Jamal Abdul-Nasir, a man of humble military background who assumed the leadership of the Free Officers during 1951–1952, when he was occupied in training the *fedayin* on military tasks. The 1952 Revolution was carried out under his leadership. A Revolutionary Command Council under Nasir's personal control was established, although nominal headship was entrusted to Muhamad Najib, whose social origins were in the military aristocracy and who was in close contact with the feudal and large bourgeois classes. The Revolutionary Command Council, Soviet authors contend, was correct in its evaluation of the balance of power whether in the country or at international level.

Radio Prague viewed the Egyptian *coup d'état* as rivalry between the imperialist powers of the United States and Britain, and produced the following analysis:

After the five bourgeois Governments which have been in power in Egypt since the beginning of the year had failed them, the US imperialists decided to take stronger measures. A coup d'état was carried out on 23rd July [1952]; an officer's clique, headed by General Nagib, took power, there have been widespread arrests among political and military leaders with British sympathies and, finally, King Faruk was removed . . . (And) the man who directed the coup d'état from behind the scenes was none other than the US Ambassador in Cairo, Caffery, with whom both General Nagib and Maher Pasha (the Regent) were in constant contact.[31]

The move by the Egyptian army on 23 July 1952 gave the outward impression that it was a normal coup executed by the highest power echelons in the country. But as future events showed, it became obvious that anti-feudal support for the coup was the manifestation of events in Egypt preceding the Revolution.

The Revolution was a turning point in the history of Egypt and the beginning of the independent development of the country. Power was transferred from the feudalists and large financial capital monopolists to the representatives of the national bourgeoisie in alliance with the middle-lower strata of society who were, in turn, close to the aspirations of the toiling masses.

At first the Free Officers had no clear set of ideas or a political program, but the members of the Executive Committee were all nationalists who believed that the deteriorating conditions of their country were due to British imperialism, the decadence of the monarchical system and reactionary oppression by the feudalist and monopolist financial bourgeoisie in Egyptian society whose power was based on British monopoly.

One of the initial main tasks of the new government therefore became the liberation of the country from foreign domination. The unconditional withdrawal of British forces from Egypt became its chief policy. The first acts of the new power-holders in opposing the main enemy, the imperialists, were the elimination of the political policy of the Interior Ministry and the seizure of its highest ranks of office. However, the Government of Ali Mahir adopted a reactionary stand in the social and economic fields. For example, in July 1952, his government issued a decree which permitted a 50 per cent foreign holding in mixed companies. This step was taken for the benefit of the foreign monopolies with which Ali Mahir was connected.

In several municipalities, the peasants, following the coup, did not wait for the Agricultural Decree to be announced and refused to pay rent to the feudalists. But Ali Mahir's government declared that it would take severe steps to punish those 'disobeying' the government decree. On 11–12 August 10,000 workers in Kirf Dawar announced a national strike and organized demonstrations demanding an improvement in economic conditions. The government's response was to send in the army and police to suppress the workers, which resulted in many casualties. By the end of August the police had made several arrests with the aim of suppressing the Communist organization.

Thus the enactments of the short-lived government of Ali Mahir contained several basic mistakes about the Egyptian Revolution. He opposed the agricultural reforms which had been prepared by the Revolutionary Council, and consequently General Najib, the President of the Council of Ministers, demanded Ali Mahir's resignation. On the same day he resigned, several high-ranking reactionary personalities were arrested. The Agricultural Reform Decree, announced on 9 September 1952, was one of the major steps which the power-holders took and was the most important and correct in principle, for agriculture in Egypt had a marked colonialist and feudalist orientation. Moreover, agricultural production was going through one of its periodic crises and was at the core of all the problems faced by the Egyptian Revolution. The historical importance of the 1952 Decree was that it was the first agricultural decree in the Arab East to lay the basis for the eradication of feudalism and these revolutionary steps, which the government enacted for the benefit of the people, had a deep-rooted effect on the new system.

The Wafd Party became the most dangerous enemy of the new system, for al-Nahas welcomed the Revolution with the disguised intention of persuading the Free Officers to accept the rule of the Wafd. At the beginning of September 1952, al-Nahas demanded the cancellation of emergency orders and immediate parliamentary elections. Following the promulgation of the Agricultural Decree, he set himself up in open opposition to the government. On 9 September a new decree was issued to regulate the political parties in Egypt, under the Minister of the Interior, who was empowered to veto the formation of a new party. In December 1952, the 1923 Constitution was suspended, and a month later all political parties were dissolved and their property confiscated. It is worth mentioning that every governmental step was directed, above all, against the right wing of the Wafd, whereas the left of the party, at different stages, sided with the Revolutionary Council. On 17 June 1953, General Najib became the President of the Egyptian Republic.

The Soviet viewpoint of the early history of the Egyptian Revolution warrants certain comment. In the first place, the role of the existing parties was nominal, if not negative, in the process of nation-building. Second, considerable attention was given to the role played by peasants rather than workers, perhaps because of the nature of the composition of the Egyptian society. Third, the army was portrayed in two different ways: on the one hand, it played the role of arbiter of power in the system; and on the other, little attention was given to its leaders, with the exception of Nasir who was shown as allying himself with the sympathies of leftist policies. The narration sees the system as being in a state of dysfunction which warranted a change and, more especially, because of their inability to rule, the overthrow of the bourgeois class. This element continued to dominate even within the army until after Nasir took power with the newly initiated social 'progressive' programs.

The ineffectiveness of the political programs pursued by the 'rightist' liberal General Najib was one reason why the revolutionary process was slowed down. Najib had associated his power, which he lacked within the corps of army officers, with the support of the Wafd Party and other former influential personalities of the old regime. But Najib had encountered the resistance of 'leftist' officers, led by Nasir, who thwarted his plans for an alliance with the old regime. In the ensuing power struggle within the ranks of the army officers those who had allied themselves with the Muslim Brotherhood were to be 'neutralized'.

The Soviet view of later changes produced a different analysis of Nasir's consolidation of the balance of power. The role played by Nasir, according to Soviet sources, was not only prominent but also produced changes beneficial to the toiling peoples in Egypt in the way of agricultural reforms, the confiscation of the King's possessions and, above all, the steps taken against the 'reactionary' leadership of the political parties. Finally, after attaining final victory against the 'bourgeois reactionaries', the new revolutionary government faced the challenge of the Muslim Brotherhood. In the clashes which followed many of its members were arrested, and because of its 'reactionary' actions the party was banned and General Najib deposed.

The new leadership had a fresh outlook and undertook reforms; the Sudan problem was solved by an Egyptian–British agreement signed in February 1953 whereby the Sudan was granted independence. In April 1953 discussions with Britain to evacuate its forces from Egypt had begun, although Britain delayed the process in its own interests. At the same time, American maneuvers came into play; its leaders wanted the region to join the SEATO military pact.

In the overall Arab political situation the emergence of the concept of Arab nationalism was noticeable, considerably assisted by Nasir, who advocated simply a new form and fresh means for Arab nationalism to combat the varied Western influences in the Arab world. The idea of Arab nationalism was an idea in which Nasir was already prominent. But, at the center of this Arab political development lay the stark reality of the existence of the State of Israel. Though Nasir had achieved his first task of changing power in Egypt, he would ultimately need the support of one of the super powers to achieve his goal. The Soviet Union, with its satellite Eastern European states, was willing to fill this gap. Thus all forms of assistance were rendered to Egypt and, in return, the Arab world was opened up to the Soviet Union. There were some practical realities generated from Arab conditions; one of these was the fact that Nasir's overall policies were diametrically opposed to Western interests. It should then be asked why the Soviet Union kept its relations with both Israel and the Arab world on an equal footing. All indications suggest that the Soviet Union was in an evolutionary period whereby both sides were a testing ground for the relatively new Arab stand that was emanating from Egypt. Thus a change in policies came from the Arab side rather than from the Soviet Union, for the latter kept its relations with the State of Israel unchanged. This meant in reality that the Arab–Israeli conflict, the heart of which was the plight of the Palestinian people, did not stand high in the Soviet Union's foreign policy objectives. This conclusion leads to the thought that even at this stage of political development one can safely argue that the Soviet Union's national interest was the crux of the matter. This conclusion explains two realities. On the one hand, the Soviet Union virtually disregarded, with only minor pronouncements, Nasir's clamp-down on Egyptian Communists. But, on the other hand, in so far as Nasir was only pursuing nationalistic attitudes and programs, socialist but not communist at heart, he upgraded the contradictions that existed between Western interests and those of Arab nationalism. He had grasped the spirit of the changes taking place and was willing to accept Soviet support to further progress opposed to Western interests.

7 The Soviet Union in the Arab world, 1953–1955

As the Soviet Union saw and interpreted the events in Egypt between 1953 and 1955, a new non-aligned policy and a refusal to enter into military alliances had emerged from the Revolutionary Council. The Egyptian government took a stand against the attempt of Western states to entice Egypt into joining military pacts; Nasir strongly criticized the Baghdad Pact, which was established in February 1955 under the auspices of the imperialist forces.

Egypt's independent foreign policy, the Soviets claimed, was clearly manifested in its participation in the historic Bandung Conference in April 1955. But the real Egyptian independence was to be seen in the establishment of cordial relations with the Soviet Union and the socialist camp. Finally, one of the frequent Soviet analyses claimed that once Egypt had gained political independence, it took active steps to achieve economic independence; one of the guarantees for the fulfillment of such a difficult task was the establishment of relations of various types with the socialist states impartially who acted as a substitute for Egyptian dependence on Western monopolistic trade.

Four major political developments occurred in 1953 which had a marked influence on the Soviet Union's foreign policy in the area: a deterioration in relations with Israel; Stalin's death in March, which resulted in significant changes in Soviet leadership, the most important of which was Khrushchev's ascent to power; Mossadezh's assumption of power in Iran, a country that shares a common border with the Soviet Union, and his abolition of the monarchical system which was totally allied with the West; and, lastly, the rise of Arab nationalism.

Early in 1953 Soviet–Israel relations worsened. In January there was the Jewish Doctors' plot against Stalin's life, a conspiracy handled with care by Soviet broadcasting stations. On the one hand they unreservedly attacked Israel's Mapai Party for criticizing Israeli Communist Party members of the Knesset; on the other hand, Soviet accusations were handled with careful editing in the sense, for example, that the Warsaw transmission to its Yiddish listeners ignored the whole affair.

On 9 February the Russian legation in Tel Aviv was bombed, resulting in Soviet casualties. The Soviet Union sent a note to Israel temporarily suspending diplomatic relations and removing the personnel of its legation to the Soviet Union.[1] The incident did not cause a major change of policy toward Israel, but this attack was intended to convey Israeli dissatisfaction with closer Soviet–Arab relations. Zhukov, writing in *Pravda*, summed up the whole incident by arguing that

> The Israeli Government has for long inspired this filthy
> campaign which however became particularly unbridled after
> the state security organs of the USSR and a number of people's
> democracies had severed the bloody tentacles of the
> international Jewish bourgeois-nationalist 'Joint'
> organization.[2]

It continued with an onslaught on Zionism and its links with Western imperialism. Soviet writers produced feature articles on the ills of the Israeli polity, in addition to the fact that it was allied in foreign policy issues with the West. A standard claim was that there was discrimination against the Arab minority in Israel and that they faced tremendous obstacles. Pronouncements against, and attacks on, Israeli policy were extensive.[3]

The nationalistic orientation of the Egyptian Officers' *coup d'état* exemplified certain anti-Western characteristics. Nationalism seemed to encompass the whole of the Middle East. This significant political development was welcomed by the Soviet Union, for not only was nationalism bound to collide with the remnants of Western colonialism – namely, Britain and France – but emerging nationalist Middle Eastern states would also have to restructure their internal economics on the Socialist model. All these developments fitted happily with the Soviet Union's predictions for foreign policy. It also meant that in particular through Egypt, the gates of the Middle East, especially the Arab world, were opened to the Soviet Union.

This nationalistic aspect of policy in Egypt under the Free Officers had in the Soviet Union's view a major impact on the latter's entanglement in Arab politics with all its inherent and future problems. Egypt, in modern Arab history, was unique in crowning the destiny of Arab political history. Nasir had emerged through the 1952 Revolution to exemplify the new spirit. He faced an Arab world saddled with mounting problems which desperately needed an energetic figurehead to achieve even partial solution. He embarked on a course which would fill that vacuum. Once power was consolidated internally, he undertook two tasks. The first was to introduce a new form of economic reconstruction in Egypt which he labeled socialism, with all its infrastructures. The second revolved around the fact that he had no choice whatsoever but to deal with the insoluble Arab obstacles from North Africa to the Arabian Gulf. This swamp of problems desperately needed some figure not to solve them but just to point out the ills. Nasir was to weaken only on the idea of Arab unity and its realization. His ambitious ideas were to encounter obstacles because of the internal conditions against which he had to work to introduce socialism in an Arab arena and because of his advocacy of Arab unity in the emerging Third World, a concept which was initiated at the Bandung conference of Afro-Asian states in April 1955. The practicalities of the situation led him, naturally, toward the Soviet Union. An alliance with the Soviet Union would not only fill the vacuum left after the expulsion of the West but would also provide the know-how for the reconstruction of the Egyptian economy on socialist lines. In a brief moment, Egypt fulfilled Soviet dreams to enter, whether alone and/or in conjunction with Eastern bloc, the Arab world. It became a testing ground for Communism spearheaded by the Soviet Union. It remains to ask whether or not the Soviet Union was equally willing to perform what was expected of it and whether it had the capability to act and whether it was willing both to proceed and endure. In deciding on its course of action the Soviet Union had to evaluate the all-important question of strategy.

The Egyptian invitation to the Soviet Union in the Arab World

In the summer of 1953, the ruling Free Officers took up the issue of the nationalization of the Canal Zone Company, which meant a showdown with Britain. The Egyptians voiced certain demands largely centered on the evacuation of the remaining British troops stationed in the Canal Zone. The Soviet Union took the stand that the Egyptian demand was just. This measure, if enacted, would have satisfied the Soviet Union's political objectives in the Arab world. Egypt would have embarked on a nationalistic course which would bring it into collision with the Western powers so that a contradiction would emerge favorable to the Soviet Union. And if nationalization were to occur, then the Soviet Union would emerge as the one important major power to side with Egypt. In the event this was the case.

Nasir had a certain political approach and orientation, which, though not communist, would in the final analysis collide with Western interests. One such approach was that he championed democratic concepts. This meant, firstly, that the Egyptian Revolution was to introduce democratic institutions in Egyptian polity, which represented a marked difference from the pre-Revolution era. The freedom of the individual in society was to be guaranteed and respected. Second, he emphasized the role of the masses in the process of making history and unmasking the yoke of colonialism – that is, the West. Third, he fixed a period from 16 January 1953 to 16 January 1954 for the Revolution to fulfill its political objectives and program for democracy. Fourth, he believed that the institution of democracy, the central idea of the Revolution, meant the destruction of colonialism and its local agents. Finally, he advocated and introduced the concept of 'democratic socialism', which meant, intrinsically, a new form for the masses to play with which in turn implied a new form of economic structure for Egypt. All this was a major turning point for Soviet foreign policy in the Arab world. Yet, from the 1952 Revolution to the Tripartite aggression against Egypt in 1956, the Soviet Union enjoyed both flourishing relations with Egypt and cordial relations with Israel. Only minor condemnations of Zionism were heard.

In February 1954[4] the Egyptian Revolutionary Council issued a statement that its nominal head, Muhamad Najib, because he had attempted to make unilateral decisions without reference to the Council, had presented his resignation and that Nasir had assumed the position of Chairman. This was a turning point for the formulation of the Soviet Union's theoretical approach as far as Nasir and the Revolutionary Council were concerned. In the middle of 1954 Nasir issued a political treatise called the *Philosophy of Revolution*,[5] in which he expounded what he considered the priorities of the Egyptian Revolution and how it differed from the monarchical era. He made several significant points. In the first Arab–Israeli war in 1948, which resulted in the defeat of Arab armies and the declaration of the existence of the State of Israel, Nasir, who had participated in the war, came to the conclusion with other army officers that the internal situation of Egypt rather than Palestine was the primary contradiction in the Arab–Israeli conflict. He came to the conclusion that the Arab armies were betrayed by their leaders and decision-makers.[6] Then he posed a rhetorical question: why was it opportune for the army rather than any other force in Egypt to take over power? The Arab defeat had left the question open as to who might carry out the expected change, and the task was laid on the effective role of the army. Thus, a major change had come about. But, he contended, after this main task was accomplished, there then remained two other tasks for the Revolution. In every course set for any people, there were two main revolutions: a political revolution whereby the people regained their right to rule themselves and cast off the yoke of the dictator who had been installed over them and the presence of an aggressive army on its soil without the people's consent, and a social revolution whereby classes struggle until 'justice' is reached. The success of the political revolution requires the unity of all the segments of *al-umah* (nation), whereas one of the features of the social revolution is the imbalance of its values. Between the two elements, conditions 'demanded that we live two revolutions: a revolution which obliges us to unite and, at the same time, a revolution which obliges us, unwillingly, to unite and, at the same time, to be disunited'.[7] This dialectical analysis and theoretical outlook was not only a major deviation of Egyptian leadership carried by the Free Officers in contrast to the dormant and pro-Western monarchical era but also laid the theoretical foundations for the Revolution. To Soviet decision-makers it must have meant a definite change of approach and evaluation of their conclusions about the probabilities of the Egyptian elite carrying out their future actions and policies which would lead to direct collision with the West. If these policies were carried out seriously, they would mean at the very least a direct confrontation with Western powers. Nasir went on to explain the objectives dominant in concerned elites. There is, first of all, the Arab situation, of which Egypt happened to be part whether it wished or not. In the second place, historical destiny had dictated that Egypt was part and parcel of the African continent where an intensified struggle for its future existed. Finally, there exists a fact that could not be ignored – namely, the fact that Egypt was a Muslim state, by virtue of which the country shared in Islamic history. Egypt's geographical position is adjacent to Arab states, and it is no accident that its livelihood is mingled with Arab destiny. Egypt, situated in north-east Africa, faced like the rest of the continent a strong conflict and struggle against the white colonialist for the exploitation of its unlimited natural resources.[8] The sort of analysis made by Nasir in setting out the Egyptian Revolution's priorities had wide implications for changes in the political conditions of the Arab world, in regional realignments and in East–West relations. It was Nasir's ideas and convictions which led the Soviet Union to embark upon a reappraisal of the situation and the policies not only of the Arab world but of the Middle East in general.

Having introduced the idea of socialism to Arab political vocabulary, thereby setting a course for the Egyptian economic structure, Nasir proceeded to the external aspect of the Egyptian Revolution. He began to activate the dormant idea of Arab nationalism. This significant element of the Egyptian Revolution was bound to lead Arab nationalist forces into collision with Western interests in the Arab world, particularly those of Britain and France, the last remnant of colonialism. Arab nationalism purported to be the idea of Arab unity, but its realization was not clarified until the trial (and failure) of Egyptian–Syrian unity in 1958. This idea of Arab unity, however, involved Egyptian entry into Arab politics in the military sense; subsequent Egyptian involvement in the Yemen is the best example. Moreover, the notion he advocated also concerned the Afro-Asian countries: the political idea that Africa, of which Egypt is part and parcel, had to struggle against colonialist exploitation, and continue the struggle against colonialism of which the Algerian war of independence against the French was an example. Nasir became the advocate of the policy of non-alignment of the African and Asian nations which met in Bandung in 1955. At the time he subscribed to the notion that Islam joined Egypt with many other countries and that this world relationship superseded political affiliation. This religious factor most certainly extended beyond the Arab world. In essence he was calling for a major change in the strategic situation to realize which there must be a drastic change in the super-power alignment and balance of power. The Soviet Union was obliged to enter into Nasir's world perceptions. Nevertheless Nasir was not a communist, either in thought or in deed, but put simply, was a new breed of Arab nationalist that emanated from the heart of the Arab world. To Nasir, moreover, the major obstacle faced by Egypt and the entire Arab world was the formidable force of colonialism; the creation of Israel was only one of its manifestations. Thus the next major step would be a direct military confrontation of Egypt by the two remaining colonialist powers, Britain and France, together with Israel as a living replica of that colonialism. It remained to be seen when, how, in what shape and to what extent this military confrontation would occur. In expectation of an occurrence of this sort, in military form and without prior and proper consultation with the United States, the Soviet Union found itself taking a leading role in championing the Arab cause, and the aggressors had to face the unexpected might of the Soviet Union.

Meanwhile, Israeli economic relations with the Soviet Union at this period operated in a natural way. For example, Dr Ze'ev Argmen, Israeli Chargé d'Affaires in Bucharest, had concluded his trade negotiations in Moscow and Israel agreed to 'deliver during this season [1954–1955] 14,000 tons of Jaffa oranges; 5–6,000 tons of Valencia oranges; 25–30,000 cases of lemons and a consignment of bananas against a delivery of 150,000 tons of petroleum and 100,000 tons of crude oil'.[9] At this point the Soviet Union's relations with the Arab world were fraught with uncertainties as far as the Arab–Israeli conflict was concerned, although its normal diplomatic channels functioned freely between the Arab states and Israel. This fact remained one of the cornerstones in Soviet relations in the Arab–Israeli conflict until the June 1967 war.

At the same time, Eastern European Jews, together with the World Council of Jews, were taking a leading role in world Jewish cooperation and unity of goals. When, for example, a conference for European Jews was about to be convened in Paris in 1954, the Jewish community in Poland held a meeting of their own to elect a delegation to attend the Conference.[10] Soviet–Israeli relations in other directions were equally harmonious. A delegation of the 'Democratic Union of Soviet Women, which attended the Israeli Democratic Women's Organization, left Israel on April 13 [1954]'.[11] The Muslim religious dignitaries of the Soviet Union held a congress in Ufa led by Mufti Shabir ibn Shaibh al-Islam Khiyaletdinov, head of the Religious Board of Muslims in the European part of the Soviet Union and Siberia.[12] The Soviet Mufti presented a report relating that he had headed a Soviet pilgrimage to Makkah, Saudi Arabia, where he told the masses he met about the absence of poverty in the Soviet Union and the conditions of its Muslim population, and at the same time, the delegation acquainted itself with the followers of the Muslim faith and Saudi Arabia.[13] A delegation of Israeli women went on a trip to the Soviet Union as guests of the Soviet Women's Anti-Fascist Association, and at the same time, access for the photographing of Jewish manuscripts available in the Soviet Union was discussed between the members of the Soviet Academy of Science and the Israeli Minister of Education.[14] Thus, at this stage of political development, the Soviet Union was in a unique position where it was granted an opportunity which enabled it to satisfy, in one way or another, both the warring factions. The Arab side, headed by Nasir and despite the mounting militarization of Israel and its closer cooperation with the West, especially Britain and France, was proceeding harmoniously in its relations with the Soviet Union.

The Soviet Union's attitude toward Nasir represented careful evaluation, though it viewed him with certain reservations. An article by a Soviet 'observer' in *Pravda*[15] dwelt on this idea, pointing out four major issues. Firstly, he argued that the Western Atlantic bloc was exerting certain kinds of pressure upon the Middle Eastern countries to join the 'aggressive' tendencies of a unified bloc that agreed with Western imperialism. Secondly, the pressures were mounting on Egypt to join such a military pact even though it did not tally with the national interests of the 'peoples of Egypt and of the other countries of the Near and Middle East'. In the third place, a reminder was issued that as far back as 1926 the Soviet government had recognized the independence of Saudi Arabia, in 1928 that of Yemen, of Egypt in 1943, of Syria and Lebanon in 1944. Thus, finally, he stated if any threat faced the Middle Eastern countries it emanated from the imperialist camp, not from the Soviet Union. According to this logic, the Arab world should strive to know and expose its primary enemy – the Western camp – for it must be clear that the Soviet Union, as its diplomatic relations with the Arab world attested, had no imperialistic designs on the region.

On the eve of the Bandung Conference of Afro-Asian countries in April 1955 the Soviet Union, through its broadcasts to the Middle East,[16] concentrated on the political reality that these states faced in opposing Western imperialism, especially in the dismantling of foreign military bases on their respective territories. The Bandung Conference offered the Soviet Union a political opportunity to act against the West. Almost all these states had in some way or another suffered from Western colonialism, and even after they gained independence, Western influence and interests were markedly noticeable. The Conference concerned itself with problems pertaining to the countries' national sovereignty, racialism and colonialism; in none of these issues was the Soviet Union involved nor had it previously played a part in them historically. The Conference therefore offered the Soviet Union the creation of a political bloc that could take a unified stand, however infirm, against the West.

That in itself was a remarkable stage of poltical development. Soviet commentators took a fresh look at events in the Arab world in which they claimed that Anglo–US rivalry for the leadership of Middle East defense organizations lay at the center of Anglo–American attention. Bocharev, for example, analyzed the events in the region in the following manner:

> The aim of such a military bloc is primarily to strengthen the
> imperialist position; therefore it is natural for each imperialist
> State to hasten the realization of the particular plan which
> accords most with its own covetous interests. One cannot fail
> to see that the Anglo–American struggle for domination in the
> Near and Middle East is not running smoothly for Britain.[17]

In January 1955 a Russian–Palestinian Association was established, affiliated to the Soviet Academy of Sciences, which concentrated basically on the history and culture of the 'peoples of the Near East'.[18] This new Soviet approach to the Arab world was basically confined to historical research, and it did not deal in practical terms with the question of Palestinian rights or the future as such.

Soviet perceptions of the general Arab political development were wide ranging. For example, on the tenth anniversary, 1955, of the establishment of the Arab League, Moscow radio beamed to its Arab listeners the Soviet understanding of the actual workings and objectives of the League which originally was the brain-child of the British; it argued that

> ... Ten years ago the Arab League was set up to strengthen
> friendship and political co-operation between the Arab
> countries for the defense of their independence and
> sovereignty, and to strengthen economic, financial and
> cultural ties between them. ... The attempts of Western

diplomacy reach a peak of crudeness whenever the League defends the independence and sovereignty of the Arab countries, according to its charter. For instance, American diplomacy dragged Iraq, a member of the Arab League, into an aggressive military alliance with Turkey, endeavouring thereby to undermine this regional organization or at least to cripple it . . . The League has expressed its solidarity with the national liberation movements of Tunisia, Morocco and Indonesia.[19]

Despite such significant political developments, especially Nasir's ascendancy, in Arab, regional and Third World political developments, the Soviet Union signed a barter agreement with Israel on 9 May 1955, whereby the Soviet Union would supply Israel 'with a further 118,000 tons of fuel oil in return for Israeli citrus fruits'.[20] Such *realpolitik* on the part of the Soviet Union indicated that it had not yet taken a definite stand on the Arab–Israeli dispute.

However, Khrushchev reached the conclusion that 'contradictions' existed in the capitalist camp, and that they could be exploited to achieve the ultimate goal of weakening the imperialist camp politically. Khrushchev's conclusion added two further points to the Soviet Union's foreign policy objectives. Power in the West, according to Soviet leaders, and the fluctuation of power amongst Western countries, had led to political changes in Western states which dictated that political reality granted the Soviet Union an opportunity to exploit the contradictions existing in the Western camp. Secondly, the Third World, or the less developed regions, presented the Soviet Union with new elements for theoretical analysis. One of the major obstacles facing Soviet analysts during the Khrushchev era was the class struggle and analysis of backward countries. However, to Soviet analysts the Arab countries of North Africa and Egypt were societies which had achieved a certain bourgeois status. It was because of this that in the Krushchev era the Soviet Union put its political weight behind some sort of political rapprochement. The Soviet Union aspired to create the anticipated class development and with it the class stratification of these backward societies. It remained to be seen to what this class stratification would lead. Furthermore, the Soviet Union was confronted by the fact that in the Arab world the proletarian class was small in number, even negligible, in relation to the size of the population and most of the population dwelt in feudal or semi-feudal societies. The agrarian question flowed into and overlapped the industrial realm. Nevertheless, Khrushchev pursued a policy in the Arab world that would 'sharpen' class struggle in these societies in the anticipation first that a proletarian class would emerge and a class struggle develop and second in the hope that the proletarian class would eventually triumph. Despite the uncertainties, the Soviet Union entered the Arab world.

Krushchev's period introduced a new style of thinking to political analysis from that seen in Stalin's time. Then the world had been divided on the basis of the 'class struggle' between two diametrically opposed international classes: the bourgeois camp and the proletariat or communist. Relations and conflicts between the two camps were to be resolved by armed struggle, and in this process one had to triumph over the other. It follows that in an international struggle of this sort the Soviet Union would be leading the proletarian class of allied states and assume their leadership. Within this rigid international theoretical outlook the Soviet Union, under Stalin's leadership, had had to direct its foreign policy objectives in the former colonies and semi-independent colonies in a manner that took into consideration the prominence of class struggle in a wide international spectrum. From Lenin's theoretical approach Stalin inherited a new and fundamental reality, concerned with the fact that capitalism in the West did *not* collapse as had been anticipated; that the workers' livelihood in capitalist countries had improved; and, finally, that the workers in capitalist countries did not declare spontaneous revolution. But, as far as the colonies were concerned, two factors in their relations with the capitalists stood out. The capitalist countries needed the colonies for capital investment and opportunities for the outflow of their capital, while at the same time the colonies were the fields from which the necessary raw materials were extracted. To Stalin there were certain theoretical experiences that evolved around his concept of war. In the first place, war was seen as an extension and an instrument of policy; violence or revolutionary change was to be the cornerstone of change. This theory was attributed to Clausewitz, from whom, it was claimed, both Hegal and Marx borrowed their notions of war.[21] In the second place, wars staged by Communists were to be viewed as 'just' wars – that is, revolutionary proletarian wars were justified when staged against imperialists. In the third place, 'preventive or aggressive' war carried out by the Communists were also 'just' wars; here, the 'class' origins of those who wage war was significant. Finally, war between Communist states and bourgeois states was inevitable. Stalin and his followers recognized that they dwelt in an age characterized by the existence of an international 'system' of states. Under Stalin Soviet decision-makers regarded the question of coexistence with capitalist states as something 'unthinkable'. Under Khrushchev this outlook changed; the policy of peaceful coexistence became a key element in Soviet foreign policy objectives. Nevertheless, Stalin's conclusions had all led the Soviet Union to give war preparations the highest priority, and this had its effects on Soviet foreign policy. Stalin's arguments for this had been declared as early as 1921 when he argued that 'four tasks' confronted the Soviet Union in foreign policy:

(1) to utilize each and every contradiction and conflict among the surrounding capitalist groups and governments for the purpose of disintegrating imperialism;
(2) to spare no pains or means to render assistance to proletarian revolutions;
(3) to take all necessary measures to strengthen the national liberation movement in the East; and
(4) to strengthen the Red Army.[22]

Stalin, however, did not deviate from Lenin's theoretical principles on imperialism, the most important element of which is that the present era is dominated by two forces: imperialism and proletarian revolution. Stalin went further and said that Leninism existed and grew under imperialism, and he went on to what he considered the logical conclusion that the existing conditions would lead to the intensification of the contradictions between the proletariat and capitalism. He also claimed that the imperialist scramble for raw materials, basically in the colonies, produced a new form of contradiction between the 'various financial groups and imperialist powers', which, in turn, would lead both to obtain foreign territory. All this would lead to wars, to the 'acceleration of the advent of the proletarian revolution' and to the inevitability of war and thus to another contradiction, between the 'handful of civilized nations' and the millions of colonial and dependent peoples of the world. The dialectical manner in which these situations evolve would 'ultimately' lead imperialism to construct industry and commerce which naturally produce a proletarian class and 'native intelligentsia'. All this would lead to the awakening of national consciousness and thence to a movement for emancipation.

Conditions in the Arab world when Khrushchev was in power were fundamentally different from those of Stalin's period. At the Twentieth Congress of the Communist Party of the Soviet Union, in February 1956, Khrushchev declared:

> The new period in world history, predicted by Lenin, when the people of the East play an active part in deciding the destinies of the whole world and have become a new and mighty factor in international relations has arrived . . . These countries, although they do not belong to the socialist world system, can draw on its achievements in building an independent national economy and in raising their peoples' standards. Today they need not go begging to their former oppressors for modern equipment. They can get it in the socialist countries, free from any political or military obligations.[23]

It was not therefore surprising that the first consignment of Eastern European arms was despatched to Egypt in September 1955, especially since Khrushchev's last alternative coincided with the peak of Nasir's power in the Arab world. Nasir maintained that Egypt and the other Arab countries could find from the socialist bloc the assistance they required in their nation-building, especially in economic and military spheres. Khrushchev's pronouncements were a clear declaration of policy toward the East in a period when the latter was on the verge of getting rid of the vestiges of the West which had dominated the East for such a long period of time. Former colonies had to embark on a new stage of international politics, which meant amongst other things that these states would play a dominating role in shaping international relations. This fact would automatically produce new crises in the world, whose outcome was uncertain except for the Soviet Union, which believed that the people of these countries would triumph in the end since they were waging a 'just' war. Khrushchev meant that the policy of peaceful coexistence had reached the stage where neither East nor West would declare war though direct military involvement in the East would be likely.

When the Egyptian–Czechoslovakian arms deal was announced, Soviet writers were loud in their praise. Maximov,[24] for example, argued that it was almost like a trade agreement – arms for Egyptian commodities, chiefly cotton and rice. The Egyptian government was guided by the fact that its independence in foreign policy decision-making must be guarded, and its desire to enhance the capability of its armed forces must be strengthened to a point where the creation of a capable army was an insurance and a sign of security and independence of Egypt. No strings were attached to the agreement which was mutually beneficial; the Western world would have much to lose because of Egypt's decision, as it aimed at preserving Egypt as a weak nation and drawing it into military pacts that would further weaken Egypt and cause it to lose control over its own destiny.

In reality, and contrary to Maximov's approach, the arms deal meant that Egypt had chosen a new course in its foreign policy which would lead, among other things, to the opening of the strategic position of the Arab world and the Middle East to the Soviet Union and its allies. More important, it was indicative of the fact that an alternative for a Third World country existed in the balance of international power. It was this last element that suited both Egypt and the Soviet Union's objectives in the Arab world, for the former was encountering great problems in obtaining aid from the West for two basic reasons. First, since Israel occupied a prominent position in the region, Egypt would have to opt out of strategic Arab and future Middle East alliances. Secondly, the United States and its Western allies would neither arm Egypt nor give it economic aid, since Egypt was the champion of Arab nationalism; one of the precepts of nationalism was to follow independent policies, including independent foreign policies, and in this respect the Egyptian concept of Arab nationalism constituted a threat to Western interests in the Arab world. The idea of Arab nationalism, which Nasir personally advocated, meant ridding the Arab world of foreign military forces; the Soviet Union, at the time, had no military presence in the Arab world.

The Soviet Union emerged from the Czechoslovakian arms deal as a major power which could sustain and fill the gap that the West had left. The alternative which the arms deal and its economic potential had created was a lesson to other nations in the Arab world that such a deal would not only be advantageous to both participants but that agreements in the military and economic spheres were not considered mere grants between the two emerging allies but were a deal made on easy terms in a relaxed atmosphere.

Arab–Soviet relations should not obscure cordial Israeli–Soviet relations. On the occasion of the celebration of the second anniversary of the resumption of diplomatic relations between Israel and the Soviet Union, the Israeli–USSR Friendship League held a reception in Ramat Gan; those present included the Soviet, Polish, Rumanian, Hungarian, Bulgarian and Yugoslav delegations representing their respective countries;[25] on the following day Israel and the Soviet Union exchanged notes amounting to a shipping agreement.[26]

When in September 1955 the Soviet Union, through Czechoslovakia, delivered its first consignment of armaments to Egypt, it was a major breakthrough for the Soviet Union in the Arab world. Nevertheless, it should not be concluded that the Soviet bloc severed relations with Israel. The issue had a different implication. The Soviet Union and its satellites enjoyed the relations which were set up by the two antagonists in the Middle East. The Soviet Union did not necessarily regard the theoretical approach and analysis of Zionism as a significant issue. The cornerstone of relations both with the Arab world, through the rising star of Nasir, and with Israel remained an issue which had two inherent objectives. As far as the Soviet Union was concerned, the question of 'national interest' remained one of the most important elements in its foreign policy objectives in the region. However, that in itself indicated that Soviet progress led to a wider issue which encompassed East–West relations in general. This period, especially the development of the Suez crisis in the following year, proved to be an arena where both East and West watched political development through the small states under their respective control in the region. It could be argued that from this moment the Arab–Israeli conflict had taken on wider international significance. Prior to the Egyptian–Czechoslovak arms deal the Soviet Union had stood on the periphery of Arab politics, for its relations with the Arab world, particularly the Arab–Israeli conflict, was confined basically to minor political pronouncements. But its intrusion into the Arab world was welcomed not only by the Arab nationalistic spirit which Nasir's leadership generated but also by all Arab nationalist parties, legal or underground, which constituted a natural political front.

In practical terms the Czechoslovak arms deal to Egypt prompted the Israelis to announce on 17 October 1955, at an exhibition in Israel of locally produced arms, that Israel had not received any similar offer from the Eastern bloc. More important still, the *Voice of Zion* emanating from Israel beamed the following message:

... Finally, there is the examination [in Israel] of ways in
which Israel's resources can be used for strategic purposes,
and significant in the context was the recent announcement
that a start had been made on extracting uranium from Negev
phosphates.[27]

This fact, of military importance, denotes a reality that the Soviet
Union ought to have taken into consideration in evaluating its
foreign policy in regard to the Arab–Israeli conflict; the simple
strategic fact that Israel now had the potential to produce atomic
bombs brought a new dimension to the whole Arab–Israeli conflict.
Setting aside the issue of the Jewish people's right to an independent
state, for Israel to obtain such weapons at a time when it was
accepted by both East and West meant that a new stage of *realpolitik*
had dawned on the Middle East scene. It was also significant that
the Soviet Union had reached a political stage in the Arab–Israeli
conflict when it had no choice but to take a balanced stand. It had
perhaps reached the stage where it had satisfied both rivals. It was
to be the continuous supplier of arms to the Arabs indirectly through
Czechoslovakia; it had been the first major power to extend *de jure*
recognition to Israel, not to mention the role it had played before the
Jewish state was established, and, more important still, it had
relaxed its laws about the emigration of Jews from both the Soviet
Union and the Eastern bloc *after* Israel had been established.
Nevertheless, Israeli press commentary on the Egyptian–Czechoslovakian deal stressed a common public stand on this development.
Al-Hamishmar argued that 'Israel should declare her neutrality in the
cold war now developing in the Middle East and not ask the West
for arms to counteract the Communist offer';[28] while *Lamerhav*
argued that 'Nevertheless, Israel's defense interests and political
position necessitate her getting rid of her one-sided dependence on
Western arms and finding additional sources of supply in the
Eastern bloc.'[29]

To Israel the announcement of the extraction of uranium from the
Negev phosphates, which meant that its nuclear capabilities were in
the process of developing, certainly had wider regional and
international political-strategic implications. In the first place, it
meant that Israel must follow the course set by the Egyptian–
Czechoslovak arms deal and obtain armaments from the Eastern
bloc and not just the West. That itself meant that Israel must have
the political capability to maneuver freely between the two blocs as

long as its relations with each bloc were historically well founded. That contained the implication that once assistance was rendered to the Arabs, Israel must be able to keep a neutral circle of friends in the Arab–Israeli conflict. None of the Arab states had such an advantage; they were at the political stage of polarization which dictated siding with either the Western or the Eastern bloc. Israel thus resorted to its final option by declaring that plans were under way for obtaining nuclear capability, and this declaration held implications for all subsequent political developments. All future events occurring after military encounters with the Arabs were to be wars gradually to fulfill the long aspired-to Zionist dream within the Zionist ideology which was sparked off by Herzl in the late nineteenth century. It left the strategic approach of the Arabs at a stage of being purely defensive gestures, for the matter only became real when applied to the question of how the Arabs would fulfill their hopes of liberating Palestine, while at the same time it took the possibility of nuclear weapons into realistic consideration. Israel's nuclear capability undoubtedly dictated a defensive strategic situation in which it would be the undisputed power in the Arab–Israeli conflict.

Nevertheless, once Soviet arms were channeled to Egypt through the Eastern European bloc, Israeli demands for US aid increased in order to equalize the balance of power in the Middle East.[30] The Soviet Union also used diplomatic channels as an intermediary for a future solution of the Arab–Israeli conflict.[31]

It must now be asked what the Soviet Union's position would be. The Soviet Union had achieved its initial objective in that it had finally been granted a golden political opportunity to gradually penetrate the Arab world through Egypt. At the same time, the Soviet Union with its Eastern bloc was in the position of having normal and cordial relations with both Middle East antagonists. Even if the Soviet position is taken on a purely theoretical basis, the Egyptian–Czechoslovak arms deal is to be viewed in the context of aiding a nationalistic trend which happened to be anti-Western. In the economic field Nasir's objectives fitted squarely with the Soviet Union's overall foreign policy objectives. This, together with the Soviet Union's intrusion into the Arab world through the arms deal, implied that the Arab world would gradually become an area in which the former would have a military-strategic position which would enable it not only to penetrate a region historically a Western domain, but also would put it in a position to be one of the most important challengers to its major rival, the United States. The traditional colonial powers, Britain and France who came out of World War II exhausted, were for all practical purposes in decline. On the contrary, the Soviet Union's *realpolitik* had national interest as its cornerstone, and all means were used to further this goal.

All wars inherently contain a political objective. To Israel, once it had added a nuclear capability to the explicit and immutable political guarantees of statehood it already possessed from both the East and the West, it followed logically that all subsequent Arab–Israeli wars would be based solely on the long-awaited Zionist expansionist designs. The Soviet Union entered the entanglement not to aid the Arabs in fulfilling their long aspired-to liberation of Palestine, but more specifically to find a role whereby it would be able to be an active member in political and strategic decision-making – a Russian dream that predates the Communist regime in the Soviet Union. The Egyptian–Czechoslovak arms deal opened a new page in Eastern bloc relations with the Arab world. Egypt signed a trade agreement with East Germany and a Czechoslovak trade mission landed in Egypt, while Syria was moved to celebrate the anniversary of the Russian Revolution and called for 'closer Soviet–Arab relations'.[32] Moreover, that a wide range of Arab states now opened their gates to the Eastern bloc was evident when Amir Faisal, later King of Saudi Arabia, had discussions with the Soviet Union and Czechoslovakian embassies while he was in Cairo which resulted in a 'Saudi Arabian mission . . . visit [to] arms factories in Prague'.[33] Both Lebanon and the Yemen reached out for mutual Eastern bloc aid; the former conducted commercial talks with Poland, the latter expressed willingness to accept arms from the Soviet Union.[34]

All in all, the Czechoslovak–Egyptian arms deal opened a new chapter in the Soviet Union's foreign policy in the Arab world, and Nasir's role in this cannot be neglected. The arms deal once concluded brought with it the idea that the existence of cordial relations with the Eastern bloc would mean in all practical senses that an alternative existed for the Arab world in the East–West balance of power; this in turn underlay another political reality, that the concept of international non-alignment does have some credibility. A short time after this development, Nasir was able to play a significant part in the non-aligned states conference at Bandung, enhancing his role within the non-aligned bloc of the Third World. But even at this point, Israel's relations with the Soviet bloc carried on normally, including trade. Trade relations subsequently flourished between the Arab States and the Communist bloc led by the Soviet Union.

According to an Egyptian source[35] Egypt had began 'thinking' about relations with the Soviet Union only two months after the July 1952 Revolution, when the Egyptian Finance Minister explained that the economic situation was deteriorating due to the inability to market Egyptian cotton. Contacts were then made with the Socialist countries for this purpose, but Egypt, at this early stage, had formed no definite opinion as to whether the socialist camp would be able to solve the problem. In this way, relations with the Soviet Union were established, which led to trade delegations and contacts being established with the entire socialist camp. The first trade delegation to the Soviet Union returned with an encouraging response to the provision of loans, the construction of factories and arms supplies. But at the end of 1953 and in early 1954, opinions were not yet clear as to how this development should be handled.

On other Arab developments the Soviet Union had definite points of view. The onset of British–American 'rivalry' in the exploitation of natural oil resources was a source of dispute elaborated upon by Soviet writers.[36] It was claimed that a 'bitter struggle' was in progress for economic, political and military 'domination' of the area, and that this rivalry had, to a large extent, resulted in a series of *coup d'état* in the Arab world brought about by the intensification of competition, especially in Iran, Saudi Arabia and the Arabian Gulf area. Oil-producing countries and agriculturally based economies were all under foreign (that is, Western) tutelage. According to V. Kapitonov, only Saudi Arabia and the Yemen had 'proclaimed' independence; the rest of the countries were British 'possessions and protectorates'.[37]

The most prominent feature of these countries was their 'backwardness'; the small industrial projects were in the 'handicraft' stage of development, while the large oil enterprises belonged 'exclusively' to foreign capital. No contribution was being made to the development of a national economy in these countries. Hence the existing conditions of the working class were characterized by misery and injustice, attributed to backwardness, of which Saudi Arabia was just one example; education was available only to the elite of these countries.

When Turkey and Pakistan concluded a military pact in 1954, the

Soviet Union came to the conclusion that the Arab world would be engulfed in a similar fashion. V. Kudryatsev, writing in *Izvestia*,[38] posed a rhetorical question about occurrences in the Arab world and asked why military questions had suddenly become central in the talks between the states of the Arab world; he pointed out that it had to be understood that the United States military policy in the Arab world was to forge out of the Arab states a military bloc to be used as an instrument of US military designs in the area. These designs were countered by the apparent 'contradiction' between the United States and Britain for influence over the Arab world; the 'disagreement' that had engulfed the Arab states themselves; and, finally, the growing 'national liberation movements' of the Arab people, which were a serious obstacle to the establishment of military pacts in the Arab world.

The question of economic agreement between Egypt and the US was viewed one way after the 1952 Revolution and in another light after November 1954 when a bilateral agreement for economic aid was signed between Egypt and the United States. K. Petrov argued that

> It is most indicative that the dollar 'aid' agreement is qualified by a number of conditions, humiliating for Egypt, which make it possible for American diplomats, generals and businessmen to force their way into the country's life and to dictate to Egypt policy suiting Washington. . . . The American monopolists intend to use the new agreement [dollar] aid to Egypt as a springboard from which to seize the natural resources of the country and crowd out ancient Britain.[39]

The author went on to state that this agreement had followed a recent agreement between Egypt and Britain on the establishment of a military base in the Suez Canal Zone.[40]

In Soviet eyes Iraq too was being drawn into a military pact with the West. When the Iraqi Parliament abrogated the 1930 Anglo–Iraqi Agreement due to expire in October 1957, a new military agreement was announced on 5 April 1955, whereby Britain joined, in the same month, the Turkey–Iraq military pact; this pact, according to the Soviets,[41] would draw Iraq into 'imperialist adventures' acting as an appendix to the Atlantic bloc of the Western alliance. It therefore came as no surprise that the Soviet Ministry of Foreign Affairs issued a statement on security in the

Near and Middle East;[42] it argued that with the collapse of the Middle East Command in 1951 a new approach had been instituted whereby regional pacts were established, such as the Turkish–Iraqi 'Military Alliance' formulated in February 1955 which replaced the Turkish–Pakistani Pact concluded in 1954. This pact was aimed at distancing Iraq from the rest of the Arab countries and at putting a strain on inter-Arab relations.

An attempt had been made by various means to draw Syria into a similar military pact. Syria was to try to influence Egypt into joining the same pact, the aim being to bring these countries into a disguised 'enslavement' and, more especially, to exploit the natural resources of these countries. Such regional military blocs were needed by the West to extend its domination over the whole area and to further its strategic aims.

The net result of all this, the statement argued, was loss of the 'independence' by these countries; eventually they would be drawn into wars. The West also produced absurd inventions about a 'Soviet threat' to countries of the Near and Middle East; the truth was that Soviet policies corresponded basically to the 'national interests of these countries'.

This statement should be treated with certain reservations. First, it was clear that the Soviet Union had not yet established itself in the Arab world. Second, the idea that the Arabs should take 'unified' or regional action against Western designs can be disputed simply because the leadership of those Arab countries had not reached the stage of maturity where they had the constructive means to carry out such action. Third, the extension of military pacts, as noted by the statement, in fact contradicts earlier contentions that a rivalry existed between Britain and America for influence in the Middle East and in the Arab world in particular. Lastly, the fact remains that, at this early stage of development, were the Arab states to abrogate or refuse an alliance with the West, the Soviet Union would, naturally, gain by filling the 'vacuum'. Given the weakness of the states in the region they would not be able to fulfill the objectives set forth in the principles governing the creation of such alliances. Soviet allegations that Israel too was being drawn toward regional military pacts that would, in the final analysis, 'convert Israel into a US base'[43] would most certainly aggravate US relations with the Arab countries. Such reasoning, however logical, would not only threaten peace in the area, but would make it impossible to maintain any such alliance.

Relations between the Soviet Union and Egypt improved markedly when Nasir, now Prime Minister, declared in August 1955 that he would visit Moscow in the spring of 1956. The planned visit was viewed in the context of a step towards an 'independent' foreign policy and carried with it the spirit of the Bandung Conference. The proposed visit was seen to relect the beneficial influence brought about by the recent easing of international tension.

The Bandung Conference and the Soviet arms deal to Egypt played a major role in the furtherance of the Soviet Union's entanglement in the Arab world. The Conference of Afro-Asian States, which took place between 18 and 25 April 1955 in Bandung, Indonesia, marked a new stage in the Soviet Union's diplomatic thrust into the Arab world, since the Arab and Muslim blocs constituted a sizeable proportion of the participants.[44] The Conference had four stated objectives. The third was crucial in soliciting and obtaining aid for the Palestinian cause. It stated that the Conference ought to consider problems of special interest to Asian and African peoples such as matters affecting national sovereignty, racialism and colonialism.[45] Most participating states had no hesitation in indulging in vituperative attacks against the 'colonial heritage'; as a corollary to this, a fundamental aspect of their belief was their assertion of political independence, particularly in foreign policy decisions.

The Arab bloc was determined to further the Palestinian cause at the Conference, and Nasir played a key role in doing so. This was an essential element in its basic political aspiration to extricate itself from polarization brought about by the Cold War. It saw the Conference as an opportunity to disentangle themselves from it, and perceived that Bandung gave them an opportunity to carry out an active independent policy in world affairs outside the limits of the Cold War. Throughout its proceedings, the Conference witnessed a new upsurge of Arab nationalism.

The main objectives and aspirations of the participants were basically favorable to the Soviet Union's foreign policy objectives in the Third World, principally its 'anti-colonial' attitude toward the West, and there were participating members who were more or less allied to adherents of these objectives; the People's Republic of China, the state of Vietnam, and the Democratic Republic of Vietnam were countries which acted as intermediaries for the Soviet Union. It was in Bandung, through the diplomatic channel of Chou En-Lai, that the Soviet/Eastern European states, mainly

Czechoslovakia, concluded the first arms deal. The Conference itself and the mere fact of the large Arab and Muslim presence added a new dimension to Nasir's image as a leader in the Third World since his country was a major recipient of Soviet aid and was fast emerging as a power to be reckoned with on the Arab and Middle Eastern scene.

8 Soviet consolidation of power in the Arab world: Suez and after

By early 1956, the United Kingdom and the United States had made moves to secure peace in the area, especially in view of the unsettled situation concerning Palestine and the Soviet Union's emerging power in the Arab world, demonstrated particularly by the arms deal with Egypt. The Soviet Union, in a statement issued from Moscow in February 1956, dealt with three basic issues: that military action against Egypt was a likelihood, and would be a violation of the United Nations' Charter; that these measures were being taken to 'safeguard' Western oil interests in the area; and, finally, that Western interests were in no way threatened. It also promised that

> The Soviet Government, true to the principles of its peaceful
> foreign policy, will continue to defend the cause of peace, to
> defend freedom, independence and non-interference in the
> internal affairs of the countries of the Near and Middle East,
> and jointly with other interested states will help to consolidate
> security in the area.[1]

The reaction from the Tripartite powers – the United States, Britain and France – was a declaration that they intended to send troops to the Middle East.[2] The Tripartite Declaration of 1950 had provided that if 'peace' was disturbed in the area, the three powers would first take action within the framework of the United Nations. The 1950 Declaration also served as a basis for interference, especially after the Soviet arms deal with Egypt. Thus the Palestinian problem served as an excuse both for Western interference in the area and, above all, for making a judgement on the Soviet commitment to side with the Arabs.

Once the Czechoslovakian arms had arrived in Egypt, the Soviet bloc also increased the supply of armaments and personnel. Fears were voiced that the Soviet Union and its allies, in the event of an Arab war with Israel, would aid Egypt and the Arab countries, thus tilting the military balance against Israel.[3] The Soviets accused both Britain and the US of instigating Israeli–Egyptian military clashes.[4]

The Soviet Union's major thrust in the Arab world in the second half of the 1950s added four potential elements to political development in the Middle East. First, it was believed at the time that with the advent of a Soviet presence, the chances of the West using military power had either diminished or were not feasible. Reliance on diplomatic channels was therefore the best approach. Secondly, the mere fact that the Soviet Union and its allies had entered the competition to supply arms to Egypt and the Middle East as a whole had changed the balance of power, militarily, in the area. Third, Nasir's role in fomenting Arab nationalism and Arab unity in the Arab world meant that a new element had entered the picture with which the Western powers would have to reckon. Lastly, Nasir's very political orientation meant that he was set on a course to combat the major political regional pacts in the Middle East, notably the Baghdad Pact. It was against this background that the Soviet Foreign Minister, D. T. Shepilov, was invited to attend the Egyptian celebrations for the final evacuation of the remaining British presence in Egypt from the Canal Zone,[5] and for further discussions on financing the Aswan High Dam project.[6]

The arms deal and the establishment of relations with Egypt were conducive to a new perspective on the Arab world, and a change of attitude occurred, especially as far as the Palestinian question was concerned. The Soviets argued, for example, that the British had fomented animosity between Jews and Arabs in Palestine, diverting the attention of the entire local populace from 'national liberation', centering it instead on the conflict.[7] The ultimate aim behind fomenting this conflict was to achieve Anglo-American domination of the area, which was rich in oil deposits. During World War II the United States had established relations with 'reactionary' Zionist leaders and had prompted Israel to carry out aggression against the Arabs. It hoped to make Israel its economic and military outpost in the region in opposition to its rivals in the Middle East, whereas the British aim in the region was to 'consolidate' its position in the Arab world with the aid of the 'feudal aristocracy'. Territorial disputes among the antagonists did in fact lead to armed clashes.

Another issue concerned the plight of the one million refugees who had fled from Palestine to neighboring Arab states but who were still living in refugee camps. A further prominent factor was Israel's policy of aggression, which provoked armed frontier clashes; this was inconsistent with its interests and some of the interests of the 'imperialists'. With the establishment of a Jewish state but with no corresponding Palestinian–Arab state, and with Israel following an independent foreign policy that was basically allied to the West, Israel had become a power to be reckoned with in its own right. The Arab–Israeli conflict slipped into the background, but the Palestinian problem remained unsolved. Although Egyptian–Soviet relations had been enhanced and had added an impetus to the latter's recognition of the problem in a wider context, the existence of Israel had not basically changed matters; rather, the Arab–Israeli conflict had taken a new direction.

When United Nations Secretary-General Dag Hammarskjöld took the first steps towards achieving a United Nations solution of the Arab–Israeli conflict, to which the Palestinian issue was central, the Soviet Union interpreted his actions as a signal for solving the problem[8] in accordance with the Security Council Resolution of 4 April 1956, whereby assurances were received from both Israel and Egypt that they would cease hostilities and would observe the cease-fire agreement on the existing demarcation line.

Hammarskjöld's step, the commentator went on to argue, was appreciated at a time when the US had adopted separate measures for the Middle East, independent of the United Nations, and had tried to influence its allies to follow suit. These plans were reminiscent of old-fashioned colonialism, but the Arab countries, in the face of such designs, were supported by the Soviet Union who shared its southern borders with them and thus could not remain indifferent. The argument was that the use of force on a bilateral basis, ignoring the United Nations' decisions, had shown that solving a problem of this nature could not be accomplished in this manner. But experience had shown that it could be handled through international cooperation based on equality, non-interference in the affairs of others and the legitimate rights of the peoples concerned. The argument stopped short of mentioning Palestinian rights and aspirations. The question of Palestine, as the Soviets saw it, was not an urgent and independent issue that warranted immediate attention but one that could be solved outside the sphere of the Arab countries' independent policy-making. As regards Israel, the Soviet Union's view remained the same, but with some hesitation so far as the idea of Zionism was concerned; the whole question was seen as having become tangled because of an 'outside' element – that is, the pressure which had been brought to bear on both the Arabs and the Israelis.

At the United Nations the Soviet delegate adhered to the argument that the issue should be solved peacefully and in accordance with the national 'aspirations of the people concerned'. Posing the question as to why this could not be applied to the Palestinians, he argued that this was because of American accusation that the Soviet Union had created a crisis by supplying Czechoslovakian arms to Egypt in pursuance of a mutually acceptable trade agreement between them, the Soviet Union and the Eastern bloc. The question had reached a critical point where the West was once again bringing back to life the Cold War in the region, an action which would result in tension that could lead to an upsurge of conflict and perhaps another war. The Soviet Union's stand remained unchanged, wanting a 'peaceful' settlement whereby the antagonists would reach a mutual solution acceptable to all concerned. This meant that if the problem had to be solved either on an international basis or in the United Nations Security Council it would mean, inescapably, a certain involvement by the Soviet Union.

Writing in *New Times*, an 'observer', generally assumed to be an official spokesman, noted on Egyptian Independence Day that the goal of independence which the Egyptians had striven for since the British 'occupied' Egypt in 1882 had been achieved after seventy years of foreign domination. He argued that the chief concern of the Egyptian leadership should be the search for social and economic 'reforms' that would enable Egypt to improve its economic development and cultural backwardness so that its independence would be strengthened. Egypt's social and economic reforms had reached the stage where agrarian reforms had limited excessive landholdings, 'repelling feudal titles' and encouraging the cooperative system; all these measures would lead to restructuring the social pattern of Egypt and the new regime had embarked on a new economic policy where the consolidation of economic and political independence was the main task. Finally, the Egyptians had set a course not only for themselves but for all Arab people who strove for independence; the significance of the Egyptian success was that a small country could set an example to other countries who could achieve independence in the same manner and, at the same time, play a role in the international balance of power.

The Soviet Union's diplomatic entry into the Arab world was acknowledged by a visit of Foreign Minister Shepilov to Egypt, Syria and Lebanon. This was the first time a Soviet Foreign Minister had toured the Arab world and an 'observer' recalled[9] that the Soviet Union had been the first power to recognize the independence of Saudi Arabia and the first to conclude an equal treaty of friendship with the Yemen. A reminder was given that the Soviet Union did not seek any 'privileges' in the Arab world, such as the building of military bases or the imposition of unfavorable agreements, nor did it wish to acquire oil rights or other concessions. In the joint communiqué which was issued by the four states, it was stated that they would not rely on their efforts alone but also on the efforts of other states which, in turn, would not lead to any doubt that relations with the Western world should be impaired or harmed in any way.

Shepilov's visit to the Arab world signified recognition of the fact that major changes had occurred in Egypt. Nasir had been installed as President of Egypt and had opened up the Arab world to the Soviet Union. This had been followed by a policy of neutrality and the Arab world had embarked on the upheavals brought about by Arab nationalism. All of these factors together had led Egypt onto a collision course with the West where matters relating to the strategic importance of the Arab world were concerned. The Foreign Minister's visit to the Arab world at that juncture underlined the fact that the Soviet Union and its allies offered an alternative to the Western powers. In all probability East–West relations were discussed, and in a situation where the Arab position was at odds with the West, the East was clearly an outlet, especially as Nasir had embarked on a course that would ultimately lead to collision with the West.

As far as the Soviet Union was concerned, the first political stage which the Arab world had to undergo had been accomplished; and it remained only to fill the economic gap; with the aid of the Soviet Union and the Eastern bloc this would be brought to a satisfactory conclusion. The Soviet Union regarded the developments that were taking place in both Egypt and the surrounding Arab countries as an opportunity that could not be ignored.

The Soviet Union had an added advantage over the Western powers at this juncture insofar as it was considered to be a latecomer politically and strategically in the region. It had no previous history of military pacts and bases in the Arab world, nor did it attempt to use force in the region to achieve its goals, whether political or economic. Everything that was happening signified a transformation in the balance of power in the Arab world, especially as the West had reached a point where its power in some of the important countries of the Arab world was about to be eroded.

When on 19 July the news came out that finance for the Aswan High Dam Project had been refused by the Americans and the World Bank, the Egyptian news media declared that 'the Western Powers' decision showed that they did not want a strong Egypt, able to stand on her feet; but Egypt will build the High Dam anyhow'.[10] The Western refusal prompted Egypt to seek the assistance of the Soviet Union, which the latter was more than willing to render. The High Dam project was thus merely the catalyst which opened a new chapter in the Soviet Union's intrusion in the Arab world, this time not confined to supply of armaments or short-term economic projects. It was significant also for the Soviet Union, since if any other Arab state contemplated any similar venture, then the Soviet Union would also avail itself of the opportunity to assist it. Soviet–Israeli relations however were not interrupted; only a few months later the Soviet State Bank and the Bank of Israel reached agreement on the extension of the payments arranged between the two states for an additional two years.[11]

On 26 July 1956, Nasir delivered a speech in Alexandria in which he attacked Britain's designs against Egypt and the Arab world which were his reasons for nationalizing the Suez Canal Company. Britain, France and Israel decided to take joint action because of Nasir's move on nationalization and its strategic implications; the US had a different opinion. The French regarded Nasir's attack on colonial powers in Africa and Asia as likely to make him an ardent supporter of the FLN in Algeria. His aspirations for the unity of the Arab world from North Africa to the Arabian peninsula and his desire to establish an Islamic unity encompassing the same area were considered a threat to French influence in North Africa. Thus the destruction of Nasir would most certainly remove a menacing power in North Africa and cut arms supplies to the Algerian revolutionaries.

The use of the Canal was vital to Western interests. The failure to internationalize the Suez Canal Company would lead to the loss of Western interests in the area. Two means were to be employed to make sure the West was not deprived of its use; first, economic and political pressures; and, second, if these failed, the use of force. Nasir's action had produced two problems for the West. If it was successful, it would be both an example for other emerging states to follow against former or existing colonial powers; and more immediately, he would be able to block seaborne movements, troops, supplies and trade to the West, the most important item in which was oil supplies. Blocking the oil supply would bring chaos to the Western financial structure, and this would have a bearing on its defense capabilities. Moreover, a weak West meant, at this stage, that the Arab world and the Middle East in general were more susceptible still to Soviet penetration and influence.

Soviet writers hailed the Egyptian nationalization of the Suez Canal Company announced on 26 July with enthusiasm. Y. Bocharyov[12] regarded it as Egypt's legitimate right, and rebuked Western commentators for leveling a 'barrage of abuse and threats against Egypt'. The US, Britain and France had sent notes of protest to Egypt, which rejected them, emphasizing that navigation through the Canal Zone would not be hampered. The whole act of nationalization, the commentator said, should be viewed in the context of an act that sought to combat the Western colonial heritage; the West's attempt at a war of nerves would fail because the age of colonialism, one manifestation of which was the use of 'punitive action', held no chance of success. Later, when the US, Britain and France sponsored a conference on 16 August 1956 to discuss Suez, Bocharyov[13] argued that the participation of the US came naturally even though it was not a signatory to the 1888 Convention.

What was not seen as natural or justifiable was the absence of the People's Republic of China and of any Arab state which had a vested interest in the Suez Canal. The argument was that Western 'weakness' in the Suez affair was due to the lack of unanimity in their own ranks, and added a reminder that

> If Western diplomats were not led away by wishful thinking
> and illusions, and if they took a more sober view of the
> alignment of public forces in the world today, they would have
> no difficulty in finding a way out of the Suez tangle . . . [and]
> the Soviet delegation to the London Conference, as its leader

> Foreign Minister Shepilov announced, will do everything possible to help find ways and means of settling controversial questions through negotiation between all the countries concerned, with the participation of Egypt, on the basis of a proper combination of her national interests as an independent and sovereign state and the justified interests of the other countries using the Suez canal.[14]

Further comment ran that a general pattern seemed to emerge from the Conference.[15] The issue had two dimensions: the act of nationalization and the assurance of freedom of navigation through the Canal. So far as nationalization was concerned, Egypt had acted within its sovereign rights, and the discussions at the London Conference had centered on the differences concerning the methods for ensuring the freedom and normal operation of the waterway – that is, the 'safe-guarding of the economic interests of its users'. Thus the first issue had been solved, but the latter remained debatable. The Soviet stand was that Egypt's nationalization of the Canal Company was a rightful act and an internal matter; nevertheless, its attitude to the establishment of an international administrative body ensuring freedom of navigation through the Canal was that this was contrary to the Charter of the United Nations and that any attempt to alter this would lead to the disruption of peace in the region.

At the conclusion of the Conference, a Soviet 'observer', writing in *New Times*,[16] put forward the argument that the Conference was not empowered to settle the problem because, not being sufficiently representative, it had no authority to do so, especially as Egypt, the main party concerned, was not represented. The most the Conference could achieve was to 'define feasible approaches' to the problem and the principles on which a settlement could be brought about. During the proceedings of the Conference two approaches to the problem were revealed: one by the US known as the Dulles Plan, and the other by India's representative, Krishna Menon, each reflecting two fundamentally different approaches. No vote was taken on either of these proposals. Western representatives at the Conference took the view that freedom of navigation through the Canal should be ensured by an international agency of some sort, but had in mind turning the Conference into a trial of Egypt to serve as an example to Asian and African countries. It demonstrated that the American position did not differ from that of the rest of the

Western powers, whereas the Soviet Union's approach was to
diminish and restrict any widening of the conflict between the
Western powers and Egypt. In holding this position, the Soviet
Union had several aims in mind. In the first place, it would be
portrayed as a power serving the national interest of a weak Third
World country like Egypt. Second, the divergence of opinion with
the West meant that there existed differences of approach and
method to the solution of international disputes. Third, the stand
taken by the Soviet Union marked the fact that Britain and France
had come to the end of their colonial heydays and that their
international power no longer existed. Lastly, the affair demonstrated that the Soviet Union had entered the Arab sphere of politics
through the Suez Canal crisis, and that by taking a 'positive' stand
to safeguard Egypt's national and international rights, the latter
would realize that there existed a new and powerful ally in the
international arena.

At the end of his visit to London for the Conference the Soviet
Foreign Minister held a press conference.[17] He summed up the
proceedings by saying it had been concerned with the twin questions
of nationalism and freedom of navigation through the Canal. He
argued with an air of concern reasoning that the whole matter had
been handled from the outset in an artificial atmosphere filled with
tension and unrest fomented by Britain and France who had
resorted to the 'imposition' of economic sanctions against Egypt.
More important, these two protagonists had made military preparations, calling up their reservists and paratroopers, and conducting
naval exercises with the aim of intimidating Egypt. At the
Conference two diametrically opposite proposals were discussed.
One was India's, supported by Indonesia, Ceylon, and the Soviet
Union, the other that of the United States, which became known as
the Dulles Plan. The first proposal recognized Egypt's sovereign
rights to exercise its will freely in the Canal Zone, assuring freedom
of navigation through the Canal, and called for a new look at the
possibility of re-examining the Constantinople Convention of 1888.
Because the Soviet Union supported India's proposal, it had
throughout the Conference furthered the idea of finding a way that
would be 'acceptable' and in accordance with international norms
(that is, through negotiations), ultimately reaching a proper approach to the Suez question which would be just and acceptable to
all the interested states. Shepilov closed his speech on the note that
the whole crisis should be considered with the utmost seriousness.

In a Soviet government statement[18] before the Tripartite Aggression against Egypt (although no mention of Israel was made at this time), it was argued that Britain and France had embarked on a course that invited military action. The convening of the NATO Council to discuss the matter illustrated this fact; the whole plan for Western military activity was made in collaboration with the US and intended to put pressure on Egypt and other Arab countries.

The statement asserted that the three Western powers had worked out a plan to establish a Canal Users Association whereby Egypt's power would be curbed, and that this plan was to be implemented by force. The Soviet Union regarded such activities as contrary to the United Nations' Charter. If Britain and France were to resort to military action, they would then bring harm upon 'themselves', and 'immense danger to the Suez Canal as well as to the oil fields located in the countries of the Arab East' would ensue. Furthermore, such action would damage the major oil installations throughout the region to the detriment of local economic conditions. It was argued that aggression against Egypt would 'arouse the profound indignation' of Asian and African countries which had embarked on a course of combating colonialism; the Soviet Union hoped and would ensure that the whole issue would be settled on the principles of equality, non-interference in the internal affairs of Egypt and in conformity with Egyptian national interests.

The statement warrants some comment. In the first place, it was remarkable that no mention of Israel was made, as if it was a party alien to the issue, to which no blame could be attributed and which would take no action. Secondly, there seems to be a lack of information as to what the Soviet position and reaction would be in the event of aggression and as to how it would view events and conduct itself if a crisis did occur. Lastly, in the event that it did interfere, the Soviet Union would set a precedent for military involvement outside the Eastern bloc, confronting the West in an area that for centuries had been considered the preserve of Western influence.

The nationalization of the Suez Canal Company by Egypt had produced a positive Soviet reaction; Nasir's act was a welcome step to the Soviets. It offered help in two areas, agriculture and industrialization, but stopped short of giving hints about, or announcing, the extension of military aid.[19] *Pravda* had a comprehensive review of the crisis but gave no indication of what would happen should Britain or other countries react with military action:

The Soviet people are convinced that the liberation movement of the peoples of former colonial and dependent countries cannot be halted by military threats, economic pressure or political blackmail. The age of colonialism, when the imperialists had a free hand in the dependent countries and did as they pleased, is slipping away in the past. Now the peoples control their own destiny. Anyone who fails to realize this and tries to oppose the will of the peoples makes himself a laughing stock before the whole world.[20]

So far as the West was concerned, Soviet foreign policy objectives during the Suez crisis, in the middle and at the end of the Cold War had a two-dimensional approach. They sought to avoid the outbreak of war in the atomic age that would increase the involvement of its military capabilities internationally and, though it seemed contradictory, it hoped for the weakening of the West through other means, in particular the weakening of the NATO alliance throughout the globe. To the West, however, particularly to Great Britain, the security of the flow of Arab oil was of primary interest. Khrushchev and Marshal Bulganin, during a visit, acknowledged both that the British economy was dependent on the continued flow of Middle East oil, particularly from the Arabian Gulf, and that Britain was willing to go to war to avert any threat to this flow.[21]

The Soviet solution proposed an 'international agency, with Soviet participation in the management and maintenance of the Suez Canal'.[22] The Soviet Union was officially invited to the London Conference attended by Britain, France and the United States to decide the future of the Canal, but Khrushchev's reaction, made public in a speech, stressed that Egypt's action in nationalizing the Suez Canal Company was a legal move and within Egypt's sovereign right.[23] No other member of the Communist bloc was invited to attend the Conference.

The nationalization of the Suez Canal Company by Egypt announced on 26 July 1956 was seen to be feared by the West as a step towards nationalizing the rich oil concessions in the Arab world. The authoritative Soviet Army newspaper, *Red Star*, asked:

How can one explain the fuss which is raised in the West? . . .
It has only one purpose: to intimidate Egypt and also other countries of the Arab East in which there are oil concessions belonging to Western monopolies. The inflexible partisans of

colonialism fear that these nations could follow Egypt's example.[24]

The Soviet Union condemned the internationalization of the Suez Canal, the point of view advocated by the London Conference, seeing this proposal as the 'beachhead of colonialism' in order to re-establish the obsolete system in the East.[25]

Prior to the French–British–Israeli military action after the nationalization of the Suez Canal Company, the Soviet Union was already warning the world that military action would be taken by the 'Western' powers. It castigated the US for failing to protest publicly against the concentration of British and French forces in the Mediterranean, and declared that Egypt would 'get the active support of all progressives of mankind'.[26] The Soviet Union also delivered a statement on the Suez to the British Embassy.[27]

Soviet gains, with war between Britain and France against Egypt imminent, were manifold. In the first place, to many nations of Asia and Africa, the Soviet Union appeared as a powerful state willing to aid a weak nation, though this did not necessarily entail direct military involvement. It was agreed, secondly, that the period after Stalin's death (1953–1954) had seen the cessation of a direct frontal attack against capitalism epitomized by the West. Third, the Suez Canal crisis proved that the Soviet Union could easily feed on the weakness of the capitalist world and, at the same time, rally its satellite nations and those of Asia and Africa as one bloc, no matter how loose their grouping, around the idea of 'solidarity' against the Western powers. The Suez crisis revealed splits in the capitalist world which showed that the bloc was not cohesive and united on one stated policy and mode of action, especially on those problems and crises that involved former colonial states. Nevertheless, and despite the Soviet stand so far as the Suez crisis was concerned, the USSR advocated the right of all nations to passage through the Suez Canal.

Israel, with the consent and collaboration of Britain and France, attacked Egypt on 29 October 1956; the Soviet Union's gains in the affair were again manifold. Firstly, the attack proved the Soviet accusation that Israel was not just sabre rattling so far as the Arab world was concerned; secondly, it diverted world attention from Soviet involvement in Hungary where ideological questions were at stake. The Soviet Union had a different view of future actions, and Khrushchev commented 'if the West attacked Egypt over the Suez,

it would be a just war for Egypt and there would be volunteers'.[28]
The Soviet government issued a statement which said, *inter alia*, that

> The facts indicate that the invasion by the Israeli forces has
> clearly been calculated to be as an excuse for the Western
> powers, primarily Britain and France, to bring their troops
> into the territory of the Arab states; notably into the Suez
> Canal Zone . . . The Government of Israel, operating as a tool
> of imperialist circles bent on restoring the regime of colonial
> oppression in the East, has challenged all the Arab peoples, all
> the peoples of the East fighting against colonialism. . . . The
> Government of the Soviet Union resolutely condemns the act
> of aggression against Egypt by the governments of Britain,
> France and Israel.[29]

The Suez crisis had helped show that the Soviet Union had been
able to maneuver politically in different ways in the area. By raising
the Suez crisis in the Security Council two further dimensions were
added to the problem. On the one hand, should US–Soviet concerns
be established, both powers could act on one course of political
action; and on the other hand, the mere fact that the United Nations
was involved and successful in achieving its objectives would
certainly enhance the organization's prestige and presence in solving
international problems. The crisis had given a glimpse of the Soviet
Union's capabilities in the area, for it had witnessed the 'non-
interference', military or otherwise, of the Soviet Union on the side
of Egypt. Although it had threatened to offer 'volunteers' to Egypt,
the offer was discounted by the West.[30] The crisis, ironically,
enhanced Soviet prestige and capabilities not only in the Arab world
but also in the newly emerging states of Africa and Asia.

Having encountered British and French vetoes at the Security
Council, the Soviet Union moved to solve the problem in the
General Assembly of the United Nations with certain objectives in
mind: the achievement of a cease-fire between the belligerents in
Egypt; the withdrawal of foreign troops from Egyptian territory; and
the creation of a 'supervisory' force by the United Nations to oversee
the execution of the General Assembly's decisions. In addition, the
Soviet Union sought to revitalize the Bandung Conference.

After accusing the three allied forces, French, British and Israeli,
of being the aggressors, the issue was handled largely within the
diplomatic channels of the United Nations. The Suez problem, after

147

it had subsided, proved that the Soviet Union had become, in its own right, a power to be reckoned with in the Middle East and, by being able to grant military aid to both Egypt and Syria, that it could make its influence felt in countries dependent upon the Suez Canal. The Soviet Union withdrew its offer of 'volunteers' to be dispatched to Egypt,[31] and the Soviet bloc took the 'credit' for the defeat of the Western powers.[32]

As relations between Egypt and Syria strengthened, especially after the Suez affair, Soviet–Israeli relations worsened. Israel was accused of becoming a 'military arsenal' threatening peace in the Middle East, especially in Jordan and Syria; Ben Gurion, the Israeli Prime Minister, was accused of preparing for another war in Egypt. Soviet Jews emigrating to Israel, it was claimed, found 'poverty, unemployment, discrimination and hostility when arriving there'.[33] The Soviets saw Israel's military role and built-up as tied in with the NATO alliance, its forces and capabilities being part and parcel of this alliance and serving NATO's strategic aims in the Middle East.

So far as Israel was concerned, the Nasirite tide was a threat that would be 'able to unite the Arabs and create a formidable force to be reckoned with the eventuality of war'. When Israel sided with the Western powers in military action it meant that Nasir would be defeated militarily. The war, which lasted from 29 October to 6 November 1956, brought a number of consequences. The British–French–Israeli fiasco over the Suez Canal brought results contrary to those intended. The Arab world rallied around Nasir, and his prestige and influence grew, while the West faced the slow erosion of its conservative allies in the Arab world. The Soviet Union, though it was involved in the Hungarian crisis at the same time, was observing events in Egypt closely. The war was a defeat for Anglo-French diplomacy and the ability of those nations to maneuver in the United Nations. The war did not achieve its objective of setting up an independent international body to administer the Canal Zone; in fact, it had produced the opposite result with an even stronger Egyptian presence.

The Soviet Union's attitude to the aggressors was expounded in official messages and pronouncements.[34] A note sent by the Soviet Union Foreign Ministry to Britain and France denounced the action of the three nations, and stated that:

In setting up closed zones that impede freedom of navigation in

the Mediterranean and the Red Sea, the Governments of the
United Kingdom and France are disregarding the decision of
the United Nations and are further aggravating the situation
in the Near East. The Government of the Soviet Union [is]
resolutely against these unlawful actions taken by the United
Kingdom and France and declares that responsibility for all
possible consequences of such actions rests with the British
and French governments.[35]

Soviet Premier Bulganin had sent a message to President Eisenhower proposing that the fighting should be stopped by joint action
of their two countries since the war in Suez was threatening the
peace of the world and creating the possibility of World War III.
The American President rejected the proposal on two grounds:
firstly, that the matter should be settled through the United Nations;
secondly, that the Soviet proposal, if it carried any weight, was
intended to divert attention from the Soviet invasion of Hungary.[36]

Ten years after the nationalization of the Suez Canal the
aggressors set out their reactions to the affair. In relating the course
of events which led to France agreeing to assist Israel in the
purchase of a patent in connection with nuclear development, it was
said that as far back as the summer of 1953, both France and Israel
had come to the conclusion that they shared a common enemy who
threatened French colonial designs in North Africa, especially in
Algeria, and the very existence of Israel.[37] The British also saw the
danger to their interests which Nasir's leadership generated. Thus
they and Israel decided to take certain military action that might
perhaps put an end to Nasir's leadership. In his recollections of the
Tripartite Aggression against Egypt, the then French Foreign
Minister, C. Pineau, argued that Nasir's prevention of free passage
through the Canal for Israeli ships had similar consequences for
French and British navies. The French reasoned that a 'feeling of
solidarity with Israel' existed because of the fear that Nasir would
extend his influence over the Algerian revolution. Two stages in the
Franco-Israeli alliance were recounted: the first was the Israeli
objective of gaining a long-term supply of arms from France; and the
second, the expropriation of the Suez Canal Company by Egypt,
which had ominous undertones and led Israel to obtain support
from France. It was related that the Soviet Union then took two
major steps. It made a proposal to the US for joint action to halt the
Anglo-French operations while it also threatened vague reprisals.

The conflict over the Suez Canal was an opportunity that the Soviet Union could not ignore since the disagreement and divisions within the Western camp gave the Soviet Union the chance to propose joint action with the United States. The Soviet Union played the whole crisis in a careful and calculated manner; it proposed the dispatch of 'volunteers' only on 6 November 1956, the day the cease-fire was announced, and it was only on 10 November that *Tass* announced that the Soviet government would not hinder the dispatch of volunteers to aid Egypt.

Seen in retrospect, the Czechoslovakian armaments deal with Egypt in September 1955 opened a new chapter in Soviet Union involvement in the Arab world. Earlier, in April 1955, the West had established the Baghdad Pact, a regional-military Middle East alliance that was an offshoot of the Cold War, which the Soviet Union regarded with disdain. The Western powers, particularly France, undertook the task of arming Israel with up-to-date military equipment. The effect of the nationalization of the Suez Canal Company was to unite France, Britain and Israel against the common enemy symbolized by Nasir. The Soviet Union made no move to rescue him other than political statements and pronouncements. Many Soviet voices condemned the Tripartite Aggression, but it was not clear to what extent the Soviet Union would execute practical steps to put an end to the aggression. The question of the short- and long-term aims of the Tripartite Aggression against Egypt remained. If the ultimate objective of the West was to overthrow Nasir's leadership in the Arab world, then the consequence was to produce a new era for it. Arab relationships had come under attack; this affected Arab attitudes to the West and so induced closer Arab–Soviet relations; subsequent economic and political Arab–Eastern European agreements were clear manifestations of such close relations.

Anwar Sadat's analysis of the Tripartite Aggression dwelt on the idea which 'divided' the Western camp on the question of aggression. He singled out the United States:

Ask yourself, America, why you changed your mind all of a
sudden about financing the High Dam Project, why Britain
and France concealed from you their alliance with Israel, in
concert with whom they used your dollars, arms and aircraft to
bomb cities and kill the innocent, why Britain used the veto for
the first [time] against you, America, on 30th October [1956],

why the war criminal Eden, at the peak of his vanity, publicly challenged you when his forces used your arms and dollars against Egypt, why Britain and France did not respond to the UN resolution of 2nd November, the resolution which you, America, presented, and why they persisted in their aggression until 7th November when they became certain that they would be severely punished for their crime. Then, and only then, did they acquiesce. Why do they resort to you today when they mocked you yesterday? Why do they kneel at your calling for help under the flag of the Western alliance? Ask yourself all these questions and find the answers before you listen to the voice of aggression and to the hissing of serpents which emanate from London today.[38]

Sadat's pronouncements tallied with Soviet Union's perception of the Tripartite Aggression, namely that 'contradictions' existed within the Western camp in which Britain and France were declining powers. The United States was the sole remaining Western power able to direct the events of the war in such a way that it at least would remain in a neutral position, if it could not exert some more positive political pressure. Sadat's phraseology was such that it neglected the role to be played by the Soviet Union whether in political measures and/or military capabilities if ever the need should arise. Such a step, if ever it were taken, would most certainly have international implications. None the less, it should be stressed at this point that the Soviet military option was not likely to be exercised for two reasons. The Soviet Union was not yet ready or willing to undertake such action on behalf of Egypt, a country that was not the least in line with Communist precepts; on the other hand, the international political pendulum was swinging in favor of Egypt, so what was needed was a certain clarification of the position.

The chronology of the Tripartite Aggression sheds some light on the Soviet Union's handling of the whole affair: Israeli forces invaded Sinai on 29 and 30 October; the British–French ultimatum to both Israel and Egypt to end the fighting was sent on 30 October; immediately afterwards, on 30 and 31 October, the British and French began bombing Egypt; they began an assault on Port Said on 5 November; finally, a UN cease-fire was accepted by Britain and France on 7 November. On 31 October, the day after the Israeli invasion, the Soviet Union called for unified action by the UN against the aggressors. However, in a practical sense, the Soviet

Union was not able to take any decisive military action, for to move against Britain and France would most definitely mean US intervention and would only serve to escalate the war worldwide. Moreover, the Soviet Union's nuclear capabilities were inferior to those of the United States should the crisis develop on an international level. But it should be stressed here that the Soviet Union would hesitate to intervene militarily on behalf of the Arabs. For one thing, the Arabs were a power 'outside' the Communist orbit. The Soviet Union would not risk getting involved directly in such a crisis; the course had been set for it to maneuver politically in the Arab world, and this was an objective which the Soviet Union wished to make the most of.

It should be stressed here that the Soviet Union had entered the Arab world during Nasir's rule by invitation, since Nasir was looking for an alternative to the former European colonial powers for assistance to rebuild Egyptian society economically and militarily. Thus Egypt's invitation to the Soviet Union was a logical step. Nasir's political outlook also played an important role in closer relations with the Soviet Union, especially his ideas on Arab nationalism, which was anti-Western. Parallel with these factors was Khrushchev's argument at the Twentieth Congress of the Communist Party of the Soviet Union in which he favored a policy of political and economic support for 'national bourgeois' ruling elite. Even though Nasir persecuted local Egyptian Communists, the Soviet Union did not find that this hindered closer relations with him. It does, however, lead to the conclusion that the Soviet Union did not use 'rigid' theoretical precepts in its dealings with emerging and mostly nationalistic countries such as Egypt. It also suggests that the Soviet Union approved the political concepts of 'national-democracy and national-socialism' that Egypt was following. Finally, Khrushchev's period witnessed the ideological friction between China and the Soviet Union which led to antagonism between the two major Communist powers over spheres of influence in the Third World, an area heading toward major changes.

At the beginning of 1957, when the Suez affair had subsided, Khrushchev granted an interview to the *al-Jumhoria* correspondent in Moscow; he accused imperialism of fomenting internal plots against the Arab countries. Khrushchev went on to argue that the Suez War had 'made it abundantly clear that Israeli leaders were imperialist tools'.[39] The Soviet Union recognized that the Arab world had entered a new phase and acquired new political status since the United States had entered the area, thus diminishing the roles played by Britain and France. This rivalry in the Western camp was a clear indication to the Soviet Union that political and economic conditions would be affected. This change of roles was expressed by the Eisenhower Doctrine, to which the Soviet Union reacted swiftly. The Soviet Union's statement on the issue argued, *inter alia*, that

> At present when a favorable situation has developed in the Middle East and when real possibilities have been created for consolidating peace and settling outstanding issues in that area, the government of the United States has come forth with a program which envisages flagrant interference on the part of the United States in the affairs of the Arab countries, including military intervention. . . . The Soviet Union's foreign policy is based on the principle of peaceful co-existence of states, regardless of differences in their social systems, and the establishment of businesslike co-operation among the nations. . . . The Soviet Union firmly denounces any manifestation of colonialism, any 'doctrine' which protects and covers up colonialism. It is opposed to unequal treaties and agreements, the setting up of military bases on foreign territories dictated by strategic considerations and plans for establishing world domination of imperialism.[40]

The Eisenhower Doctrine was proclaimed in January 1957 to ward off what was then termed as the Soviet threat of Communism to the region; in the Middle East it also sought to curtail Nasir's sweeping influence in the Arab world.

In an attempt by the Soviet Union to counter the Eisenhower Doctrine, the Soviet Foreign Minister, Dmitri Shepilov, addressed the Supreme Soviet, and Russian notes were delivered to the three Western powers containing two suggestions. The implication of Soviet aims were as follows:

> On the one hand, the 'Shepilov Doctrine' seeks to displace the 'Eisenhower Doctrine' with public opinion in the Middle Eastern countries, by suggesting an agreement to refrain from interference in the area. This would, in fact, mean obtaining a suspension of Russian arms deliveries to Egypt, Syria and the Yemen, and of Soviet encouragement to anti-Western feeling

153

in Arab States, at the price of Britain's withdrawal from the Baghdad Pact and perhaps from the South-East Asia Treaty Organization, of Turkey's withdrawal from the North Atlantic Treaty Organization, of the recognition of Egypt's sole authority over the Suez Canal, and the dismantling of American and British bases in Libya and Saudi Arabia. Simultaneously, Soviet policy is aimed at a renewed attempt to see whether it cannot turn the disunity of the West to good advantage.[41]

What Shepilov was, in essence, asking for was a declaration by the four powers – Britain, France, the United States and the Soviet Union – to aim to achieve several goals. In the first place, 'peace' in the Middle East should be achieved by negotiation and peaceful means. In the second place, some sort of guarantee of non-interference in the internal affairs of the countries of the Middle East and respect for their sovereignty and independence should be established. Thirdly, the implications of all this were that the countries of the Middle East should be involved in regional military pacts, which would mean the abandonment of the Baghdad Pact and SEATO, which would entail in return the withdrawal of Pakistan from the Pact and finally the withdrawal of Turkey from NATO. Fourthly, and consequent upon the preceding, foreign bases should be liquidated and foreign troops withdrawn from the Middle East. This would have entailed the abandonment of US military bases in Saudi Arabia and British military bases in Libya. Fifthly, there should be an out-and-out renunciation of the supply of arms to Middle East countries. This would curtail Western arms supplies to allied Arab countries and Israel. Lastly, a degree of cooperation in the economic field should be established toward the development of the region, without infringing upon the sovereignty of Middle Eastern countries. In a nutshell, what the Soviet Union was proposing was the diminution of Western power in the region in general and the Arab world in particular. Shepilov's six-point proposal placed certain political reservations on all parties concerned, especially the Western powers. Two major questions existed about the political situation in the region:

(1) How ... could a plan for neutralization of the Middle East be made self-enforcing? That is, how could the United States guard against the obvious possibility that its

withdrawal would merely open the doors, and let the
Soviets in?

(2) What would be the strategic effect on the United States of
the loss of its bases in Saudi Arabia and Libya? On the
British, if abandonment of Cyprus was also involved?
What compensating sacrifice of Soviet strategic position, if
any, would be forthcoming?[42]

The whole conceptualization and approach advocated by Shepilov
was aimed at dislodging the West from its strategic position in the
Middle East. The Soviet Union was a power in search of a political-
military role in a geographical area that was ceasing to be the
domain of the Western powers. The political gates of Egypt had
been opened to the Soviet Union; it remained only for it to pursue its
objectives in the Arab world. These were furthered by close relations
with Egypt and the role played by Nasir's overall political objectives
in the Arab world and the non-aligned camp. Both partners had
common political objectives that complemented each other over a
wide range of issues. In view of the prevailing international situation
in the Arab world, it is quite logical that a certain political
rapprochement should have developed between the Soviet Union
and Egypt. It remained to be seen how close the relationship might
become.

At the time the West viewed the Soviet Union's political,
economic and military offensive in the Arab world, through Nasir's
leadership, as a development to be taken seriously and combated
through Arab conservative regimes. What was then termed the
Arab Cold War had its repercussions for some time. The prevailing
political situation demanded an overall strategic consideration of the
Arab world. The Soviet Union was a newcomer to that world in the
sense that this was still an area in which the Western powers
exercised their influence. The speed with which the Soviet Union
was entering the scene alarmed the Western powers, and hence the
Arab world was compelled to suffer the last waves of the Cold War,
whose repercussions and imprints were to be seen for years to come
in the political forms of East–West relations. The euphoria of the
anti-Western Arab nationalistic feeling wrought several changes in
the political map of the Arab world in content and in general
outlook. It was within this outlook that the Soviet Union perceived
the general path for Arab political progress. Arab nationalism had
clearly become a rallying point in the Arabs' search for an identity of

155

their own, and in this search the Soviet Union and its bloc were available and willing to aid the Arabs in overcoming the obstacles, both military and economic, placed there by the West. In an official statement the Chinese government voiced its support for Shepilov's six-point proposal, stating *inter alia* that

> Although the armed aggression by Britain, France and Israel against Egypt has been stopped, Israel, supported and connived at by the Western powers, still refuses to withdraw, in according with the resolutions adopted by the United Nations General Assembly, all her invading troops from the Egyptian territory which it occupies . . . Undoubtedly, the realization of the Soviet proposal would also help the countries of the Near and Middle East to advance towards economic prosperity through peaceful construction and independent development. Therefore, there is no reason whatsoever for the Governments of the United States, Britain and France to reject this reasonable proposal of the Soviet Government.[43]

After this development, all the Communist bloc countries took a unanimous stand on the Soviet Union's proclamations on the Middle East situation in general and the Arab world in particular. Such Communist unanimity against Western powers was a unique development, only possible because the Sino–Soviet dispute had not yet come into the open. Nasir in particular reaped the advantages of this unanimity.

However, it would be mistaken to view the Arab world as a single cohesive entity. The Arab world was undergoing major political changes, and the Soviet Union's entrance to the Arab world further intensified East–West rivalry in the region. In a *Pravda* editorial dealing with the Arab situation in general and giving certain facts about British, French and Israeli aggression against Egypt, vituperative Soviet attacks on these powers were expressed in an unmistakable fashion. It was one of the rare occasions that anti-Israel sentiment was clearly stated. It argued that

> The Soviet Union, which has advanced a programme for safeguarding peace in the Middle East, fully supports the just demands of the Arab countries for the unconditional and immediate withdrawal of the Israeli forces from the Gaza Strip and the coast of the Gulf of Aqaba. The violation of the United

156

Nations decisions by Israel has raised the question of applying
sanctions against the Israeli aggressors in accordance with
United Nations Charter. The Soviet Union supports the
demand for sanctions against Israel if Israel does not
immediately withdraw its forces from Egypt.[44]

The Soviet Union's pronouncements against Israel should be
viewed in the perspective of the new phase of cordial, close
Soviet–Egyptian relations. To understand the implications of the
Soviet attacks on Israel one should examine the remarks from the
Arab point of view. In the first place, to single out Israel for such
vituperation would imply that the danger facing the Arab world was
not coming only from the Western powers. In the second place, the
Soviet arguments implied that the three aggressors had acted in
concert and had had agreed political objectives. Finally, the Soviet
Union stated its readiness to impose sanctions if an agreement
should be reached. It was not clear either what form these sanctions
would take or how far-reaching they would be. This uncertainty
implied that if these sanctions were ever imposed the Soviet Union
would abide by them; at least, this is what can be inferred from the
Soviet Union's declarations and political commentary. It is in this
context that the Soviet foreign policy objectives should be taken into
consideration if one is to view the Soviet Union's reaction to events
in a pragmatic sense. It is important here to estimate the reaction of
the Western powers and how this would have influenced the general
East–West relations in super-power policies towards the Arab world
if the Soviet Union had imposed certain sanctions on Israel. This
development in the Soviet Union's relations with the Arab world
should be seen as a consequence of the preceding events in the
Arab–Israeli conflict and of the Tripartite Aggression against Egypt.

Nasir's role in all of this is far from negligible. What he had
achieved in East–West relations was to make use of the Soviet Union
as an alternative provider of aid in various fields. This approach
threatened Western interests in the Arab world, for the West had a
long history of involvement in the area, one aspect of which was
military and it had sliced the Arab world into political zones that
were, not infrequently, useful for military occupation. The West was
not willing to depart from this strategic area voluntarily, and the
Tripartite Aggression against Egypt was a clear indication of this. In
its unwillingness to relinquish the Arab world the West reinforced
the existing divisions by several means, amongst them the military

regional alliances, such as the Baghdad Pact. Nevertheless, this period in the history of the Arab world witnessed the gradual erosion of Western power, which was considerably weakened by the emergence of Arab nationalism and by the Arab search for a political and military alternative to the Western powers. The Soviet Union was *invited* to play this role by the Arabs, to an almost limitless extent. It was initiated by an arms deal and then proceeded via cultural exchanges to economic cooperation. This political change in the Arab world affected its international strategic and political alliances with the balance of East–West relations and within the Communist bloc itself. Additionally the Arab world carried with it what was then known as the non-aligned bloc of nations.

The Soviet Union's perception of events in the region was dealt with in a *Tass* statement which argued that

> It is stated in leading Soviet circles that the Soviet government
> has been and remains a resolute opponent of the use of force
> against Middle East countries, as in international relations in
> general. New aggression against Egypt would create a
> dangerous situation and a direct threat of a large-scale military
> conflict, with dire consequences for the peace. That is why
> these circles resolutely condemn the stand adopted by
> extremist circles in Israel, and also in France, who instead of
> assisting the peaceful settlement of the situation in the Middle
> East, are artificially and deliberately exciting passions,
> aggravating the situation and preparing a new and dangerous
> war gamble.[45]

On the Arab side, conservative Arab regimes were alarmed by the Soviet Union's entrance into the Arab world and saw it as synonymous with the 'threat' of Communism in that world. King Hussein of Jordan voiced this fear when he stated that a link was in existence between international Communism and Tel Aviv and that Tel Aviv was 'the center of communism in the Middle East and the communists in Jordan are brothers and collaborators of [these] communist Jews'.[46] The King's unfounded and distorted allegations corroborated the West's general allegations of the 'threat' of Communism. In the face of such unfounded accusations the Soviet Union was making great strides in furthering its relations in the Arab world, aided by the towering presence of Nasir. The Arab strategic position in the balance of power was another factor that could not be avoided in the political interactions of Arab–Soviet interests. Arab political objectives at the time were drawing closer to embarking on a neutral and non-aligned movement, and Nasir was the personification of this political trend. This political movement made it necessary for the Arabs to find an alternative source of military aid. The Soviet Union was available to fill this gap. Lastly, prominent Arab regimes embarked on their own form of economic restructuring, labeled 'socialism'. This in turn led certain Arab regimes to extract from the Soviet Union expertise on economic systems. Nevertheless, the official Arab form of socialism was devoid of the elements of class struggle which is the core of Marxism-Leninism. It was a form of socialism forced on the Arab world through existing political-economic objectives. Arab and Soviet interests coincided.

In April 1957 the Soviet Union sent notes to the American, British and French governments regarding the political situation in the Middle East. In June the US government replied, stating, among other matters, that

> Opposition to the use of force in the settlement of disputes anywhere has been and continues to be a cardinal element of the United States . . . Rather than a repetition of existing obligations, what is necessary is loyal implementation of the principles of the [UN] Charter. It was this conviction – not, as the Soviet Government alleges, a desire to divert attention from serious solutions – which prompted the United States Government to refer to Hungary in its note of March 11.
>
> The United States Government notes the assertion of the Soviet Government that its concern about conditions in the Middle East arises from the close proximity of this area to Soviet territory . . . if the Soviet Union sincerely desires to contribute toward the establishment of peace and security in the Middle East, it could do so by working constructively within the United Nations for the solutions of fundamental problems in the area among which the Arab–Israeli dispute is outstanding.[47]

The US note clearly pointed out several aspects of Soviet foreign policy objectives. Though it mentioned the US stand on the Soviet invasion of Hungary the year before, it also pointed out a strategic reality of the Arab countries: their proximity to the Soviet Union.

The importance of this position constituted a rather heavy burden for the Middle East since that area had become a region in which East–West contradictions were likely to spill over. It was also the area where both East and West were compelled to test the political credibility of their allies within the region. Finally, the note attested the fact that both East and West had demonstrated their prowess and ability to steer events in the region.

The British government's reply to the Soviet Union's note was clearly expressed, and it argued that

> ... In particular, HM Government reject as unfounded the Soviet Government's suggestions that the Western Powers over the years favoured one side or the other in the Palestine dispute with regard to arms deliveries. They deny, and the Governments of other countries concerned have already denied in official statements, that the territory of any member of the Baghdad Pact was made available for aircraft engaged in the action taken by HM Government and the French Government last November [1956] to bring about a cessation of hostilities between Israel and Egypt. They also deny emphatically that the Baghdad Pact is used to undermine the sovereignty of countries of the region or for interference in their internal affairs. .... If the Soviet Government are seriously concerned about the possibility of hostilities in the Middle East they will agree that it is important to define the main focus of tension which is likely to lead to such hostilities. As a result of the interest they have recently shown in the Middle East and from their study of its problems they cannot have failed to perceive that the main focus of the tension in fact lies in the Arab–Israeli dispute.[48]

This British note distorted major historical facts concerning the region in general and the Arab world in particular. For example, nothing was said that concerned the British role in the creation of the State of Israel in Palestine. Its justification for the Baghdad Pact was contrary to the facts for which it was created. Finally, the Western powers' attempt to reduce political tension in the region was neither clearly argued nor defined. The Soviet note to the three Western powers had aspired to achieve an agreement on a unified East–West approach to tackle Middle Eastern questions and problems. Such a proposal was not accepted by the three major

Western powers because they feared that the Soviet Union would gain markedly. If the Soviet Union's proposal had been accepted it would undoubtedly have meant that it would have had a larger role to play in the region. The Western powers proposed, rather, to deal with Middle Eastern questions through the proper channels of the UN. The Soviet Union had been pleading for the world powers to 'renounce the use of force in the Middle East and pledge non-interference in the internal affairs of the Arab states'.[49] But Soviet leaders continued to fulfill their pledge in supporting Arab nationalism and went to further their earlier stand in supporting Egypt economically as had been requested.

Soviet leadership was unanimous about supporting Arab needs; meanwhile it denounced Israel as being a 'tool for executing imperialist plans'. This policy was in conformity with Nasir's nationalist and neutralist policies of the period. It also accused Jordan of surrender to the United States under the 'shadow of the guns of the [United States] Sixth Fleet and under pressure from American companies and petroleum monopolies'. These Soviet arguments were rejected by Western powers because of their firm belief that the region was within their influence. In this phase of Soviet foreign policy the main concentration centered on three basic areas: the first was Europe; the second, Asia; and the third, the Middle East. Syria at the time was leaning toward leftist tendencies internally and drawing close to the Soviet Union and its bloc in foreign policy. In August 1957 the visit of acting Syrian Defense Minister Khaled al-Azem to Moscow and Prague[50] indicated that the Syrian regime was approaching the Communist bloc more closely still, and was especially interested in acquiring arms. However, East–West polemics intensified as far as events in the Middle East were concerned. An official Soviet government note sent to the government of the United States challenged the latter's 'aggressive' tendencies in the region; it stated *inter alia* that

> It is common knowledge, however, that the existence of the United Nations Charter did not prevent, for instance, Britain and France from undertaking, jointly with Israel, an armed attack on Egypt, or the United States Government from undertaking a military demonstration of the American Sixth Fleet in connection with developments in Jordan, thus resorting to a threat to use force. The 'Eisenhower Doctrine' directly provides for the possibility of American armed forces

being used against the Middle Eastern countries. The
intervention of the British armed forces in Oman represents a
gross violation of the fundamental principles of international
law and of the United Nations Charter. The United States
Government in fact supports this aggression against the people
of Oman.[51]

An official Soviet note to the British government of 3 September
1957 was more emphatic in tone and dealt with various aspects of
Soviet policy in the Middle East generally and the Arab world in
particular. The note emphasized the following amongst its more
general points:

> The Soviet Government points out that having taken a
> negative attitude toward the proposals to denounce the use of
> force in the Middle East and failing to put forward any
> concrete proposals which would tend to normalize the
> situation in the Middle East, the Government of the United
> Kingdom has now again resorted to the use of force, this time
> in Oman and Yemen ... In its Note the Government of the
> United Kingdom contends that the main source of tension lies
> in the Arab–Israeli dispute. This does not correspond to
> reality, however. The principal menace to peace and
> tranquillity in the Middle East stems from the interference of
> the colonial powers in the affairs of the countries of that area.
> ... Unquestionably the Arab–Israeli conflict would never
> have been so acute, and practical prerequisites for its peaceful
> settlement would have appeared, if the United Kingdom, the
> United States and France had refrained from using Israel as a
> tool of the colonialist policy.[52]

Meanwhile, the Communist parties of the Middle East proceeded to
Moscow for consultation on the events in the region. The Secretary-
General of the Israeli Communist Party, Mikunis, who was at the
same time a member of the Israeli Parliament, was present, along
with representatives of Arab Communist parties.[53] Prominent
among them was the Syrian Communist Party, under the leadership
of Khaled Bakhdash, who at the time was playing down the anti-
Islam stand of the Communists and advocating the policy that
Communists should be regarded as nationalists. Normal diplomatic
and trade relations between the Soviet Union and Israel suffered no

disturbance.[54] The Soviet Union's presence in the Arab world was already well established. Egypt, the heart of the Arab world, Syria at the north-east corner of the Mediterranean and the Yemen at the mouth of the Red Sea were all Arab states that had cordial relations with the Soviet Union. Their strategic importance could not be neglected, and they could offer the Soviet Union their anti-Western outlook and strong anti-colonialist feelings, one of the salient features of all the most important Arab countries. Moreover, the Soviet Union was a newcomer to the region with no known involvement in internal Arab affairs. The Soviet side therefore had to deal carefully and strictly with the Arab world. Soviet advances in the Arab world were viewed with alarm in the West, Western observers seeing in them a threatening element that endangered oil supplies from Saudi Arabia and the Arabian Gulf.[55] Western fears emanated from two sources, the first being the internal political changes in the Arab world itself, and the second the willing availability of Soviet Union assistance. That in itself indicated that the regional balance of power was changing. These impending developments naturally had their political and military consequences.

The Soviet proposals for the Middle East centred on five principles: that Middle East disputes should be settled peacefully and by negotiation; non-interference in the internal affairs of local countries; non-involvement in great powers' military blocs; disarmament of the region; and finally, 'economic aid without strings'.[56] The proposals were not to find any welcome from the Western powers. If they were agreed it would mean that Western power in the region would dwindle. It would also mean that the Soviet Union would have an outlet for exercising its powers there. In the final analysis, the acceptance of these Soviet proposals would mean a major shift in the foreign policy of the Arab states concerned and implied the reception of Communist potential in their own world.

In his appeal to the Western powers on this five-point approach, Khrushchev attached importance to Western socialist parties by sending them similar notes.[57] Khrushchev's letter to the British Labor Party and other NATO countries' socialist parties argued that the major political-military trends in the Middle East were dangerous and would lead to future military confrontations:

A small peace-loving and democratic state, Syria is being

subjected to a serious threat of military aggression. Foreign troops are concentrating on the Syrian coast, ships of the US Sixth Fleet are being assembled. . . . Under the wing of the Turkish authorities, reactionary Syrian immigrants have congregated in Istanbul. . . . Renewed attempts are being made to set Arab countries against each other to unleash a fratricidal war of Arab against Arab. . . . After Syria, the organizers of the plot intend to settle accounts with independent Egypt, and then one by one with the other Arab States, both republican and monarchical, which have gained independence since the end of the war.[58]

Khrushchev's letter sought to persuade the British Labor Party to pass a unanimous declaration against what it considered the dangerous elements who carry out policies counter to the interests of the people of the Arab world. Under Khrushchev's chairmanship, the Soviet Union uttered vehement attacks against Israel and Zionism, and went so far as to claim that Soviet Jews emigrating to Israel faced discrimination and humiliation.[59] However, the reaction of the Scandinavian countries to Khrushchev's letter expressed the same tone as most of the British press.[60] The Soviet Union's attitude to the alleged Western powers' military attempts on Syria through Turkey was explained by an article in *Trud*:

Nowadays, when socialism has become a world system, when more than one thousand million people have cast off the colonial yoke and when the forces of the peace supporters have grown immeasurably, any attempt to set ablaze the conflagration of war can only end in a disaster for the instigators of war. . . . The spokesmen of American imperialism have now been given the task of lulling public opinion and of presenting things as if Syria were not in the least threatened with an attack and as if the exposures made by the Soviet Union and Syria were, perhaps, fabricated in Moscow.[61] [emphasis in original]

Needless to say, the Western powers were annoyed at Khrushchev's open letter to these countries. Some elements in the West certainly considered that the whole affair would produce several developments. In the first place, the Soviet political move was aimed at opening a rift in the Western camp. Secondly, given the fact that the Middle East constituted a bridge to Asia and Africa, then

Communism could easily be transferred to this geographical region. In the latter part of the 1950s these fears were a natural assumption of the Cold War era. Thirdly, the West realized that the Soviet Union's penetration of the Arab world meant that it had itself lost the ability to resist Soviet advances. Fourthly, the West was not ready for the 'neutralization' of the Arab world. Such a political move would mean the abandonment of the Baghdad Pact and the scattered Western military bases in the Arab world. Finally, the West could not let go of the Arab world's rich natural resources – namely, oil. In essence, Khrushchev's notes to the Western powers were not acceptable in either form or content. The Cold War had indeed entered the Arab world in full strength. Even Israel kept a low profile in its military relations with Jordan; at the same time there was a Western drive to isolate Jordan whose interests lay with the West, particularly the United States, from other Arab states which also maintained relations with Egypt and, by implication, with the Soviet Union. However, this political stage of Arab development favored Israel in the sense that political attention was diverted from the Arab–Israeli conflict to the wider question of East–West relations.[62]

Another major political development occurred when the Iraqi monarchy was toppled in mid-July 1958 by a coup under the leadership of 'Abdl-Karim Qasim and 'Abdl al-salam 'Araf, Premier and Deputy Premier respectively. This political change in Iraq also led to its closer relations with the Soviet Union.

The Soviet Union's views of the developments in events regarding Syria are worth observing. In the eventuality of a war against Syria and in the light of the lessons of the Suez crisis, the Soviet Union feared that Syria would be facing 'aggression' from the Western powers. To a large extent the appeal was directed towards socialist parties, rather than any other grouping or official agency, for two major reasons: first, these parties were the opposition parties within their own countries; second, their foreign policy platforms expressed an abhorrence of the use of military means for the conduct of foreign policy. Moreover, the Soviet Union's attacks on Turkey reflected the former's attack on both the NATO alliance and the Baghdad Pact. By then Syria and Egypt had merged in unity and both were allies of the Soviet Union. Relations between Syria and the Soviet Union improved in the military and economic fields; Syria entered the Cold War on the side of the Soviet Union.

It is significant that the most important elements in the overall political foreign policy objectives were expounded by Khrushchev himself. In an interview the Soviet leader summed up the situation in the Middle East and the Arab world.[63] Once political independence had been achieved, he claimed, economic independence must follow; it would be through the Soviet Union's help that the economic situation would be strengthened. The struggle for national independence would force the colonial powers to make concessions, but these gains would be resisted by the colonial powers who would devise a number of ways to prevent them from occurring. This accounted for Britain's actions, which had been met by revolt and uprising, and, finally, by the clash with the 'colonialists' that had ensued. Thus a new stage would emerge in which a developing nation must consolidate its political gains to achieve two main objectives; the first being to withstand the intrigues and maneuverings of the colonial powers, the second being to mature the internal economic structure. He argued that Arab history – that is, the history of Egypt and Syria – was going through such stages, and a clash with the former colonial powers was inevitable. The Middle East had two assets that the Western powers wished to control: its strategic situation and its wealth of natural resources. The new form of colonialism stemmed from a new imperialism of which the Eisenhower Doctrine was one manifestation; the former colonial powers in this case, Britain and the United States, agreed with the current force of imperialism to re-distribute roles. The Suez affair of the year before had failed because of the revolt of the Arab people and the Soviet intention to implement its military might in the ensuing conflict. Thus the United States had been able to 'squeeze' Britain and France out of the Middle East and undermine their influence. By a variety of means this new form of colonialism had confronted the Arab world with a number of problems; if these states showed any sort of resistance then the imperialists would resort to alternative methods such as the *coup d'état*.

It is noteworthy that Khrushchev mentioned Israel only once, and then in passing, by implying that it was a 'stooge' of the West and that its actions were not independent of the Western powers. The idea of 'liberating' Palestine was never mentioned, nor was Israel regarded as a power in its own right. He went on, however, to argue that Soviet foreign policy towards finding a solution to the Middle East crisis was one of 'peaceful coexistence'. On the other hand, when one of its allies was faced with imperialist intrigues, it would supply material and moral support to that state, and should conditions warrant it, it would threaten military intervention.

Khrushchev's remarks require some comment. In the first place, though the Soviet Union was willing to lend moral and material support to Arab countries which engaged in a struggle against the West, it nevertheless fell short of condemning Israel or even thinking that Israel was taking independent action. Secondly, he was not specific as to what this material support would be; and if it were granted, what its size and limits would be. Thirdly, he left unclear what the Soviet reaction would be should the West grant Israel tacit and concealed support, as subsequent events showed it did. For the Arab–Israeli conflict had wider implications than its application to an isolated case confined to these two antagonists. Finally, his whole argument centered on the role which 'outside' powers played in the region and the means by which they exploited the Arab world. In a sense, local Arab leadership did not have any responsibility in the affair. This last element shed some light on the workings of the Arab world, the most significant of which was the fact that local Arab leadership was not in a position to direct and implement its policies, with the exception of 'inward' orientation on which the Soviet Union did not take a direct stand – as the suppression of Arab Communists, for example, was to show in the future.

The noted Soviet writer G. Mirsky,[64] commenting on the aftermath of the Suez crisis, argued that the West had resorted to a new and different method of putting pressure on Egypt – namely, the imposition of an economic blockade to be achieved by a boycott of the Suez Canal and the exertion of financial pressure. To achieve the first objective, two factors were considered: the first was a plan for the construction of large, extended oil pipelines that would obviate the need to transport Gulf oil in tankers; the second was the building of 'super-tankers'. Thus, the argument went, Egypt would be obliged to reconsider its economic position, especially in its relations with the Western powers. Discussing the results of an economic war against Egypt, Mirsky argued that the US, France and Britain had already yielded to economic expedience and had permitted shipowners to use the Canal on Egyptian terms. More important, the Western organizers of the blockade did not foresee that their action would result in the stimulation and development of Egyptian domestic industry and the forming of a new policy of self-reliance. It is noticeable that Mirsky considered that Egypt had entered its second stage of economic independence, from which two concomitant elements followed. One was that Egypt must follow the idea of self-reliance, and the other was that if the West were to embark on an economic war against Egypt, the latter should and could easily reverse the situation by entering into more extensive cooperation with the Soviet Union and the Eastern bloc. Were this to happen, the Arab world would be opened up still further and would enter a new stage of development *vis-à-vis* the Soviet Union, a stage in which the balance of power would be tipped and the Soviet Union would have a new role to play. The Arab world, through Egypt, had become entangled in a new era of the Cold War whereby the balance of power would be dramatically adjusted. A new phase had dawned.

On the subject of Soviet–Arab relations, Y. Bochkaryov[65] argued that current Soviet foreign policy was formulated in accordance with Lenin's earlier precepts and policies in which the struggle for national liberation was to proceed to the second stage of economic assistance after liberation; the Soviet Union and its allies could fulfill this requirement of the development stage. This Leninist approach, he argued, had laid the groundwork for an enhanced relationship between the Arab world and the Soviet Union, but the author asked why it had reached this stage only in recent years. His answer was that, while Soviet policy had not altered, major changes had occurred on the Arab side, the most important of which was the emergence of independent Arab states and the advent of new rulers who were shaping the future of the Arab world. The Soviet Union, he went on, had followed a policy toward the Arab world on the basis of non-interference in their internal affairs and had embarked upon broad economic cooperation that would be beneficial to both sides. The agreement between the Soviet Union and Syria was just one example of this. Finally, he argued that 'unequal' agreements between the Western powers and the Arab states were no longer an 'inevitability', for the fact was that no longer could only the West assist in the economic sphere. He presented a comparison between United States and Soviet economic assistance, whereby the former had concentrated, it said, on the purchase of armaments and the latter had directed its aid to projects for raising the 'economic and prosperity standards'.

The argument on which Bochkaryov dwelt was that the Soviet Union posed an alternative to Western aid, providing the Arab world with an option; if the Arab world was refused by the West it could easily resort to assistance offered by the Soviet Union and its bloc. This aid, moreover, fulfilled the economic needs of a Third

World country such as Egypt. His argument was based on the fact that the agreements signed between the two countries indeed indicated that the terms were favorable. In either case the Soviet Union had entered a new phase of development, one repercussion of which was to open a new road into a volatile region that had for years been considered one of the areas that lay within the West's sphere of influence. And if the Soviet Union could open up or in some other way make an inroad into such a region, it would be one of the new spheres whereby it could extend its influence in an area that was both strategically important and also rich in natural resources. Finally, the Soviet Union would be in a position to exploit the existing 'contradictions' that might ensue in the future between the West and the Arab world.

Egypt and Syria (UAR), united in February 1958, turned to the Communist bloc for aid in various fields of the economy, culture, education, finance and scientific and military assistance. A new era had dawned with Nasir's alliance and the cooperation of the Arab world. Cooperation in political and other fields took a variety of forms. Nasir, for his part, had established a sort of African Cominform with other Afro-Asian states in Cairo, whereby these newly emerging states could not only aspire to political independence but also find foreign aid and alignment to steer them on their course for independence. The African continent was therefore witnessing a new gain in its journey of political self-realization; the political course was especially directed against the West. The political map of the Arab world and the Middle East at large was about to see new changes coming on to the horizon.

The British role in Aden, the unstable monarchy of Iraq, and above all the situation in Palestine, were all areas where Nasir could play and maneuver politically with Soviet assistance. If the Soviet Union emerged aggressively as one, if not the only, power-protector of Palestinian rights and political aspirations and thus force out the Western powers, notably Britain and the US, its political gains would be immense in the Arab world. Until this period, the Palestinian problem was a cause centered around the charismatic leadership of Nasir, whether exercised in the Arab world or in Afro-Asian and East–West relations. In the absence of any 'independent' Palestinian movement or organization, Egypt, under Nasir, dominated the problem, in particular its leadership and aspirations.

The tone adopted during Nasir's visit to Moscow at the end of April 1958 was one of 'independence' from the Western powers; that

Egypt (UAR) was steering a course opposed to military pacts, alignment, and the establishment of foreign bases; and finally, that a newly emerging state must depend on its own resources.[66] The visit had several objectives in mind. In the first place, it was aimed at tipping the balance of power strategically. The strategic approach served the Soviet Union's long-range objectives in the Middle East as a whole and the Arab world in particular. Secondly, the benefits of a closer alliance with the Soviet Union, if the visit were successful, would mean to a newly emerging nation that alignment with the Western bloc was not the sole choice in the calculation of that balance of power. Finally, the opening up of the Arab world to the Soviet Union meant that its Eastern European satellites would follow suit. Cooperation meant that new political, economic and cultural spheres would be opened up less dependent on the Western powers. The Soviets knew well that the Egyptian Communist Party had been declared illegal and that Nasir was prosecuting Communists; none the less, the overriding objectives of Soviet interest in Egypt as a state took precedence over other localized interests. Furthermore, with the merger of Egypt and Syria into the United Arab Republic, Nasir, in reality, could negotiate outstanding economic issues for both countries. He also represented a force in the Middle East and the Arab world that had to be reckoned with; thus the visit was both symbolic and realistic.

Soviet and Egyptian sides exchanged views and ideas. On 30 April 1958, Khrushchev was the host at a banquet for President Nasir in Moscow where he set forth several points concerning the Soviet Union's foreign policy in general. Starting from the non-aligned nations of Bandung and the Conference of Afro-Asian countries recently held in Cairo, Khrushchev advocated that these nations should aim at fulfilling their aspirations for national independence. Next, he criticized both the US and British policy of nuclear armament and explained how the Soviet Union had followed a worldwide policy of nuclear disarmament. Similarly, the Soviet Union was pursuing a course of peaceful coexistence among nations. Then he pointed out that the West had exploited Arab oil and advocated an independent oil policy. Finally, he said, the Arab world could rest assured that not only could it rely on the Soviet Union but also on 'all progressive mankind'.

In reply, Nasir said that the visit was a new chapter in cooperation between the two states and that 'further' cooperation, in due time, would strengthen their relations; a new era had started.

The UAR was undergoing a new stage of 'national liberation' and that once national independence had been accomplished, the UAR and fellow Afro-Asian countries would follow neutral policies on the global scene, especially in regard to East–West relations. Finally, Nasir directed attention to a new and different element when he said:

> It was a pleasure for me, Mr Chairman, to hear you say *that you understood the struggle of the Arab states for freedom and independence, that you understand the danger threatening the Arab states from Israel, in view of the fact that Israel is a bridgehead of imperialism.*[67] [emphasis added]

The main political topic discussed in Moscow, other than bilateral relations, was that which Nasir considered to be the central issue, the crisis regarding Israel: the rallying of all-out Soviet support for claims against Israel and for the Palestinian Arabs' right to their former homeland. Nasir's immediate concern during the discussion was the liberation of Palestine and the reinstatement of the Palestinians. His statements and views 'covered three points: [that] Israel represented frank aggression against Arab rights; second, Israel entertained expansionist ambitions; and third, Israel amounted to an instrument of imperialism'.[68]

The joint statement of the Soviet Union and the UAR covered a wide range of areas and issues pertaining to current developments, and devoted a large section to the exchange of views on the questions and problems confronting the non-aligned nations of Asia and Africa. It said that:

> the two governments examined the problem of the rights of Arabs in Palestine and the question of their expulsion from their native places of residence. . . . Both governments reaffirm their full support for the legitimate rights of the Arabs in Palestine.[69]

It was in the context of how and by what means the two powers should embark on the problem and its solution that the Palestinian problem was seen. The Palestinian question was still viewed as a 'refugee' problem; if any solution was to be presented it should be dealt with by the various Arab states under the leadership of Nasir. There was a final reference to the problem in the joint communiqué

171

issued before Nasir left Moscow. It stated:

> Both governments considered the question of the plight of the
> Palestinian Arabs and their expulsion from their homeland.
> They have also considered the question of the violation of
> Human Rights and the threat to peace and safety in this area
> that had resulted from their expulsion. *Both governments affirm
> their full support of the legitimate rights of the Palestinian Arabs.*[70]

It is significant that this was the first time that the Soviet Union had revealed such an understanding of the Palestinian question in an official high-ranking statement; it was mostly due to Nasir's championship of Palestinian rights, and it came, moreover, almost two years after the Suez crisis.

So far as the UAR was concerned, the visit had several outcomes. It had shown that Nasir was the recognized leader of the Arab world and could play a positive role in the Afro-Asian bloc. It also had reaffirmed his policy of 'neutrality' in the global balance of power. So far as Egypt was concerned, an undertaking was received that there would be a reduction in 'the price of arms that have been purchased by Egypt and Syria',[71] and Nasir was able to obtain a price reduction of between 20 and 30 per cent of the price of the various military items bought by the UAR. He also obtained a '15% reduction in the price of industrial equipment his government had ordered from the Soviet Union under the terms of a huge Soviet credit to the United Arab Republic'.[72]

These achievements, primarily the bi-lateral ones, were the basic motives which had inspired Nasir's visit to the Soviet Union; the other agreed points in the joint communiqué were political matters that concerned regional, Arab and international aspirations in which the policy of neutrality had the highest priority. If the visit resulted in anything worthwhile, it was more and closer cooperation between the Soviet Union and the UAR in cultural, economic and, to a limited degree, scientific fields.

The record of Soviet–Egyptian (UAR) relations confirms Soviet claims; when the West froze Egypt's foreign assets after the nationalization of the Suez Canal Company in 1956, the Communist bloc bought Egypt's cotton and supplied machinery, oil, etc, in return. When the West denied arms to Nasir, the Communist bloc stepped in and furnished the necessary aid. When the Tripartite attack on Egypt took place, the Soviet Union threatened to take action, although it was never clear how and to what extent this would be implemented. When Third World countries such as Egypt needed to industrialize and initiated an industrialization program, the Soviet Union came through with the necessary capital. Finally, after the West refused to provide the capital needed to finance the Aswan High Dam project, the Soviet Union filled the gap.

Thus by the end of the 1950s the Soviet Union had achieved several objectives in the Arab world through the medium of Egypt. In Soviet–Egyptian relations there were certain points both of strength and of weaknesses. The strength lay in Nasir, who had emerged as a leader to be reckoned with in the Third World, had enhanced his prestige as a political leader in the Arab world, had stood up to the Tripartite Aggression against Egypt and had been able to thwart that aggression. From the Bandung Conference onwards he was able to rally support for the solidarity he needed for any political alliances or upheavals that might involve Egypt. The Soviet Union recognized this fact. He was emerging on the Arab scene as one of the prime exponents of Arab nationalism whose energies and designs ranged from Arab unity to opposition to Western imperialism. And he was able, through Soviet and socialist bloc assistance, to find a substitute for the Western powers in his schemes for economic reform, thus setting a fine example to the rest of the Third World.

Nasir was above all an Arab nationalist, not a Communist; the vituperative encounters he had with Arab Communists in both Iraq and Egypt were looked upon by Khrushchev with disdain. Nasir's alliance with the Soviet Union and the socialist camp was both a lesson for the emerging states of the Third World and stressed the fact that any Third World country would be able to do likewise. Experience had shown what could be achieved and what the repercussions might be.

9 The Lebanese crisis, the Baghdad Pact, neutralism and the Soviet attitude, 1958–1959

During this period the Soviet Union made several gains, some the result of changing political conditions, others the result of deliberate decisions. It gained another ally (Iraq), it had plenty of opportunities to denounce the West (mainly through Lebanon), and it drew economic links with Egypt closer when it finally agreed to finance the Aswan High Dam.

Although relations with Israel remained no more than usually tense, the Soviet Union had to reconsider them in the light of the many complaints about conditions there received from emigrant Jews. On the whole, however, the years 1958/9 were a time of consolidation and advance.

The Lebanese crisis erupted in the summer of 1958. After President Chamoun had asked for President Eisenhower's assistance, American troops landed in July with a force twice the size of the Lebanese army. Chamoun faced two problems at the time. Firstly, the Muslim population was increasing in numbers, due to a higher birth-rate among the Muslim population and to Palestinian immigration; this was threatening the equilibrium and the balance of Lebanese society. Secondly, the idea of Arab nationalism had its appeal to the Lebanese people.

Chamoun also faced a constitutional dilemma. He was not eligible for re-election when his term ended in 1958, and he had tried to alter the constitution, hoping that the US would come to his aid. He wanted to align Lebanon with the Eisenhower Doctrine, a policy which the Lebanese Parliament had rejected, objecting to the establishment of foreign military bases. In February 1958 the union of Egypt and Syria had been announced and the move found some support in Lebanon. The deteriorating internal situation in Lebanon threatened the eruption of civil war, and at both the Arab League and the United Nations Security Council Chamoun accused the UAR of instigating disturbances in Lebanon; the United Nations sent a group of observers to Lebanon.

Civil war did, however, break out; as it gathered momentum Chamoun requested US forces under the Eisenhower Doctrine. Anxiety increased when in July 1958 a military coup toppled the monarchy in Iraq. Chamoun was succeeded by Fouad Shahab in July, and by October the American Marines had left Lebanon.

The American landings in Lebanon and British aid for Jordan following the toppling of the monarchy in Iraq in July were viewed by the Soviet Union as 'aggression against the Arab East and a threat to universal peace'.[1] Khrushchev sent a message to Eisenhower, British Prime Minister Harold Macmillan, Charles de Gaulle of France and Jawarharlae Nehru of India, proposing that a conference of heads of states meet in the presence of United Nations Secretary General Dag Hammarskjöld to work out specific recommendations for ending the military conflict in the Middle East. The Soviet proposal not only involved the major Western powers and the United Nations but also included a major Third World figure who was a close associate of Nasir, both of whom played an important role in the Third World. It was an opportune moment for the the Soviet Union to play a role, however indirectly, in a Middle East conflict on the same footing as the West.

When the Baghdad Pact members met on 28–29 July 1958 without an Iraqi representative, the Soviet Union made great play of the occasion and claimed that Iraq had set itself on a new road to independence. Asking why the meeting should take place in London at this particular moment, *Pravda*[2] argued that the members of the Pact were planning conspiracies against both Iraq and the UAR; the US and Britain having 'intervened' in Lebanon and Jordan, they were now planning further 'aggression'. For the first time *Pravda* singled out Israel, stating that although not a member of the Pact, it was a state that lent support militarily to the United States and Britain by allowing the latter's transport of logistical items. It added that if Iraq was the object of 'aggression' by the Pact's members, Iraq would receive aid.

Iraq's later secession from the Baghdad Pact (February 1959) strengthened the Soviet belief that it was now on the road to

175

independence, and so two Arab countries, the UAR and Iraq, had become valuable allies of the Soviet Union in the Arab world. The Iraqi Communist Party was activated within the country and gathered strength, a move which the Soviet Union approved with considerable satisfaction. The news of the withdrawal from the Baghdad Pact was welcomed by the Soviet Union without reservations,[3] for not only had it withdrawn from its commitments to Western allies but Iraq was seen as a state which could play an important role in Arab regional politics, thus weakening the position of the West in the Arab world. The Soviet Union viewed military pacts with great reservation, especially the Baghdad Pact, which was seen as a 'supplement' to the NATO alliance and which had held a meeting at the end of 1957 – at a time when the policy of peaceful coexistence was becoming an issue to be reckoned with.

The idea of the Baghdad Pact, as seen by the Soviet Union, was to 'divide' the Arab world; its signatories had participated in the aggressive policies of the Israeli–British–French attack on Egypt, and such pacts had become a 'tool' of the colonialists who sought to dominate the Middle East. US maneuverings in the area had the sole aim of 'uniting' the military blocs of NATO, the Baghdad Pact and SEATO under one organization with definite military goals in the area, the two latter being under the leadership of the first. This design would result in constant 'material sacrifices', an increase in the burden of taxation and further strains on the economies of these countries, leading to a further deterioration of living standards.

The Soviet argument was that the current situation in the Middle East differed from that of the recent past. A number of independent states had emerged which had freed themselves from the 'colonial' stage and gained political independence, and those states had embarked on a new method of economic independence. Novel ideas were showing themselves among those countries which were trying to find their own political role. For example, the Afro-Asian Solidarity Conference held in Cairo in May 1958 had supported the trend to struggle against colonialism and had condemned the imperialist policies followed by the Eastern world which sought to establish and enlarge military groupings in the Middle East.

The course of events in these countries was significant for the Soviet Union since they had passed through the first stage of economic independence, a sphere in which the Soviet Union could assist. The political alignment of these Arab countries with the Soviet Union derived basically from their long political experience with the West. It was natural that the Soviet Union, with its military and political potential, should offer an alternative to the West. The Arab world had therefore entered a new stage of political development in East–West relations, and this new stage imposed on the Soviet Union a fresh orientation of its foreign policy in the area, for the demands and responsibilities laid upon a major power that had undertaken regionally to tackle the economic backwardness of the Arab world were immense.

When Marshal Abdel Hakim Amer, Vice President of the UAR, paid a visit to the Soviet Union in October 1958, he declared in a speech at a reception where Khrushchev was present that the UAR had embarked upon a course of 'positive' neutrality in its foreign policy reflecting the principles set forth by the Bandung Conference which called for a spirit of peaceful coexistence despite differences in social systems. He emphasized that, since his last visit, following the British–French–Israeli aggression of 1956, the stand taken by the Soviet Union as leader of the socialist camp had played an important role in thwarting aggression and securing victory for Egypt. A policy of positive neutrality, he claimed, abhorred adherence to military blocs and opposed the establishment of foreign military bases.

Khrushchev, in his reply, stressed that the Soviet Union also adhered to policies of peaceful coexistence. He then linked this to economic aid and reconstruction that would lead to two results: first, to the development of the Egyptian economy, thus achieving real independence and freedom from dependence on some other strong economy (namely, that of the West); second, that aid, once given, should enable the UAR to 'increase their economic and political [potential] . . . strengthen them and help them to stand on their feet'.[4] Thus, according to Khrushchev, the economic issue constituted a fundamental basis for real independence; the Soviet Union had designed a plan, in contrast to the West, that would enable those states to achieve their independence. It was remarkable that Khrushchev's speech avoided mentioning the role played by Israel in the area although it expressed the willingness of the Soviet Union to establish relations with all countries. This was in marked contrast to a speech delivered by him during Nasir's visit to the Soviet Union. The visit of Marshal Abdel Hakim Amer resulted in an agreement between the two states on the request made by Egypt (UAR) for aid in the construction of the first section of the Aswan Dam, to replace the United States which had refused assistance.

This Soviet aid made a noticeable contribution to the economic reconstruction of Egypt.

Writing in *Izvestia*[5] V. Kudrayavtsev argued that events had unmasked the true nature of US foreign policy in the Arab world, where at the time of the Anglo–French–Israeli adventure it had tried to pose as a friend, then took advantage of its actions and attempted to seize Arab territories. United States policy was obvious in the Dulles–Eisenhower Doctrine; the Arab peoples had realized that there was a difference between the American brand of 'imperialism' and that of Britain and France and that in the guise of economic aid, the true purpose was military and the construction of strategic-logistic elements. When Egypt had approached the US for aid for the Aswan High Dam Project, the latter had dictated conditions that 'nullified' the independence of the former. By contrast, Kudrayavtsev argued, the Arab states had been shown the 'selfless' support which could be found in the Soviet Union and the socialist camp; this aid would enable Egypt to attain economic independence which was one step further towards real independence. Such aid had already taught the Arab people, over the previous two years, a lesson leading to their 'maturity' in the political sphere from which they had drawn the appropriate conclusions.

With the conclusion of the agreement on the Aswan High Dam, the Soviet Union had achieved three goals for its foreign policy. Firstly, it set a precedent for Third World countries, namely, that if conditions were attractive, it would be willing to come to their aid. This aid could be either economic or political and its nature would be based on mutual advantage. Secondly, when the West refused aid to a particular Third World country, the Soviet Union, as the leader of the socialist camp, could easily fill the gap. In this case the refusal had emanated from the American side. Lastly, on the same note, the Soviet Union, in providing economic aid to a Third World country, would be able to reconstruct its economy, thus bringing about a stage of economic maturity that was a step towards complete independence. By this time the Soviet Union had reached a stage of total involvement in the Arab world through its aid to Egypt (UAR) and through assistance envisaged for Iraq which by then had achieved its political independence because of its withdrawal from the Baghdad Pact.

As far as Israel was concerned, the Soviet Union still maintained its diplomatic relations but it had exposed the negative side of developments there (especially in the economic sphere) and Israeli economic and cultural reliance on the US. As the Soviet Union viewed Israel as a loose ally of the Western camp, particularly of the United States, the diplomatic approach was negative. However, the emigration of Soviet Jews to Israel which provided the manpower that Israel needed so desperately had not been halted.

Relations between Egypt and the Soviet Union were not absolutely harmonious. Some disagreement arose because of Nasir's suppression of local Communists, and minor polemics started to be exchanged, though mildly, between the two countries. An observer argued in *Pravda*[6] that the unity of the Arab people had been enhanced because of their aspirations, their struggle for national independence and the emergence of common goals. The strength of this 'solidarity' had played an important role against the colonialists; and it was pointed out that the support they received from the socialist camp headed by the Soviet Union had been of the utmost importance. Nevertheless, there was some surprise at Nasir's attacks on the Soviet Union which claimed that the support he had received was basically because of the will of God, that no help was rendered in this world from any person and that the Egyptian people relied on themselves. In defense of these allegations, the author pointed to the aid given to Egypt by the Soviet Union, China, the socialist countries, and a number of other Asian and European states; he went on to question the logic of mixing religion with 'earthly' matters. Nasir's claim of self-reliance and the will of God dealt a blow to Soviet support for Egypt, especially since it came at a time when Soviet influence in the Arab world was beginning to show its strength and was gathering momentum not only in the UAR but also in Iraq where the Iraqi Communist Party was gaining strength.

Soviet annoyance with Nasir extended to a wide range of issues. In particular, the Soviet Union accused the UAR, and Nasir in particular, of fomenting 'propaganda' against the Soviet Union, local Communists, international Communism, the socialist camp and Iraq.[7] The timing of the Egyptian attacks, the Soviets argued, had coincided with 'internal difficulties' in the UAR during which the Syrian sector and its leaders had been fomenting disunity among the Arabs. It would be naive to ascribe these difficulties to Communist intrigues, and any such allegations were refuted by Soviet pursuit of a policy of non-interference in internal affairs. What these internal difficulties did do was to weaken Arab nationalism and the unity of the Arabs in their struggle against imperialism. 'Mechanical' unity of the Arabs was not necessarily a universal objective and would not be realized by the UAR. The question of Arab unity should be solved 'voluntarily' only by the Arabs themselves, but its realization would not occur until the economic and political conditions were 'ripe' for it. 'Premature' unification, the argument went, would undermine Arab abilities in this process and would only benefit the imperialists. Unity between the UAR and Iraq would not strengthen either under the present circumstances because the conditions were not yet ripe. Iraq was undergoing a process of economic and political change that was basically anti-imperialist and 'progressive' in its own right. The 'progress' of Iraq had shown that it had consolidated its national independence and national unity and was set on a course that was anti-imperialist in character, in which the Arab people and the feud between the UAR and Iraq served only the ends of the 'imperialists' in the area.

To the Soviet Union in the late 1950s a rift among the Arab states at a time when the Arab world was groping towards political independence would pose a threat to the likelihood of further internal cooperation in their search for independence. As the Soviet Union saw it, both Iraq and the UAR had already achieved their first objective in the second stage of economic independence to which the Soviet Union could contribute. One of its many results was the signing of an economic cooperation agreement between Iraq and the Soviet Union.[8]

Zhubov, writing in *Pravda*,[9] argued that the 'colonialists' had a traditional policy toward the Middle East which contained three basic elements. Firstly, they relied on 'corrupt feudal' leadership, of which they represented the elite. Secondly, they operated the principle of 'divide and rule', which made Arab unity unrealistic. Finally, they interfered 'directly' in the internal affairs of these states through subversive activities or direct military intervention. In addition, they followed the policy of 'foreign aid', of which the Eisenhower Doctrine was only one example, aimed at stopping the Arab national liberation movement. This approach had been demonstrated to be fallacious and the West had to re-evaluate its policies in the region in the hope of regaining its influence. Plans had been made by the West for a new counter to the Eastern bloc's aid to the UAR and the Arab world, and if this did not work out then it would resort to military intervention. The third element of the Eisenhower Doctrine had proposed reliance on local reoriented 'feudal' leadership to achieve its goals. The West's new economic policy, called 'interdependence', whereby it provided capital funding in return for cheap and much-sought-after oil, meant in the long run Western domination. The West, so it was argued, had clearly demonstrated its 'bankrupt' policies when it refused to finance the Aswan High Dam project, whereupon Nasir, having been unsuccessful in the international market, turned to the Soviet Union.

During this same period Soviet mass media carried reports from Israel on the prevailing conditions of Soviet Jewry in Israel, the different aspects of life they were encountering in the new promised homeland and their stated desire to return to their country. *Trud*[10], for example, carried the contents of a letter sent by a group of Soviet Jews to Kliment Y. Yoroshilov, Chairman of the Presidium of the Soviet Union Supreme Soviet, which contained an appeal for permission to return home and a description of their disillusionment. They had arrived in Israel, the letter stated, at two different times between 1946–1948 and 1956–1957 with the promise of a better life in Palestine but had been misled by Zionist propaganda regarding the promised land; most of the emigrés had returned to Poland. To them, Zionism was the ideology of the large bourgeoisie which served the interests of the Americans, the French and the British. Israel, having been transformed into a US 'military base', had fallen into total financial and economic dependency on the United States and it lived on the 'contributions' of the latter. The economy lacked a developed form of industrialization, and imports and foreign debts constituted a burden on the people. All the capital funds collected by Jews worldwide were used for military objectives and in 'exploiting' Jewish emigrés, which meant that the situation of the working people was gradually deteriorating. Finally, Eastern European Jews who emigrated to Israel were treated as second-class citizens. Thus, it claimed, many had a great desire to return home to the Soviet Union. As far as the Arab inhabitants were concerned, in addition to their meager existence, they lived under military administrative rule and were forbidden to travel freely through the country. The local authorities prohibited the mingling of Arab and Jewish populations and it was difficult for Arab inhabitants to acquire jobs freely. He ended the letter on the hopeful note that peace might endure between Israel and its Arab neighbors, and 'constructive' relations should be established between it and the Soviet Union.

This description by a Soviet author of Jewish conditions highlights a number of points concerning immigration. Firstly, the emigrant Jews suffered serious disadvantages, some practical, others psychological, one of which was disillusionment. Secondly, Soviet Jewry was discriminated against as Eastern Jews; this formed the basis of their disenchantment and stimulated their desire to return. Finally, the hopeful note that peace might prevail between Israel and its Arab neighbors still constituted an aim in its own right. The fact remains that the attainment of peace, in the prevailing circumstances, was a far-fetched hope, given the attack on Egypt, the very establishment of the state of Israel, the dispersal of the Arab inhabitants of Palestine and the view that Israel had much in common with the West in the region. Nevertheless, the narrative proposes that Israel, as a state, should face new changes that would help to further the livelihood of the working class and the unity of both Arab and Jew in the process.

But between 1958 and 1959 there occurred major Arab changes with repercussions on Arab–Soviet relations. Commenting on the Iraqi Revolution of 1958 which put an end to the monarchy, M. Heikal argued that

> Following the Iraqi revolution there was an uproar in the
> Western world. American marines landed in Lebanon, British
> paratroops in Jordan, and the US Sixth and Seventh Fleets
> were on the move. . . . But suddenly all this battle of arms
> abated . . . the US government recognized Qasim's
> Government. Britain and other Western camp countries, even
> Turkey and Pakistan – closest friends of Nuri as-Sa'id and
> partners in the unlamented Baghdad Pact – followed suit.
> Them came the strange time of comparing Abd an-Nasir with
> Qasim.[11]

In another detailed analysis on the plight of Arab nationalism Heikal dwelt on a different outlook from which the following paragraphs have been extracted:

> In short, the future of either peace and war in the region
> depends on the battle taking place between the remnants of
> 19th century and the vanguard of the new power emerging in
> the second half of the 20th century, in other words between the
> West, which willingly or reluctantly is bid or dragged by the
> States of old imperialism, and Arab nationalism, which has
> awakened after a long night to find the world and the

circumstances changed . . . The important thing is that the fate
of peace and war in the region depends on the battle which is
taking place between the West and Arab nationalism. The
serious thing is that this battle is now passing through its
decisive phase . . . What was the starting point of the battle
now taking place between the West and Arab nationalism.
Was it the Palestine war and its traces? Or was it the Egyptian
revolution and its consequences? Was it the Baghdad Pact? Or
was it the Gaza raid? Could it have been the arms deal or
withdrawal of the offer to finance the High Dam? Or was it the
blow of the Suez Canal nationalization and the events which
followed it, beginning with the aggression, then the
Eisenhower Doctrine and the attempt to isolate Egypt, union
with Syria, the revolution in Iraq, and what has recently taken
place in Khartoum, the triangle capital in the south? This
really is a problem, a great problem. . . . Events later followed
to indicate that Israel was the reason for the battle between the
West and Arab nationalism, which tried by every means to
improve Israel's existence and compel the inhabitants of the
region to recognize it. . . .

Another scene is Khrushchev's office at the Kremlin. Round
a big desk sat Khrushchev, Bulganin, Zhukov and Shukri al-
Quwatli, then on an official visit to the Soviet Union during
the triple aggression against Egypt. Quwatli spoke about the
situation in the Middle East and said that something should be
done to assist Egypt in its battle. Quwatli said, in conclusion:
'Unless the Soviet Union proves in deed and not words in this
crisis that it supports the Arab struggle, its respect will be lost
and its position in Africa and Asia will be dealt a great blow.'
Marshal Zhukov here said to Shukri al-Quwatli: 'I would like
to ask if you can tell me the best way to help Egypt in the
battle?' Quwatli replied: 'Marshal Zhukov, do you expect me to
tell you – the highly renowed military expert and experienced
leader – how you can help Egypt in the present battle? What
do you say?' This is also another thrilling scene and a true
one.[12]

By the end of the decade the Arab world had witnessed sweeping
political changes affecting the whole scene, especially after the
Egyptian Revolution of 1952 and the end of monarchical rule there;
in 1955 the Sudan gained its independence from Britain; in the same

year Tunisia was freed from French domination just as earlier Syria too had gained its independence from France; finally Iraq overthrew the monarchy. In 1958 Egypt and Syria announced their unification.

These factors combined contributed to the rise of Arab nationalism under Nasir's leadership. It was a sweeping force that awakened Arab sentiments against the traditional colonial powers. One of the thorniest issues at stake in North Africa was the French presence in Algeria. Britain began to reassess its position in the Arabian Gulf. All of these political developments assisted the entrance of the Soviet Union to the Arab world. It was an opportune moment for the Soviet Union. It remains to ask how the Soviet Union executed its policies in the Arab world. Armaments first were supplied to the Arab world through Egypt, a gesture reciprocated by the Arab world, because of conditions there which facilitated Soviet penetration through other means, mostly economic. The Soviet Union, finally, grasped this opportunity to enter an area of the world that was basically a Western domain, especially of the old colonial guard. By the latter half of the 1950s the global importance of the Arab world had been upgraded from localized disputes to international status. Concomitant with this fact is the elevation of the Arab–Israeli dispute, which became one of the major focal points of the international balance of power, to a political and strategic level where the US entered the scene. When this happened it was important for the West to strengthen the status of Israel as a power which acted as a counter-balance to the Arab world, especially the Arab states adjacent to its borders. Arab nationalism, in essence, achieved its prominence only through Arab local military officers who happened to come to power, starting with the Egyptian Revolution of 1952. Almost all other important changes of the political structure at this period emanated from such forces, with minor exceptions in North Africa. The Arab world was experiencing a wave of major changes that assisted the Soviet Union's entrance to it. And at this particular juncture the force that was important for Arab political conditions was beginning to emerge on the Arab political scene. That by itself implied a new political international reality which the Soviet Union exploited in a way that influenced the direction of events. The Soviet Union was able to further its objectives through its Eastern bloc – for example, by a small-scale supply of armaments and trade relations. Both these channels witnessed a new Soviet offensive in the Arab world.

Perhaps it should be noted here that two theoretical facts were observable. On the one hand, national interest overrode Marxist-Leninist precepts, and, on the other hand, outside the confined spheres of the Communist regimes of Eastern Europe, the Soviet Union welcomed the nationalistic upsurge in Third World countries. The Arab world was proceeding through this phase with Nasir as its spearhead. He was faced by the very real change in political realities brought about by Arab development whose most prominent aspect was its anti-imperialist nature. The West, personified in the British and French presence, was facing eclipse because of the political development of the Arab world. Yet Nasir's socialist orientations, and for that matter those of any of the emerging Arab leaders, were neither communist nor were they radical in the economic sense; they were, rather, animated by the objective necessities of each country's economic and political realities. The Soviet Union was willing to override the interests of the Arab Communist movement. Soviet objections to and reservations about Arab suppression of Communist parties were confined to innocuous political commentaries that did not seriously affect Soviet decision-making in relation to its normal Arab channels. Thus attacks on the Syrian and Iraqi Communist Parties were launched by Soviet writers at the beginning of 1959, for there were Soviet reservations about the unification of Syria and Egypt, despite the fact that it afforded a further opportunity for Soviet expansion. The Soviet Union concentrated on building up the arsenals of Egypt and Syria, the former because it was the heartland of Arab political force while the latter possessed considerable strategic value because it bordered Turkey.

10 The advance of Soviet power in the Arab world, 1960–1966

This period is characterized by minor developments. The Soviet Union was not hesitant in proclaiming its stand on internal Arab political developments. In 1961, an incident which produced a certain frigidity in UAR–Soviet relations originated from the murder of the Lebanese Communist Party's leader, Farajallah al-Hilu. *Pravda* accused the UAR (Egypt–Syria) of the assassination. The UAR commentator, Kamil al-Shinawi, wrote an article dismissing Soviet allegations and touchng upon the issue of Soviet financial aid to the UAR. He wrote.

> In its campaign against us, *Pravda* quoted an old Arab saying
> to reprove us. The saying goes that one should not cut the tree
> which shades him. *Pravda*, of course, is hinting at Russian
> loans to us. We have never denied getting loans from Russia
> . . . We treat Russia as a bank. The bank which grants me a
> loan has no right to interfere in my own affairs. All that a bank
> can do is to ask for the settlement of the loan if the date of the
> settlement is overdue. Our relations with Russia, as a bank, do
> not entitle it to claim that it is doing us a favour. The benefit
> which the bank gets from the client is not less than the benefit
> which the client obtains from the bank.[1]

However, in general the Soviet Union's relations with the Arab world proceeded normally. On the Arab side, Egyptian relations with the West, especially West Germany, took a turn for the worse, but this only encouraged closer relations between the Communist bloc and the Arab world, considerably helped by Nasir's leadership.

It was not until mid–1965 that certain political changes and developments manifested themselves.

The year 1965 opened with several unresolved military and political conflicts: the Congo, Vietnam and South Arabia, to name but a few. The international situation was further clouded by the state of East–West relations on nuclear disarmament, Berlin and the Cold War, all of which were intermingled. At the outset these issues were basically the concern of the two major powers, but their effects were soon felt more widely. Moreover, the unevenly balanced economy of the globe (the split was between the industrialized powers and the former colonies who were the suppliers of basic raw materials) was a disadvantage to the latter which in turn created new forms of instability. On the Arab scene the Palestinian question was far from being resolved.[2] The year witnessed the first proclamation of military action by Fatah against Israel. Despite the Palestinian Resistance Movement, small as it was, the Palestinian question had not fared high in Soviet–Arab relations. Of the Communist bloc only China came forward with the much-needed aid for the Palestinian Fatah.[3] Relations between the Soviet Union and Egypt had improved by the beginning of 1965 when Alexander Shelepin, Soviet Deputy Premier, visited Egypt on a state visit. After inspecting the High Dam he said that

> ... We are satisfied with the close co-operation between our
> countries and governments in the international arena as well.
> ... Our positions coincide on many most important problems.
> These include the efforts for peace, support for national-
> liberation movements, the struggle for elimination of the last
> vestiges of colonial regimes, the struggle against foreign
> military bases for the discontinuation of nuclear tests, for
> disarmament and a number of other vital international
> questions of principle. In our speeches and talks with UAR
> leaders, we emphasized that the Soviet Union regards as just
> the struggle of the UAR and other Arab countries for the
> solution of the Palestinian problem with due consideration for
> the interests of Palestinian Arabs.[4]

A wide range of international issues were of common interest to Egypt and the Soviet Union. The former was emerging as part of the non-aligned bloc of nations with an anti-colonial outlook; at the same time internally it was devising and putting into practice its own version of socialism. The Soviet Union meanwhile was careful not to indulge in vituperative accusations against Israel, doing no more than state its views on 'Palestinian rights'. Such generalizations on the Palestinian question (rather than the rights of self-determination) were at the time vague concepts. Although the formal structure of the Palestinian Liberation Organization (PLO) was in existence, it was not capable of making its presence felt and the Soviet Union and the Eastern bloc could keep a low profile on this development. The Soviet Union saw the Palestinian question as only one of several questions facing the Arab world, not the key point in the Arab–Israeli conflict, and was more concerned that the Arabs should not lag behind in anti-colonialist policies or the internal establishment of socialism. It was easy to coin the phrase 'the Palestinian problem', but quite different to argue for Palestinian rights and/or self-determination or even the liberation of Palestine. It can be argued at this point that the 'question' of Palestine, as Soviet phraseology went, did not occupy a high place in Soviet foreign policy. This, most likely, is due to the Palestinian Resistance Movement itself and, more precisely, to the Arab conditions through which it operated.

In the mid-1960s the Palestinian Resistance Movement had not yet surfaced independently as a viable force within the Arab political spectrum. Even within certain Arab quarters the Palestinian question was treated as one concerning refugees rather than as one concerning the existence of an independent Palestinian Liberation Movement. The Soviet Union simply followed the general Arab official line on the Palestinian question. Al-Shukeiry announced on 22 May 1965[5] that the PLO had created its own army called the Palestine Liberation Army of which he was the head. This new military structure was to constitute its first form of military build-up, but al-Shukeiry achieved little noticeable assistance from Arab regimes. China, alone of the Communist countries, declared its support. The Soviet Union did not extend any military assistance. This was perhaps due to three factors. Firstly, the PLO was an organization created by Arab governments, a fact that would naturally lead to the imposition of Arab political demands and priorities. Secondly, to the Soviet Union the existence of the State of Israel was a political reality. To topple Israel was unthinkable. Finally, and perhaps most important, the conceptual framework of the PLO was something methodologically unacceptable. It was a nationalist movement, far from being Communist-oriented.

Al-Shukeiry undertook to establish the infrastructure of the PLO with all its various committees and military, financial and cultural apparatus. In its initial years the PLO was greatly influenced by Nasir. However, it lacked the possibility of 'independent' action since it lacked, among other things, the operational areas where it could take military action in a relatively free way against Israel. This limitation constituted a burden on its relations with non-Arab countries and was evident to the Soviet Union. The Soviet Union's silence on the growth of the PLO had wider ramifications. Firstly, Arab governments' domination of the PLO, especially Nasir's, was of such magnitude that the political consent of Arab 'host' states was almost certain to be guaranteed before it embarked on any political or military activities. If the Soviet Union decided to aid the PLO militarily, it must also obtain the consent of the host Arab state. This difficulty was encountered over China's military assistance to the PLO when Nasir was in power. Secondly, the Soviet Union's reservations on the PLO could be attributed to the political reality that the mechanics of the idea of the liberation of Palestine from Zionism were shrouded in mystery. It was not known at the time how the PLO would carry out this task. Thirdly, the PLO was a nationalist movement rather than a Communist one. This political adherence to nationalism acted as a constraint not only on the Soviet Union itself but also on the entire Communist bloc with the exception of China. Even in this realm, the Chinese had embarked upon a polemical dispute with the Soviet Union. On the part of China therefore there was a strong tendency to aid and support national liberation movements. Combined with this factor, moreover, China and the Soviet Union had embarked on a polemical charade which dictated checks on national liberation movements' receiving aid from both countries. Fourthly, the Soviet Union's preference for dealing with Arab states was obvious at this juncture since it found itself in the Arab world and its state-to-state relations had priority over other considerations. Fifthly, the Soviet Union still maintained diplomatic relations with Israel. This factor could not be taken lightly. It meant that the Soviet Union was not able to pursue policies in two diametrically opposite directions. China did not face this choice, because after the Communist take-over in 1949 China refused to have diplomatic relations with Israel. The Soviet Union, however, was faced with a difficult choice. Sixthly, if the Soviet Union embarked on the risky task of supporting the formidable force of an Arab national liberation movement this would have immense political repercussions. It was significant in this sphere that the PLO was engulfed in a sea of political uncertainties whose outcome was unpredictable. It was uncertain whether the PLO could conduct military operations from some of the Arab states bordering Israel, such as Syria, Jordan and Lebanon. Strategically Egypt remained a different question. The towering figure of Nasir was a political cloud over the PLO and slowed its progress, particularly in the first half of the 1960s which was governed by different political and strategic considerations. The Arab struggle against the remnants of colonialism (Britain and France) produced changes in the Arab political map, and the main political actors by 1965 were the United States and the Soviet Union.

Once relations between Egypt and the Soviet Union strengthened, the Eastern bloc also embarked on new relations with the Arab world which took many forms, though basically centered on economic[6] and cultural agreements. This new Arab–Eastern European rapprochement took place at a period when in general Arab–Western relations were not improving. The Soviet Union and Eastern Europe were an alternative for military supplies to the Arab world, a fact which introduced new political implications, the most important of which was the *freedom* to choose between East and West. This strategic element in East–West relations played a fundamental role in policy formulation toward the Arab world, especially that concerned with the Arab–Israeli conflict, which thereafter had new bearings on East–West relations in the Middle East. Both abstract issues and political realities took different directions. The outlook of both East and West on the Arab–Israeli conflict manifested itself in the sophistication of armaments delivered and the speed with which they were supplied to both antagonists. The outcome of East–West relations would be of military significance should a confrontation take place. In a practical sense, the military arsenal of both East and West was being judged, and the military preparedness of the two antagonists was, in a sense, the yardstick, for in the event of war its outcome would have serious implications for the two antagonists acting on behalf of the super powers. The strategic factor meant that the Soviet Union had to decide how far it was willing to interfere with its Arab allies. Such action would be the testing ground for future military and political developments.

The complex conditions prevailing in Egypt – namely, Arab nationalism, non-alignment and the invitation extended to the

Soviet Union and its bloc – were all considerations that imposed a heavy burden on Egypt since its leadership of the Arab world was at stake in the outcome of these developments. Furthermore, in the event of a military confrontation, not only would the military capability of the two super powers be tested, but the victor would also acquire unprecedented opportunities to dictate its conditions for the future. The whole capability and credibility of the Arab world would be put to the test. For the Arabs, therefore, it was one thing to put forward the notion of liberating Palestine and another to consider the means of achieving this goal. The task of liberating Palestine was laid upon the newly established PLO. But even this contained within it certain fundamental problems, since the PLO was operating in a sea of dilemmas which in turn imposed certain political constraints upon it. Furthermore, the PLO followed a political platform which extended beyond the goal of the liberation of Palestine. The PLO's platform was content with a general political orientation; other detailed strategic considerations were left open-ended, and would have to be dealt with in the future. Such confusion within the PLO led it to overestimate its capabilities while its inflated objectives made the governments of countries bordering Israel move cautiously in their support of the 'total' liberation of Palestine.

The Soviet Union found itself on an uncertain path. In a sense, if the Soviet Union were to back the political objectives of the PLO whole-heartedly then the question would assume wider international dimensions. It became even more complicated if the Soviet Union's foreign policy were viewed as ruled by Marxist-Leninist principles. Because the PLO was inherently a nationalistic movement, there was little freedom of maneuver for the Soviet Union, and it was for the Arab side to handle Arab–Soviet relations rather than the other way around. The Arab world, divided politically as it was in the first half of the 1960s, would not and was not able to offer the Soviet Union the political luxury of having the entire Arab world under its direct domination. Even Nasir could not arrange this for the Soviet Union.

Nasir steered his foreign policy carefully so as to be as independent as possible of both Eastern and Western camps. His neutral policy was encouraged by the fact that all local opposition parties were suppressed. The Egyptian Communist Party, for example, could not threaten his power. Neither were there Communist military bases in either Egypt or in any other Arab country.

Nevertheless, the Communist bloc supported Nasir in building up his armed forces and arranged several joint economic programs, and his choice between East and West was clearly demonstrated. Nevertheless, Nasir faced an unenviable political situation in the Arab world. Syria's secession from the UAR, three years of involvement in the Yemen war, the emergence of King Faisal in Saudi Arabia as a noted Arab leader, and, above all, the internal difficulties of the Egyptian economy combined to leave him a prey to the fear of war with Israel. At the same time the rest of the Arab world was plagued with problems and obstacles that hindered any political stability there, not in any way diminished by a Turkish uprising and resistance to the authority of the Iraqi central government.

The Soviet Union found itself involved in the tangle of Arab political, economic and military troubles. It was bewildered as to how it might deal logically with these awkward political developments, for the Arab world, particularly Egypt, was neither Communist-oriented nor totally Western in its political and economic outlook. It remained for the Soviet Union to calculate its own various moves in accordance with existing conditions. The Soviet Union had also to observe how the Western powers maneuvered in the Arab world from a strategic point of view, and the results of these cogitations formed the cornerstone of Soviet behavior in the Arab world. Furthermore, the Soviet Union found itself dealing with Arab regimes which were, to say the least, unstable politically. Arab instability led, ironically, to further Arab reliance on the various forms of Soviet aid, and this added a new international dimension to the Soviet Union's entanglement in the Arab world. The West, led by the United States, also found there fertile ground to enhance its powers. At this stage of political development, the Soviet Union did not accept the Arab desire for the 'total liberation of Palestine'. This ambivalence remained a salient feature of Soviet policy in the Arab world. The 'peaceful' approach adopted by the Soviet Union implied another factor in the Arab–Israeli conflict in that it negated the 'revolutionary' Arab solution to the dispute of the conflict with Israel. However, at this stage the Soviet Union did not offer any 'constructive' solutions to the Arab–Israeli conflict. It was, more precisely, involved in achieving an overall strategic position in the area on the world political scene.

In the international political development of Egypt, there existed three main stages.[7] The first was characterized by the dominant presence of the United States on the world political scene after World War II. This domination was expressed in its possession of atomic power, which made it the leader not only of the Western world but also of the Western powers at the United Nations. Europe was weak after World War II and thus had to yield to the dictates of the US in dealing with major international problems and had itself to accept aid, in the form of the Marshall Plan, to revive its economy and revitalize its status. The Soviet Union tried to resist the indisputable supremacy of the US by strengthening its armed forces internationally and furthering the capabilities of its allies. The second stage was demonstrated by the eruption of the Suez Canal affair in 1956. Even then the United States was still supreme in world affairs, and demonstrated this supremacy and power by its attempt to create a containment policy against the Communist world. An arms race ensued and the Soviet Union embarked on building its military arsenal of which the launching of inter-continental ballistic missiles was a manifestation. The Soviet Union aimed at crippling the United States' freedom by massive retaliation, and its wider objective was to render the Western military pacts in Europe, the Middle East and the Far East useless. The third stage had witnessed other significant developments. Among these were the after-effects of the crisis facing the Iranian regime of 1947, the revolution of Marcos, the strengthening of the international Communist movement in Eastern Europe and the success of the revolution in China. Lastly, the Soviet Union broke the US monopoly of atomic weapons. None the less, the United States embarked upon a policy of containment of the Soviet Union, and encircled it with various military pacts, regional and/or international.

These developments were crowned by the emergence of two facts. On the one hand, national revolution in the former colonial countries was gathering momentum. On the other hand, there appeared on the world political scene a tendency towards neutrality and non-alignment. Against this background the Suez Canal crisis occurred, which led, among other things, to the 'defeat' of the Tripartite aggressors. At much the same time, moreover, an unfounded uproar was created for the diversion of the Jordan waters, over which Israel threatened to go to war. The international political situation stood at a clear demarcation line between the military poles of West and East separated by an elastic grouping of

193

states known as the non-aligned nations. Nevertheless, Soviet aid to Egypt at this point increased in every possible form and led to noticeable involvement in the Arab world. The latter, mostly led by Nasir, was by then at a political stage for it to choose between alternative alliances. The increasing polarization of forces became markedly noticeable when Egypt embarked on internal socialist reconstruction.

This socialist element in the reconstruction of the Egyptian economy led to further involvement of the Soviet Union in the Arab world and had its effect on the political polarization of East–West involvement in the region. This played an important role in the course of the Arab–Israeli conflict. The dispute acquired an international dimension. Both East and West found themselves on the testing ground of their client allies. It remained for the two antagonists to demonstrate their logistical military strength in an open show of military capability. The defeat of a client of the contending states would confront one or other camp with new realities. The anticipated show of power was the decisive factor in the appeal of the Arab–Israeli conflict as the testing ground for their credibility in the Middle East at large. At this juncture Nasir had set in motion a pro-Soviet drive, which alienated him totally from the West. This occurred at a period when his Arab policies were witnessing certain setbacks and when his troops were tied down in the Yemen war. His ideas about Arab unity and the struggle for the liberation of Palestine were facing too marked a resistance for them to be realized. Despite this he was contemplating the occurrence of war with Israel although it would have to be delayed for a while. At the same time, he was not able to find remedies for the ailing Egyptian economy.

Within the Soviet Union, foreign policy in the world at large and in the Arab world in particular as part of the Afro-Asian bloc was expounded by various Soviet authors. A *Pravda* editorial argued that the most characteristic feature of Soviet foreign policy was that it aimed at peaceful coexistence between different social systems throughout the world. This policy was a revolutionary one stamped by firmness and yet following a Leninist international line; it imposed the necessity for Soviet support for revolutionary movements, based on the cardinal principle of opposition to all forms of imperialism. These world revolutionary movements, it was argued, together with the Soviet attitude towards them, was based upon Maxist-Leninist analysis. And one deviation from this

Marxist-Leninist analysis was the emergence of an international alignment of class forces and the 'key objective factors of world politics'. It follows from this argument that the unfolding of crises dictates certain political negotiations in order to reach the ultimate goal of victory. Peaceful conditions should be adhered to so as to insure the final victory of socialism. It was argued that the 'most important trend' in Soviet foreign policy was its attempts to create conditions conducive to peace, to follow a policy of peaceful coexistence between states with different systems, the strengthening of world socialism and the unity of the socialist camp. All these developments, it was argued, could be achieved because of the unyielding position of the Soviet Union. It was further stated that both the Soviet Union and other socialist countries must support the national liberation movements in the world and that, at the same time, the former should forge links of solidarity and cooperation with the independent countries of Asia, Africa and Latin America. Finally, the argument dealt with more pressing tasks at hand by arguing that

> The USSR has never been indifferent – nor will it ever be indifferent – to the aggressive actions of colonialists which threaten the independence of peoples. The Soviet state has always opposed the imperialist policy of 'exporting counter-revolution'. It has given and continues to give the broadest assistance to people fighting for their freedom and independence against colonialism and neo-colonialism. The Soviet Union always bases itself on the right of each people to free and independent development as a sacred right: the desire to end imperialist aggression is profoundly legitimate and completely justified. When the imperialists compel them to take action, the peoples reply with all available means of struggle, including national liberation war, to imperialist attempts to deprive them by force of their sacred right . . . The Soviet Union is playing an enormous role in the economic development of countries fighting for their liberation from imperialism.[8]

Economic and political development in Arab states which had close relations with the Soviet Union was welcome news to the latter. In Soviet coverage of the Syrian economy, N. Smetanin, writing in *Pravda*, reported on overall Arab political and economic 'progress' in the region:

The Arab press notes that the intensification of private capitalist tendencies in the economy since Syria's withdrawal from the UAR has caused great damage to the country. One of the consequences was that major capitalists transformed their profits abroad, which reduced the funds needed for industrial development. . . . In Algeria the self-government sector has taken firm positions. In July of last year [1964], banks, insurance societies and companies, and enterprises of several industries were nationalized in Iraq. The Soviet public is following with sympathy and compassion the struggle of the Arab peoples, who resolutely oppose imperialism and neo-colonialism and are advancing along the path of progressive and economic transformation.[9]

Moreover, the Soviet press was critical of Israel and its military provocation of neighboring Arab states. One instance of such Israeli provocation occurred in May 1965. Soviet commentators dealt speedily with this development. Y. Primakov argued the case, *inter alia*, by posing a rhetorical question:

What are Tel Aviv's 'motives'? Two of the three points where the invasion was made are situated on the Arab bank of the Jordan River. Israel has already begun the unilateral diversion of the River's waters and is doing everything it can to prevent the Arab countries from undertaking acts of retaliation. Tel Aviv apparently is not guided by considerations of an economic order. . . . Tel Aviv has apparently decided to use the problem of the Jordan River to put pressure on the Arab states. Perhaps this is the reason why the Israeli invasion was timed to coincide with the conference of the heads of government of the Arab countries in Cairo.[10]

The Soviet Union welcomed, by this time, the various political Arab developments. Amongst these was the political route taken by Arab Communist parties, in particular the Syrian. Attention was given to the Syrian government's nationalization program in the Syrian economy. This economic change, which led to state ownership of the means of production, was viewed by the Soviet Union as a real step toward socialist 'progress'. It was within the economic sphere that the Soviet Union was encouraged to further various forms of aid to what it termed 'progressive regimes' in the Arab world. Added to this, Syrian programs in releasing political prisoners and holding local elections in Syrian trade unions were considered as another indication of progressiveness. Political solidarity between the Syrian Communist Party and the Soviet Union reflected the strengthening of worldwide Communist trends.[11] To the Soviet Union all this indicated that certain Arab regimes had embarked on a new form of political development which logically led to closer Arab–Soviet relations, and, at the same time, it meant that certain Arab states had made their choice between an East or West alignment. This had repercussions in the international sphere. East–West relations and their impact on Arab conditions, where the Arab–Israeli conflict was the key point, dictated its own conditions in the region. For example, the military preparedness of either the Arabs or the Israelis meant that in case of war, the outcome would have its impact on the term imposed by the victor. Moreover, the result of testing the armaments of each side would affect future developments.

The political situation of the Arab world implied also that the Soviet Union was involved in inter-Arab relations. At this point Egypt was engaged militarily in the Yemen where, in Soviet eyes, imperialism played its role, but Egypt encountered difficulties in the management of the crisis. Attention was paid by the Soviet Union to the role played by Saudi Arabia in this war, and accusations against the latter were levied when Y. Primakov, a *Pravda* correspondent, argued that:

> A halt in intervention from Saudi Arabia, for which Cairo is
> now striving, is an important condition for establishing a
> stable peace in the Yemen. Allusions are being made here to
> the possibility of reaching an agreement on this question,
> regardless of the considerable influence exerted on Saudi
> Arabian policy by the USA and Britain. In the event the UAR
> fails, it will be forced to deal a blow to the bases from which the
> aggression against Yemen is being committed.[12]

In the Arab world at the beginning of the second half of the 1960s, independence became an aim. However, the Arab world was far from being cohesive politically, and the Arab political pendulum swung wildly from one extreme to the other, from nationalistic trends to the growing leftist tendency. It was therefore misleading politically to speak of a unified political outlook or course of action.

As a divided geographical entity, the Arab world vacillated as a result of the prevailing objective conditions. One could easily conceive a political situation where foreign powers played a leading role in the division of the Arab world and, with the entrance of the Soviet Union into it, political demarcation lines became more pronounced than ever. The Arab world was the prey for both East and West. Whereas the latter had a much longer history of involvement in the region, the former, inherited in the Arab world both the remnants of this long history of colonialism and neo-colonialism and the political uncertainties which the Arab world was encountering. Within these uncertainties the Soviet Union had to operate. The Arab world was influenced by both the East and the West, for it was a region ripe for political experimentation. Arab nationalism emerged from this awkward situation as a force to be reckoned with. The issue of Arab survival became an issue in its own right, and it followed that the desire to fulfill the precepts of nationalism came itself to be a goal. That led certain Arab states under Egypt's leadership to support the cause of non-alignment enthusiastically, for it was a choice that was neither Western or Eastern in orientation. This political course coincided on general lines with overall Soviet foreign policy. Non-alignment was a movement that aimed at blazing a particular independent political trail in international politics.

Arab nationalism was aimed at the achievement of Arab unity, even though the experiment was tried and failed. The idea of unity remained a cornerstone, and its failure was attributed partly to the influence of outside powers. The stark fact remained that it was conceivable for it to happen. Secondly, related to the above, was the achievement of national independence. It was a period that necessitated some sort of national independent action. Coupled with the previous factors was the reality that national progress was attainable. That involved the various strata of the polity – not only its political orientation but also its economic and social dimensions. And, among the precepts of progress, it was generally held in certain Arab quarters that the routes of progress lay in the realm of state socialism.

The Arab world added a new dimension to international politics because it possessed oil, which provided a further opportunity for international rivalry. The scramble for oil among Western companies was an element to be reckoned with for any future economic development that affected Arab oil-producing countries. Arab oil policies, especially those centered on the value of oil and the demands of certain Arab countries for its nationalization, were welcomed by the Soviet Union even though the question of nationalization was, for all practical purposes, dormant at this period. Where it was practised, however, nationalization meant that certain governments had taken an economic route that led to socialism. However, this socialistic tendency was not universal; socialism was only one means to further progress in an assertive way and combat the backwardness of some Arab states. The Arab world was far from accepting Marxism or following a Marxist route in state-building. Nevertheless the existence of a unified Arab world would pose a threat to Western powers rather than to the Soviet Union and its bloc. Such a threat would be basically strategic, for, in addition to its situation the Arab world was covered by Western military bases. Some Arab states were also involved, at one stage or another, in Western regional pacts, many of which were directly concerned with anti-Communist states. But, internally, those Arab states which chose socialism as a political means for achieving certain national goals embarked on their own forms of state ownership, and they found the desired assistance in the Soviet Union and its allies.

The Arab–Israeli conflict was not the only source of instability in the region. There existed, for example, undemarcated boundaries and serious unsettled border questions. Uncertainty and change made the whole region an easy prey to super-power influences and rivalry. It was one thing to choose a certain goal for internal developments, and another task to elevate entire issues and sources of conflict to an international level where East–West alliances played an important role in fomenting disagreements and disputes. Egypt, Syria and Iraq had now established close relations with the Soviet Union, whereas other major Arab states sided with the Western powers. However, the extent of Soviet penetration of the Arab world, compared with the influence exercised by the Western powers, had not noticeably widened since 1957 and, although there was observable progress in economical and political aid, the military dimension remained open.

The United States and Britain were at this time the most notable military powers in the Arab world. It was one thing to speak about political alliances and another to have military bases stationed in Arab countries; military alliances favorable to Western powers were not uncommon. One of these was the Central Treaty Organization

(CENTO) whose object was to deter the Soviet Union from extending its influence in the region. One commentator thought such alliances had an added dimension in that 'their primary purpose is a more local one: to safeguard the flow of Middle East oil, to prevent or check conflict in their own immediate area and to provide a base for British military intervention in other areas close at hand'.[13] A large segment of the Middle East had become a solid military appendage of the West. The Soviet Union embarked upon a program of economic aid and became a covert supplier of arms to Arab countries who were part of the non-aligned nations.

On the Arab scene, meanwhile, the PLO was on more solid ground even though its political aspirations were still overshadowed by Nasir's leadership. It was set on a course that transferred it from the path of Arab internal politics to the international scene, a path that naturally encountered the swings of the Arab political pendulum. The PLO was the creation of Arab governments and the initiative of Nasir; it was not an 'independent' organization or movement. The Palestinians expelled from their native homeland had need of some sort of official Arab recognition. The earliest period of the PLO's history coincided with that where the prestige of Nasir was at the center of the whole inter-Arab Cold War. It remained to be seen how Nasir would maneuver and how the PLO would handle the very wide sphere of action open to it, for the range of available options was one of the main stumbling blocks for its future actions. Militarily, the PLO was land-locked, and in the event of future military action against Israel, the approval of the 'host' Arab country would be necessary, because such action would undoubtedly antagonize Israel. This required the Arab governments bordering Israel to make a decision on how far each was willing to go. The extent of this involvement remained the point of departure for future political and military developments in the Arab–Israeli conflict. However, efforts to find a peaceful solution, such as President Bourguiba's proposal to recognize Israel which he put forward in 1965 were not likely to be fruitful since the Arab world was not ready for this kind of settlement. The general Arab line of thought was crystalizing in the opposite direction and the armed forces of the Palestinian Resistance Movement were heading toward militarization and a military showdown. These political developments indicated that the Palestinian question had become the central issue in the Arab–Israeli dispute although the 'liberation' of Palestine remained open.

The exact way in which Palestine would be liberated had not yet been clearly defined. The Soviet Union had still not become directly involved in the issues of the Palestinian question and, if it ever did, then it would have to be through a third party, probably Egypt. There were no direct Soviet–Palestinian relations so that there could be no 'independent' decision-making by either side. Soviet hesitation to deal directly with the PLO at this juncture is to be attributed to several factors. Firstly, as was stated earlier, laying the foundations of the PLO was the affair of Arab governments. Secondly, the specific political orientations of the PLO did not make clear what sort of an organization it was. Thirdly, the Soviet Union could have hardly accepted the Palestinian concept of 'liberating' Palestine. If this were ever to occur, it would mean direct Soviet involvement in the Arab–Israeli conflict from which it was restrained by its wider relations with the West. Lastly, the Soviet Union and the Eastern European bloc still retained normal diplomatic relations with Israel, a political fact that could scarcely be ignored in relation to the Arab–Israeli conflict. Only China, within the Communist bloc, extended unequivocal support to the Palestinian cause.

It should be stressed here that the Soviet Union had first-hand information about the Palestinian cause. For, in 'Amman, Jordan, the Soviet ambassador had contacts with the PLO. It was reported on July 7 1965, that Shukeiry had conveyed to the Soviet ambassador, "the Palestinian people's thanks for Soviet support for the *Arab* viewpoint on the Palestinian question at the UN Security Council and the General Assembly".' [emphasis added][14] But on (for example) military grounds the Soviet Union's contribution was negligible; Al-Shukeiry had been aiming to penetrate Soviet silence on the question. He had to be satisfied with a simple political denunciation of Israel and the general appeal for 'Palestinian rights'. The Soviet Union expressed its attitude through normal Arab diplomatic channels, although its vociferous attack on Israel was carefully aimed and administered.

At the United Nations the Soviet Union paid due consideration to the issue known then as that of the Palestinian 'refugees'. The Soviet representative, A. I. Blatov, in the Special Political Committee of the United Nations General Assembly argued for the implementation of the UN resolution concerning the plight of the Palestinian 'refugees'. He declared at the session of this Committee that

The USSR attaches great importance to the problem of the refugees. Only recently, in September [1965], the Soviet Government, jointly with the Government of the United Arab Republic, condemned imperialist policy in the Middle East. It was emphasized that the Soviet Union expressed its full support for the struggle of the Arab peoples against the policy and fully supported the unalienable lawful rights of the Palestinian Arabs.[15]

It is clear from the above that Egypt played a major role in helping the Soviet Union to understand the plight of the Palestinians. At this time, when the PLO was under Al-Shukeiry's leadership, the Palestinian question was gaining wide international diplomatic recognition. He associated the Palestinian people with other Third World peoples. At a press conference in Baghdad he is reported to have said:

The Vietnamese people will triumph in the end and the force of colonialism and imperialism will be defeated ... On the Southern Rhodesia situation, he denounced Britain's stand towards the Southern Rhodesian problem and that the Southern Rhodesian problem was a replica of the Palestinian tragedy. The Southern Rhodesian colonial regime would be removed from power only by military force.[16]

The international outlook of the PLO leadership added a new dimension to the Palestinian cause, whose attempt to identify with world revolutionary movements was only one of the manifestations of the general outlook of the PLO leadership. This international political orientation of the PLO was to bear fruit in the future and it meant that the Palestinian cause had been upgraded to an international level.

The year 1966 began with a carefully calculated article by M. H. Heikal in *al-Ahram*[17] in which he took the overall situation of the Arab region with the Arab–Israeli conflict as his point of departure. He then touched on the international situation of the Arab world strategically, and commented that between 1952 and 1956 Egypt had spearheaded resistance to Western powers which had embarked upon an aggressive trend against it because it was seeking an independent foreign policy. Egyptian determination to follow such a course had been strengthened by the marked influence such a decision had on the remaining Arab countries. This path had led to major changes in alignments between East and West. The Arab world was on the threshold of major changes. Thus, it was not surprising that the Arab road towards nationalism and non-alignment emerged as a natural consequence of the existing conditions. It would have been unrealistic if the Arab world had not chosen this route. Conditions imposed rules. It became natural for the Arab world to be anti-Western, for the West had a lengthy history of domination over the area and the sentiment was similar to an Arab uprising against foreign domination and internal decadence. Outright Egyptian rejection of the Western powers set a political example to other Arab states, and marked the beginning of an upsurge of Arab nationalism.

These manifestations of nationalist sentiment were an obstacle to the Soviet Union in its relations with the Arab world and because they were also manifested in the Arab-Israeli conflict they became more of a menace still. Within this sphere the Soviet Union did its best to fill the gap in Arab preparedness to combat Israel, even though its willingness to aid Egypt and other Arab states placed a heavy burden on its capabilities. The Soviet Union, moreover, was a super power which could, to a certain extent, affect the outcome of events. It had set out to divert the course of events in the region. But it was left to the Arab states to choose the degree to which the Soviet Union might become involved in their affairs. At the time, the Arab–Israeli conflict constituted the key to all political issues facing the Arab world, and it posed a dilemma for the Soviet Union. Although the Soviet Union had working diplomatic relations with Israel, it was nevertheless critical of the precepts of Zionism. Most Arabs were confused and bewildered by this behavior; it was incomprehensible both to the masses and at governmental level. But the formidable weaknesses of the Arab world could not be corrected without aid, and requests for help continued to be laid before the Soviet Union. One of its requirements was military aid which, when granted, naturally led Arab countries to embark upon speedy militarization. Although both super powers carefully guided events in the region to avoid direct military collision, the antagonists in the Arab–Israeli conflict were, meanwhile, heightening tensions so that the conflict might reach a climax. But it was difficult at this point to predict whether or not a military showdown would take place.

To Egypt, relations with the Soviet Union were of prime importance both internally and externally. At the first level, the

Soviet Union had rendered noticeable assistance to building the Egyptian economy, for which Egypt was grateful. Nasir, in an interview with *Izvestia*, summed up the importance of the Aswan High Dam project to his country when he said:

> At the outset of the project, the High Dam was the cause of aggression against us, and the Soviet Union stood by our side in our battle against the aggressor.[18]

On Egypt's foreign policy objectives, Nasir reiterated his previous idea of three circles in the Egyptian revolution, and he dwelt on Arab unity, the struggle against colonialism in Africa and the road the Muslim world was taking. At the same time, Egyptian relations were developing speedily with the Eastern bloc in various fields of trade, technical cooperation and military agreements. These developments provided an incentive for both sides. Nevertheless, Nasir was threatening Israel and declaring that if Israel developed its nuclear capabilities, then Egypt must take 'preventive' action against the achievement of this goal.[19] Shimon Perez, Israel's Deputy Defense Minister, was quick to respond to Nasir's message in which he declared that 'there was no peace in the Middle East because the necessary conditions for establishing peace are inadequate. Israel's only enemy . . . is the policy followed by Abdul Nasir.'[20]

The strategic element of the Soviet Union's foreign policy in the Arab world became, by this time, an overriding element in its overall perception of the importance of the region. One manifestation of the strategic use of the Arab world was the Soviet Union's attempt to use its navy for military exercises in the warm waters of the Mediterranean with Egyptian ports as its anchorage which alarmed the West.[21] However, at this early period of development in Arab–Israeli relations, several commentaries were tinged with the scare of impending war in the region. The military build–up of both antagonists continued to be an indication of the likelihood of military confrontation.

Internally, Egypt was carrying through its socialist form of reconstruction, although the ruling elite remained aloof from accepting Communism as a guiding force in furthering what it termed a revolution. In an article, M. H. Heikal mentioned the various stages through which the Egyptian policy was proceeding and their wider implications for Egyptian foreign policy. Heikal attempted not only to dispel the fear of Communism in Egypt which he asserted Egypt could ignore in its national reconstruction, but also to assure the general readership that Egypt was making progress despite all odds. Nasir sought such reassurances as would confirm him in his view that the path he had chosen was correct.

It had yet to be seen what course Egypt would adopt towards Israel. Although the Arabs had scored notable progress within the non-aligned and Communist blocs, the stark political reality remained that none of these accomplishments affected Israel in any way. After the collapse of Egyptian–Syrian unity, it remained for Nasir to deal with the tattered situation of the Arab world. The task was monumental, and it was left entirely to Nasir to consolidate his 'victories' and rectify his failures.

In this climate of uncertainty the Soviet Union had to evaluate its priorities and put into action its short- and long-term objectives in the Arab world. In the short term the restricted run of normal international diplomatic achievements seemed rewarding even if Arab diplomatic movements against Israel had witnessed little success. The Soviet Union's achievements were, however, facing certain obstacles. Communism, for example, was not acceptable to the Arab world and in the circumstances there was little more the Soviet Union could do to further its involvement there. This placed the Soviet Union in a dilemma. Although certain Arab states welcomed the various forms of Soviet aid, they rejected its ideological buttress. The overwhelming mood in the Arab world under Nasir's leadership was in favor of Arab nationalism, and the Soviet Union could not achieve more than to cater to these sentiments and aspirations. It was not, however, an unwelcome trend, for Arab nationalism was in direct collision with Western goals; the Arab world wished to eradicate the remnants of the bygone colonialist era.

The Soviet Union, meanwhile, had accomplished its short-term economic objectives; it welcomed the Arab world's own brand of socialism and it provided certain constructive means towards its implementation. Nevertheless the Soviet Union could not proceed beyond a certain point and it became observable that the Soviet Union, as a super power, found itself entangled in a region that belonged to neither the Eastern or the Western camp; the Arab world remained divided both in its mode of economic reconstruction and, especially, in foreign policy objectives. Within the Arab political spectrum one could find all sorts of political trends, except the existence of an Arab entity that seriously entertained, and adhered to, Communist ideology as a guiding force.

In May 1966 the Soviet Premier, Alexsei N. Kosygin, arrived in Cairo on an official state visit, an event whose implications were considerable. It was the second visit from a Soviet Premier within two years, and it indicated not only how much weight Egypt carried within the Arab world but also the extent to which it was the bridgehead between Asia and Africa. The most significant aim of the visit was to confirm the Soviet contribution to the building of socialism in Egypt and to emphasize the political undertones of the worldwide alliances of the Soviet Union with the non-aligned bloc. Kosygin's trip to Egypt was his first outside the Communist bloc, and was an indication of the importance the Soviet Union attached to the role played by Nasir in the region. But there had already emerged a conservative trend in the Arab world headed by Saudi Arabia which attempted to form some sort of Islamic pact while other countries besides Egypt declared themselves to be radical, socialist Syria in particular. The Soviet Union was in fact on strong ground in the Arab world since the entire region was the scene of East–West rivalry. Israel was a power which threatened both these trends. Although the Soviet bloc maintained normal diplomatic relations with Israel, Israel remained a problem which no Arab regime could solve. The Arab regimes had not yet recovered from the military defeat of 1948, and many countries were still, even in the first half of the 1960s, so backward that they were handicapped in making any united approach to solve the problem.

At the beginning of his visit the speeches Kosygin exchanged with Nasir were carefully worded. On one of these occasions, his approach was milder than Nasir's, and he put marked emphasis on Soviet–Egyptian relations.[22] In international politics both sides were in agreement in denouncing American military intervention in Vietnam. Nasir asserted that one of the basic tasks facing the 'progressive' forces in the world was to counter and spearhead the struggle against imperialism. It was understood that the United States was the target of this accusation. The Arab world constituted a region where all major foreign world powers played some sort of political and strategic role and it had simply to react to the intermingled but unsolved questions of the time. It was a case where political conditions dictated the rules rather than of the Arab world being free to choose its destiny. The Arab world had become a stage on which outside powers might experiment – though the experiment appeared to be leading to a confrontation with Zionism. A significant part of the Arab world was expecting Soviet assistance in various forms, which proved to be both valuable and necessary to counteract the barrier of Arab conservatism being constructed by the West and its efforts to build up the arsenal of Israel.

Kosygin, while in Cairo, met the PLO Chairman Ahmad al-Shukeiry; the talks were described as 'important'.[23] Indications, however, were that the Soviet Union had not yet formulated its final decision on how to handle the Palestinian question in its own way. The question was viewed by the Soviet Union as a cause furthered by its official Arab allies – notable among them, Nasir – and it considered that the PLO was maneuvering politically under Nasir's political umbrella. But while the Soviet Union might oppose Israel as a bridgehead of Western imperialism it was a completely different matter fully to support the PLO as an independent political entity. The Palestinian cause, from the Soviet point of view, had neither its own independent military infrastructure nor its own political independence. Before the PLO could further the Palestinian cause either internally and/or internationally it had to build a much-needed infrastructure, and to this only China in the Communist bloc rendered solid political and military assistance. The joint communiqué issued at the end of the visit was carefully worded on the Palestinian question. It simply stated that:

> The Soviet side fully supports the legitimate and indivisible rights of the Palestinian Arabs. It supports the struggle and the efforts made by the Arab states against the aggressive intrigues of the imperialist forces which are seeking to exploit the Palestinian problem in order to increase tension in the Middle East.[24]

The Soviet Union's stand on the Palestinian cause was markedly different from that which it had adopted on other Arab liberation movements – for example, Aden and the Arab south, where the struggle was against British colonialism. Furthermore Soviet hesitation in singling out Israel in its condemnation of events surrounding the political developments in the region is evident. Although Nasir played an important role in furthering the Palestinian cause, it remained to be seen how far the Soviet Union was willing and ready to go in providing its much-needed support.

The PLO had been brought into existence by decree of Arab governments. Because it had the official blessing of Arab governments the Soviet Union was placed in an awkward political situation. If it chose to recognize the PLO it was simultaneously acknowledging the legitimacy of the Palestinian cause, and the consequences of this support would be of great magnitude. Recognition by a super power is no small matter, for by implication it would carry with it the possibility of military assistance. Moreover Soviet support would also carry with it that of the other countries in the Communist bloc. Repercussions on the international scene would be immense.

However, the Soviet Union at this point was not willing to extend full political and military support to the PLO because its specific political platform and orientation was not clear and the Organization was far from reaching political maturity. It was not practical to simply proclaim the broad political slogan of Palestinian rights, for such a political agenda became obscure when applied to political reality and concealed a number of difficulties. It was not clear for example, what Palestinian rights meant: a return to the 1948 borders, or to part of Palestine? It was not clear what was to be done if the Arab–Israeli conflict were resolved in a bilateral situation without the PLO's participation. There was also the separate question of what weight the PLO carried as a power in its own right. To a large extent Soviet hesitation to deal independently with the PLO emanated from the fact that the PLO was not capable of independent action. It seems that Nasir was not aiming to obtain more from the Soviet Union than its approval for the relatively vague political slogan of 'Palestinian rights'.

It was in fact too soon for the Soviet Union to give military aid to the PLO, for if it did, the consent of the Arab 'host' country would have to be requested. Were Soviet military aid to be rendered, even the Soviet Union did not know how far it was willing to go in jeopardizing its relations with the 'host' Arab country. All these considerations led the Soviet Union to tread warily in giving any indication of support for the Palestinian cause. While the Arab side never questioned the validity of the phrase 'Palestinian rights' and it seems that the PLO also was content with this vague wording, it was a slogan for internal consumption only. It was insufficient to satisfy the Soviet Union.

It was reported by Palestinian sources[25] that Ahmad al-Shukeiry relayed to Kosygin in Cairo that while the spirit of the Tashkent Agreement which had dealt with the Indian-Pakistani dispute over Kashmir was the prevailing spirit internationally, this spirit did not apply to the Palestinian cause. The sources assert that the reason for this was that Israel had occupied and usurped Palestinian territory and turned the Palestinian peoples into refugees. Al-Shukeiry went on to speak of the remarkable stand taken by China in supporting the Palestinian cause politically and militarily.[26] It was obvious that al-Shukeiry was aware of the Sino-Soviet rift. But since his main concern at this point was to discover how much support the Palestinian cause could muster internationally he could not afford to take sides in this conflict. At the time, the PLO was building up its infrastructure, one aspect of the task being to enlist help from abroad, another al-Shukeiry's organization of the election for the National Assembly of Palestinians outside Israel.[27] The PLO needed friends in every available quarter.

However, Iraq reported that at the meeting of al-Shukeiry and Kosygin on 18 May 1966 the former had asked the Soviet Union to terminate its diplomatic relations with Israel and put an end to Soviet Jewish emigration to Palestine. On both counts the Palestinian request placed a heavy burden on the Soviet Union. For it to take such steps, the Soviet Union would have to disregard certain historical facts, the first of which was the major role it and the Eastern bloc had played in the creation of Israel. Secondly, even if the Soviet Union could forget the past, there was the more general problem of East–West relations, where what was at issue was not simply the Arab–Israeli conflict *per se*, but the ramifications and repercussions of this problem in global politics with which it had become entangled. The separate but related question of the emigration of Soviet Jews to Israel implied widespread Arab dissatisfaction with the Soviet Union, for the latter was supplying Israel with its much-needed human element. These two questions are really one, the most remarkable in Arab–Soviet Union relations. It was an aspect that was brought to light by the Arabs, and it remained an issue for those Arabs who were spearheading an anti-Soviet movement. If the Soviet Union were to curtail or completely stop Soviet Jewish emigration to Israel and were to break off diplomatic relations with Israel, then it would dramatically lose ground in the Middle East. This is not to say that the Soviet Union was benefiting from the existence of Israel. But the argument against such action would center on how much the Arabs had to offer the Soviet Union given that their political development was uncertain. It was more rewarding for the Soviet Union to keep all its options open, for in fact there was little to lose. As long as it enjoyed a solid alignment with Nasir it occupied an assured position in the Arab world. However, Arab armies whose states received Soviet military aid had to adapt themselves not only physically to changes to new military equipment but also politically to changes of alignment. Nasir's brand of Arab nationalism constituted a threat to Arab monarchical regimes, notably in Jordan and Saudi Arabia. The latter headed an Islamic movement which spread across the Arab world and to which Nasir was opposed. This political imbalance affected East–West relations in their respect objectives in the Arab world.

One of the sharpest antagonisms dividing Arab states was the arguments which arose over the question of armaments. The Soviet Union supplied a significant proportion of this weaponry although some, mostly the so-called conservative Arab, armies were equipped and supplied by the Western powers. No Arab state was self-sufficient in this field. Thus it followed naturally that the Arab world became an 'experimental' field where foreign powers had a role to play, and this led to the polarization of forces in the Middle East as a whole. Israel was able to exploit this inter-Arab contradiction, in addition to the development of its nuclear capabilities.[28] An Israel with nuclear power implied that it would stay in Palestine. Arab pronouncements concerning the liberation of Palestine fulfilled the dreams of the Arab world, but the search for a solution to the problem only led to inter-Arab rivalries and disputes. There was a point at which efforts to solve these differences should have taken precedence over the pursuit of the Arab–Israeli conflict, for it would have been sensible to establish priorities on the problems that faced the Arab world. But logic has no room in Arab politics. Submerged obstacles facing the Arab world surfaced slowly and when they did the Arab world was handicapped in the process of dealing with them. Aspirations to Arab unity were one thing, but it was another matter to advocate a unified Arab struggle against Zionism. The former meant, among other things, that all internal Arab questions were capable of resolution, whereas the latter implied that all Arab states believed in a unified military solution to the Arab–Israeli conflict. Arab priorities, as always, fluctuated in their importance.

The Soviet Union could not avoid the problems of the Arab world, but its involvement in that world had come about by invitation and while it contributed to the economic reconstruction of the Arab world, it also lent a hand in the Arab military build-up. The various forms which Soviet aid took helped the extension of its spheres of influence in an area still regarded as a Western enclave. Soviet penetration of the Arab world was a step towards the intensification of the Cold War in the Middle East, for the West did not yield easily to Soviet advances there.

War clouds were gathering when Nasir declared his intention to launch a deterrent attack on Israel should the latter build up its nuclear arsenal.[29] Yet it was not clear how this war was to be conducted. Was it to encompass all Arab states sharing borders with Israel or just with one of these Arab countries? The uncertainty behind a war desired by the Arab side would have its international significance. It was a war which nobody expected to happen for the balance of power on paper appeared to be numerically favorable to the Arab side. Nevertheless though not taken seriously it was a topical issue. The language used, however, was far from being precise, and threats to use force by the Arabs were common, mostly couched in phrases associated with the liberation of Palestine. Belligerent terminology filled certain Arab psychological gaps.

From the Soviet Union's point of view there were international questions that were more pressing at this time than the Arab–Israeli conflict. Amongst them were the American military involvement in Vietnam, and the East–West military build-up in Europe. These two questions assumed overriding importance in Soviet foreign policy objectives, even though the Arab–Israeli conflict was taking a fresh turn for the worse and absorbing the interest of the Arab world. Once the PLO was certain of official Arab support it embarked on a two-pronged objective, the furthering of the Palestinian cause internationally and intensified effort to build its internal infrastructure. The military aspect of the liberation of Palestine dictated new practicalities, centered on the need for the availability of Arab forces capable of countering Israel's military might. On the face of things this was not a task likely to be accomplished. To achieve it the Arab–Israeli conflict became the central point in internal Arab politics and the Palestinian cause overshadowed all other Arab questions, including economic recon-struction, the regional questions which had led to an Arab Cold War, and East–West rivalry in the Arab world. None of these could be solved immediately.

The Arab world as a whole was puzzled as to what to do with the Palestinian refugees herded together in camps in Jordan, Syria, Lebanon and the Gaza Strip administered by Egypt. New Pal-estinian political orientations began to surface in the wider Arab scene, ranging from ultra-right to the extreme left. Arab states were at a loss as to how to handle the emerging political orientations. Already with nothing left to lose the Palestinian refugees began to feel the further effects of disparate Arab official policies. The Soviet Union already entangled in the Arab world, became also a super power involved in inter-Arab disputes and this led it to tread more carefully still in the wider Arab–Israeli conflict. Despite the pitfalls and uncertainties about the future it seems that conditions were still favorable to the Soviet Union; the divisions of the Arab world provided more room for the Soviets to maneuver within it.

In the sense that it advocated a military solution to the Arab–Israeli conflict, the PLO was from its creation, a threat to Arab countries sharing borders with Israel, notably Jordan. The regime in Jordan was one of the PLO targets. At the same time, the PLO was acting under Nasir's protection and he, in turn, was leaning on the Soviet Union internationally. The Soviet Union at this juncture, though voicing a few criticisms of Zionism, had come nowhere near endorsing the PLO's political program. Such Soviet hesitation was, perhaps, due to the PLO itself. It was a movement without solid ground on which to operate and the Soviet Union could not offer to operate in a vacuum. If Egypt chose to aid the PLO then it would mean that the Soviet Union must extend aid indirectly to the Palestinian cause. It was an awkward situation for the Soviet Union.

It should be stressed that the main aim of the PLO on its creation in January 1964 had been to gather together the Palestinians scattered over the Arab world. It had no political coloring and was simply a nationalist movement. By 1966 it was little more.

But in one of the most remarkable incidents in PLO history, Ahmad al-Shukeiry, Chairman of the PLO, asked King Hussein of Jordan to abdicate.[30] This dispute revealed the extent to which the PLO was allowed to function from Arab bases. A statement issued by al-Shukeiry dwelt on the difficulty of maneuvering effectively on the wider Arab scene and put forward the PLO's inability to deal with the Arab–Israeli conflict. It set out the following points which it hoped the King would take into consideration:

(1) Compulsory military service be applied to all citizens in Jordan in conformity with the request of the Unified Arab Command.
(2) Liberation Army battalions be formed in Jordan in

accordance with the plans earlier set out by the Unified Command.

(3) The PLO be given full opportunity to apply the popular organization system approved by the National Congress at its meeting in Cairo.

(4) The Palestine Liberation Organization should be allowed to organize camps for young people and students in Jordan.

(5) The Palestine Liberation Organization should be allowed to hold free public elections in Jordan for the National Council according to the system laid down by the organization.

(6) The 'liberation tax' system in Jordan as ratified by the National Council in Jerusalem and the arming and fortifying of the front villages must be enforced.

(7) Complete liberty be accorded to the organization in shouldering its national responsibilities for the mobilization of the Palestine People's powers, the unification of their ranks and preparation for the liberation battle according to the decisions of the Cairo Arab Summit Conference.

(8) The organization has an independent entity; it represents the Palestine people inside and outside Jordan, just as any Arab Government is the representative of its people: Arab governments have no mandate to exercise power over the Palestine people.

(9) Neither Jordan nor any other Arab country is entitled to interfere with the organization's affairs. The organization's Chairman is directly associated with the Palestine people in whatever he says or does. The fact that he remains chairman of the organization is subject to the confidence of the Palestine people: he is not protected by a King or President.

(10) A statement should be issued by King Hussein announcing his ratification of these principles and all prisoners and detainees should be released at once.[31]

The complicated situation surrounding the Palestinian cause sheds some light on the ultimate political goal of that cause. It was easy to say that Palestine must be liberated but totally different to put such a statement into effect. Among other things, the PLO laid a heavy burden on Arab regimes in its readiness to engage in inter–Arab politics, especially in Jordan. It seemed logical that the Soviet Union would have certain reservations about the PLO, largely because the PLO had not gained a final and unanimous official consensus on the means for the liberation of Palestine with the Arab regimes so that Soviet foreign policy in the Arab world was left in an unresolved state. For if the Soviet Union threw its support and international weight behind the PLO as the sole representative of the Palestinians there would be political changes in the region. The military side of the PLO was also still vague, so that it was not clear to the Soviet Union to what extent it should proceed to give military aid to the PLO. Even if military aid were extended it was still not clear how this should be handled if the consent of the Arab 'host' country were not given. Furthermore, in building up PLO military apparatus the Soviet Union would be dealing with a Palestinian threat to a particular Arab country. Nevertheless, from time to time it was convenient for the Soviet Union to launch an attack on Zionism, and one of the remarkable aspects of Soviet policy at this period was that it did not share the Arab desire for the liberation of Palestine. The PLO hoped to receive military and political support from the Soviet Union similar to that offered by the Chinese, but its relations with the Soviet Union were not such as to achieve this. Part of the reason for this lay with the aims of the PLO itself. To an outsider the idea of eradicating Israel from the map went contrary to history, and the Soviet Union was such an outsider. In Soviet eyes, its own attacks on the idea of Zionism were not the same as adopting a policy similar to the PLO's aim of eliminating Israel, and in any case the Arab–Israeli conflict was only one among many. None the less, Soviet coverage of Israeli policy was becoming negative because of developments in Israel itself. Great attention was paid to the various stands and pronouncements of members of the Israeli Communist Party.[32]

In April 1966, a *coup d'état* was carried out successfully in Syria. The new regime emerged with a pro-Soviet outlook. Afterwards a high-ranking Syrian delegation arrived in Moscow to debate means of furthering relations between the two countries. A joint communiqué was issued at the termination of the visit which emphasized that

The two sides reaffirm their solidarity with the Palestinian Arabs and support their legitimate rights in the just struggle

214

against Zionism, which is used by the imperialist forces to exacerbate tension in the Near and Middle East.[33]

By the end of 1966 the Soviet Union had four allies in the Arab world: Egypt, Syria, Algeria and Iraq. Geographically, Syria was the nearest to the Soviet Union and thus close cooperation between the two states was viewed with favor. Geo-politics played an important role at this point. During this period, Soviet commentators began to be alarmed at Israeli military attention focused on Syria. Israeli military preparedness against Syria had, in Soviet eyes, wider international implications.[34] On the occasion of an Iraqi delegation's visit to the Soviet Union headed by the Iraqi Prime Minister, Abd Rahman al-Bazzaz, the two sides reviewed the international situation and paid special attention to the overall Arab situation. The two sides confirmed their support for Palestinian 'rights' and their support for South Yemen's struggle against the British occupiers.[35] However, the Soviet Union's mass media concentrated on the Israeli military presence on the Syrian borders. An Arab–Israeli military encounter was judged by the Soviet Union to threaten stability in the region[36] and the general Soviet opinion was that the Arab–Israeli conflict was about to flare up. Meanwhile, Israeli–Soviet relations were deteriorating.

11 Conclusion

From the start of the Bolshevik Revolution in 1917 to the recognition of Israel by the Soviet Union in May 1948, Soviet foreign policy in the Arab world was confined to theoretical analysis of Arab developments and limited to pronouncements about the plight of the Arab masses. At the end of World War I the world balance of power, in Soviet eyes, was such that international capitalism was personified by Britain and France. These two powers had reached, as Lenin put it, their highest phase of capitalism – that is, imperialism – whose main characteristic was the plundering of their former colonies. The Arab world, as the Balfour Declaration and the Sykes–Picot agreement testified, had become one of these domains. It had become common to portray imperialism as a French and British manifestation, and it followed that the Soviet Union would champion the aspirations of the masses in these countries.

Political indications of Soviet behavior in the Arab world were abundant in Soviet writings from Lenin's time to the end of the period with which this study concludes. In the early stages of the establishment of the Soviet Union it was pointed out that the salient features of the East differentiating it from the capitalist world was that it lacked an industrial base and therefore also lacked any formidable proletarian class. Furthermore, it was expected that wars would occur between the capitalist-imperialist nations, the more so since this period was characterized by the scramble for the natural resources of the colonies. Political opposition to this form of colonial exploitation was held to be the responsibility of the proletariat in the industrialized Western countries. The Western proletariat had two tasks to accomplish: to avoid its own internal exploitation and to oppose the exploitation of the colonies by the imperialist powers. To achieve either implied that it would have to attain power in its own country. Meanwhile, in all revolutionary objectives conditions had to exist that would warrant a new phase characterized by political change.

In the absence of such an internal situation a new element had surfaced in the colonial societies the most prominent aspect of which was the role played by what Soviet theoreticians called the national democratic forces in the exploited colonies. The basic task of these so-called national democratic forces was to oppose the capitalist-imperialist powers and, at the same time, the internal reactionary forces. None the less, Lenin, other Soviet leaders and later Soviet theoreticians did not discount the role played by the idea of nationalism in these colonies. If it were to occur in the future – as it did under Nasir, in the 1950s – then the natural political outcome of nationalistic appeal would be a collision course between the nationalists and the imperialist-capitalist powers. The Soviet Union devoted considerable consideration to this 'natural' progress of political events.

Neither Lenin nor later Soviet theoreticians, however, foresaw the significant role which might be played by local military forces in steering the course of history in their own country. Political changes in former colonies were anticipated only in terms of rigid and conventional Marxist-Leninist formulae: what in fact happened when local armies took the lead and spearheaded the changes was very different. Neither could what social and economic policies these colonies would follow be anticipated, and by the mid-twentieth century the question was complicated by the division of the world into two camps, socialist and capitalist.

The backwardness of the East and the absence of a proletariat was a problem to Lenin and his comrades, which left them bewildered as to how the revolutionary process should be carried out. The only glimpse of hope lay in the upsurge of nationalism which up to a point compensated for the fact that the proletariat was to all intents and purposes non-existent. Nevertheless, the East was bogged down in problems that rendered it an area ripe for revolutionary upheavals and transformations. More importantly perhaps, the East was experiencing its initial political formation: national independence was not a term in its political vocabulary at the beginning of the twentieth century. Lenin's aim to achieve the international unity of the world's proletarian classes through a world Communist movement was difficult to apply to the East. Its socio-economic basis was predominantly agrarian and the economic structure feudalistic. Furthermore, its class structure and its external relations deviated from the normal political processes which guided Marxist analysis, factors which imposed certain practical constraints on the young Bolshevik Revolution.

Nevertheless, the world political map was on the threshold of major changes. The old colonial powers, France and Britain, were slowly declining, especially after World War I. The Arab world was still in the grip of Western colonialism, and to the young Bolshevik Revolution this reality was all-pervasive. It was left to the Soviet Union, in the absence of any formidable opposition in the East, to spearhead both the leadership of an international Communist movement and, at the same time at an international level, to combat imperialism which was seen to have reached the acme of capitalism. It is within this context that the Soviet Union's foreign policy should be analyzed.

Lenin's great gift was that he was able to grasp and analyze the historical changes taking place at this period. But the Soviet Union was in its formative stages, and so the toiling masses of the East had to be left to form their own Communist parties. But, as future developments were to prove, these emergent Communist parties were to receive their directives from Moscow. At this early period Arab Communist parties encountered several obstacles; the backwardness of the Arab world, particularly because of the Muslim religion, and the absence of a proletarian class being amongst the most important. The Arab peasantry was far from being at a stage of political maturity which would permit it to undertake revolutionary changes. Arab Communism was still only in its formative stages as a mass movement, although this does not mean that Communist ideas were not circulating amongst Arab intellectuals. These Communist ideas were basically inspired by the Soviet Union, and although in Lenin's time Arab Communism was still embryonic, it was reinforced later on under Stalin.

From the outset the Bolshevik Revolution, under Lenin's leadership was against the idea of furthering, let alone accepting, Zionist political aspirations. Zionism was seen by Lenin as the embodiment of British imperialism, and it was this imperialism which granted the adherents of Zionism such legitimacy as was conferred by the Balfour Declaration. However, Lenin and his comrades had reached the conclusion that in facing imperialist 'oppression' *both* Jews and Arabs would unite against imperialist undertakings. But this argument negates important elements concerned with the absence of antagonists in Palestine: it negates the assumption that there was no dividing line between Zionism and the Arab nationalistic outlook and approach and it negates the fact that both the Zionist and the Arab ruling elites derived their existence and legitimacy from the Western powers. In the Marxist-Leninist sense no anti-British imperialist sentiments existed in the region. But, even if they were non-existent, it was thought that the masses of impoverished Jewish immigrants to Palestine would turn out to be political revolutionaries and so, by its own intrinsic nature, Palestine would generate its own revolutionary process.

Against instability and the ever-changing political spectrum – from conservatism, leftism and nationalism – the Soviet Union had to face and adapt to all the changes so that it might deal effectively with the political conditions prevailing in the Arab world. At the same time, in its dealings with the Soviet Union, the Arab world had to recognize – indeed, contend with – the fact that it was face to face with the cradle of the Marxist-Leninist theoretical approach and that clear-cut Communist perceptions governed the Soviet approach to the East. Lenin believed that the East was confronted by the power of the remnant of Western European colonialism. In this light it was essential for the East and the Arab world in particular to embark on a revolutionary course to solve its internal agrarian question. Lenin and his comrades considered that the East must achieve an agrarian revolution as an essential preliminary to a successful social revolution. It was considered, moreover, that once this stage had been accomplished the East would then be ripe for total revolution. The emphasis on the role to be played by the peasantry would compensate and substitute for the absence of a proletarian class in these societies. The initial stage was to counter the colonialism which dominated their societies. This element so necessary to success was grasped by the Soviet Union, and the magnitude of the problem of achieving the implied political changes was significant in the formulation of its overall political objectives. The opportunity to enter the Arab world came to the Soviet Union with the upsurge of two internal factors in combination, Arab nationalism and anti-colonialism.

The creation of the State of Israel in 1948, for which the Soviet Union had worked and to which it was the first state to extend *de jure* recognition, was, ironically, the USSR's initial foothold in the Arab world. Soviet recognition reinforced the reality of its existence at the international level, while at another level the natural links between the two countries were in practical terms very real indeed. The Soviet Union and its Eastern European allies provided Israel with the much-needed Jewish manpower which was of the utmost importance for its continuity. Ashkenazi Jews were the founders of Israel, and on them lay the responsibility for nation-building in an area that suffered from a combination of internal backwardness and Western colonialism. The Soviet Union was thus presented with an opportunity to exploit whatever might be favourable to it in the situation which had come into being.

Two major factors connected with the theory of the 'natural link' appear to have influenced the Soviet Union's decision to be the first state to extend *de jure* recognition to Israel in May 1948. The first had to do with the sheer size of the physical presence of Soviet and Eastern European Jews in Palestine which dictated a new reality. It was a body assembled in Palestine for certain political objectives and which was definitely socialist in outlook. This early Zionist socialist orientation was regarded by the Soviet Union as the best justification for the Jewish presence in Palestine. The foundations of the much sought-after State of Israel were based in socialist thinking and sprang from the conditions surrounding the Jewish presence in Palestine and their previous existence in socialist countries. Zionism had one goal: the establishment of a Jewish state in Palestine, and in its early stages the building of Israeli society was much influenced by socialism, even though the socialist orientation of Zionism was not communist. As things stood in May 1948 Zionism was more advanced and more workable in Soviet eyes than the conditions which prevailed in the surrounding Arab countries. The 'natural link' theory would suggest that recognition was the result of a logical sequence of events; it would have been 'unnatural' for the Soviet Union and Eastern Europe to act otherwise. Stalin, moreover, found in the newly established State of Israel an alternative solution to the internal Jewish question. But brute military force was a basic tenet of the Zionists, who believed that the Palestinian population had to be evicted; Soviet and Eastern European Jewry thus founded their state on the ruins of the Palestinian people.

In May 1948 therefore the Soviet Union entered the Arab world in a way that had not been anticipated; from the outset its policy towards Israel was a question of legitimizing the existence of the Jewish state in Palestine, the strongest justification for which, in Soviet eyes, was the socialist orientation of Zionism. It should be noted that while by 1948 there were over half a million Jewish immigrants in Palestine whose presence was, to the Arab inhabitants of Palestine, one of the crudest forms of colonialism, the Arab world was still politically retarded internally and externally was dominated, directly or indirectly, by the Western powers. These facts which would seem to be a disadvantage were in fact to be turned to Soviet advantage since the diaspora of the Palestinians in the end produced its own eventual reaction, just as the immediate reaction of the Arab states to the foreign body settled in their midst was to declare war. This, the first Arab–Israeli conflict, introduced certain Arab officers to radical ideas and they later instigated a *coup d'état* in Egypt which overthrew the monarchy.

This change of power in Egypt in 1952 engineered by the army officers produced grass-root changes in the Arab world. Internally Nasir propagated a set of socialist changes which affected the whole structure of Egyptian policy, a welcome departure for the Soviet Union. Externally, Nasir generated and radiated the sentiments of Arab nationalism and embarked on the creation of what became known as the non-aligned bloc of Asian and African nations. Both these developments were intrinsically anti-colonial and, by inference, anti-Western. The Soviet Union could not ignore these changes and was indeed invited by the Arabs to participate in Arab politics, thus affecting the balance of power in the region. Soviet involvement in the Arab world imposed on it the political necessity of taking sides in the Arab–Israeli conflict, and its started with anti-Zionist pronouncements. This change of attitude is to be attributed to the role played by Nasir.

Nasir's book, *The Philosophy of Revolution*, noted the three circles of Egyptian revolutionary orientation he proposed to implement: the first was the Arab circles in which the Arab–Israeli conflict held first priority; the second revolved around the Third World with its policy of neutrality; the third revolved around co-operation with the Soviet Union and the Socialist camp. The third option was introduced largely because of the West's unwillingness to aid Egypt though it increased aid to Israel. These concentric circles were more than agreeable to the Soviet Union for they not only opened up the Arab world to it but also made it an ally in both East–West relations in the Middle East and in Third World politics. Nasir's abhorrence of a regional military balance that was in any way tied to the West added to Egypt's image as a politically independent emergent nation. These three circles were to introduce fundamental changes in the Arab world, the most important of which occurred in 1955 when Egypt was drawn closer to the Communist block through an arms deal with Czechoslovakia. This act was, in a sense, imposed on Egypt because it had no choice in arming its forces. Given Egypt's experience with the West, it became natural for it to gravitate towards the Soviet Union and Eastern Europe. It seemed that at this juncture of political development the interests of both the Soviet Union and Egypt coincided and ran parallel – from the Revolution of 1952, to the arms deal to the Suez Canal crisis and finally to the policy of non-alignment. All these new dimensions furthered relations between the two states, whether bilateral, regional or international. It marked an era of development. This approach by Egypt was initiated out of necessity, for its revolutionary leaders were destined to climb high in Arab politics.

The Revolution of 1952, the aims of which included ridding Egypt of 'colonialism' and British bases, was an essential part of the nationalist movement. To achieve these aims, Egypt had to look for foreign aid in both the economic and military fields, and it was natural that attention should be paid to the socialist camp in the light of the position adopted by the West, especially that of the United States. Egyptian foreign policy was directed towards the Soviet Union from 1953 and matured fast until its culmination in the arms deal of 1955. Soviet assistance was based on the proposition that in order to fight 'imperialism' and the remnant of 'colonialism' in the Third World, national liberation movements, whether established states or organizations, had to be aided. Over and above the ideological factor, the strategic importance of Egypt and its role in the Arab world, its location on the African continent and its importance as a link in East–West relations should not be ignored, for all this had an effect on Soviet foreign policy in the Arab world. This combination of theory and pragmatism had helped persuade Egypt to accept Soviet aid; not only were the conditions conducive to the furthering of relations, but they also enhanced Egypt's position in the Arab world.

It must be asked how the Soviet Union regulated its foreign policy priorities in the Arab world. At first it chose to maintain a direct relationship with an Arab enemy, namely Israel. The Soviet Union had normal diplomatic relations with few Arab countries at the time of recognizing Israel, and it lacked then the means by which to further these relations. Arab Communist parties were both illegal and politically dormant. Unlike Israel, where a form of socialism was in existence and where the Israeli Communist Party was operating legally, the Arab side could hardly claim that socialist tendencies were in existence in the Arab world before 1954. The Soviet reaction to Arab conditions was one of puzzlement and uncertainty, made more confusing because a socialist state *had* sprung up in the middle of an area that the Soviet Union considered to be politically backward. At the same time, it remained uncertain how it could penetrate the Arab world and propagate socialist ideas.

Nasir, however, provided this opportunity. His leadership combined the sentiments of both Arab nationalism and anti-Western colonialism. The political objectives of young Arab leaders gave them the leadership of emergent Arab socialism. This was not Marxist, but since the Arab world was politically unstable it opened up new opportunities and imposed new priorities on the Soviet Union. By the time the consequences of the changes in the Arab world had been worked out the Soviet Union had become a super power. This situation brought its own constraints, which must be set against global strategic realities. All together, the different factors forced the Soviet Union to calculate its political and military moves at a level befitting its new status.

Moreover, the 1950s witnessed tremendous upheavals in the Arab world, both internally and in its external relations, that affected the course of history in the region. The 1952 Revolution brought great changes not only to Egypt but also to the Arab world, to which the Soviet Union at the beginning paid little attention, its attitude being ambivalent. Despite the fact that Nasir was in the limelight, Soviet publications only later bestowed on him the leading role in the events which led to the success of the Revolution. Egypt, once on course to change the map of the Arab world, could not be ignored. Soviet inroads into the Arab world began in earnest at the Bandung Conference, where Chou En-Lai of China played the role of broker for the first Soviet arms delivery to Egypt. Again, this was a breakthrough; Egypt, under Nasir's leadership, played a pioneering role amongst the non-aligned nations. Neither was it possible to discount Egypt's importance within the region, within the wider Arab world or within the still wider spectrum of the African continent where Nasir's leadership had an immense effect. Egypt followed a program of economic development to which the Soviet Union lent the necessary assistance; it culminated in the construction of the Aswan High Dam (to which the US had refused assistance) – a project of social and economic importance equal to the significance of the 1955 arms deal. Overall, the economic development program fitted the

Soviet Union's perception of a state aspiring to achieve 'complete' independence – that is to say, once the political objective had been achieved, the era of economic independence would follow.

Nasir had not long emerged on the Arab political scene when the Tripartite Aggression of 1956 was carried out against Egypt. Nasir's 'wait and see' policy proved successful. The Soviet Union condemned the aggression; when the crisis had virtually subsided the Soviets threatened to send 'volunteers' to aid Egypt. In its wider aspects, the war had different objectives for its different participants. To the French and the British the question was confined to limiting Nasir's Arab nationalistic appeal, since this was a force which threatened the interests of both Western powers in the Arab world. The status of the former colonial powers was entering a new phase in the area; on the western flank of the Arab world France was embroiled in Algeria while the British had fundamental interests in political and economic developments elsewhere. Nasir's basic objective in the 1952 Revolution had been to enable Egypt to embark on internal reconstruction and cure its stagnant economy. Essential to this was the establishment of socialism. Because of the peculiar position of Egypt as an Arab, Muslim and Third World country Nasir was assisted to achieve the political objectives of his three circles. His aims, however, were a direct threat to Britain and France. In this situation the Soviet Union could offer constructive help – for example, towards the establishment of socialism in Egypt – while at the same time Nasir's international perceptions and objectives assisted the Soviet Union's more general policies in the Arab world. Thus on the one hand the Soviet Union was able to demonstrate that it was a 'true' and reliable friend and ally of the Arab people, while, on the other, the Suez Canal crisis was a unique moment for it to see that an emerging state could play a significant role in the balance of power in the Middle East.

Nasir's gradual changes to Egypt's political course did indeed have wide implications for the Soviet Union's involvement in the Arab world. Nasir, though a socialist in a broad sense, was not a Communist – and, indeed, persecuted Communists. The Soviet Union largely ignored this, probably because its political and strategic role was of overriding importance. Through Nasir, and because of Arab rapprochement with Egypt, the Soviet Union was able to extend its contacts throughout the Arab world extending from North Africa to the Arabian Gulf. Nasir's political stature in the Arab world and the conditions there facilitated the Soviet advance. The demise of the former colonial powers meant that the balance of power in the Arab world was changing to reflect the status of the world powers – namely, the United States and the Soviet Union. This polarization had its political and strategic effects on the Arab world. The Soviet Union seized on the opportunity afforded by the events of the Tripartite Aggression to declare itself and deliver pronouncements against the declining Western powers, although it remains unclear how far the Soviet Union involved itself directly in the crisis. Outright military intervention was ruled out in favor of the political option. However, whatever the degree of involvement, the Soviet Union had been led to participate indirectly in the Arab–Israeli conflict. By this time it already condemned Zionism although it did not take the necessary practical steps (for example, military) to tip the balance of power in favor of the Arabs. It should, however, be noted that the Soviet Union had resorted to arming its Arab allies, and this led Israel to rely on Western military supplies. The Arab world, with the Arab–Israeli conflict, had become a factor in the international balance of power. One of the implications of this development was that both Eastern and Western weaponry was to be put to the test.

When in 1958 Egypt and Syria merged, the Soviet Union was still further involved in the Arab world while the latter was under the direct rule of neither East nor West. Later in the same year the monarchical system in Iraq collapsed and the Baghdad Pact came to a virtual end. The Soviet opposition to this military pact was well understood. Meanwhile Nasir's courtship of the non-aligned nations began to produce results beneficial to the Soviet Union. The majority of this bloc, if not all of it, had one way or another experienced the force of British or French colonialism and non-alignment was a new form of political protest against Western domination in Asia and Africa. The Soviet Union could not ignore such a political opportunity. The Western world was henceforth on trial.

Soviet commentary on Arab conditions paid a great deal of attention to the role played by Britain in the region, which it regarded as the most significant motivating force behind the many upheavals taking place there. The Soviet Union saw the Arab world as the prey of both the colonial powers and its political situation so divided as to leave the concept of Arab unity as little more than an imaginary notion to the masses. The Soviet Union was therefore bewildered as to how it might penetrate this world, for Arab mass organizations, particularly the Communist parties, were for all practical purposes powerless and lacked the structure that would one day enable them to reach and uphold power in an Arab state. In their turn these powerless Arab Communist parties, whose directives came from the Soviet Union, were puzzled as to how to comprehend the fluctuations in the Soviet stand on Arab conditions and its changing policy. From the theoretical analysis of the East propounded at the Baku Congress to the recognition of Israel in May 1948, to the first involvement in the Arab world through Nasir's leadership, the Soviet Union had come full circle in its relations with the Arab world and its actions there were conceived as policies which might be those of a super power. They thus influenced countries outside the Communist bloc.

Israel remained a thorny question in Arab–Soviet relations. Although the Soviet Union objected to Zionism, it nevertheless maintained normal diplomatic relations with Israel and this despite the fact that Israel, now a power in its own right, posed two challenging questions for the Soviet Union: that of Zionism and that of the existence of a polity which embodied a Jewish political entity. There were objections equally to the Jewish nature of the country and to Zionism as a political movement. This dual problem, however, was difficult for the Soviet Union to explain since to Arabs there was no difference between the country, Israel, and the creed, Zionism. The Arab states, especially Egypt, which were aligned with the Soviet Union, overlooked the Soviet differentiation. More seriously, however, the Arab world (which reflected the East–West political pendulum) and the Arab–Israeli conflict were becoming increasingly important at international level, even if initially little attention was paid to either the Palestinian Resistance Movement or the PLO. Moreover, the Soviet Union never fully worked out the implications of the existence of the Palestinian refugees, the true coin in which the diaspora was paid, and for a long time after 1948 it trod a thin line as far as the Palestinian–Arab regimes were concerned. Even in 1964 when the PLO was established and in 1965 when Fatah emerged the Soviet Union kept a low profile in its relations with the Palestinian Resistance Movement.

The position of the Arab world in the wider spectrum of its alignments in East–West relations is also important. Although the Soviet Union perceived that the disunity in the Arab world hindered the development of mass-based organizations and left the notion of Arab unity as a meaningless concept to the Arab masses whom it would benefit, it was prepared to seize every opportunity to promote the new currents of thought sweeping the Arab world. The help it offered was unconditional but it was not offered without first being requested. Here Nasir was the moving force, and thus he was the major focal point for the Soviet Union's entry into the Arab world which, stretching from North Africa to the Arabian Gulf, afforded a strategic opportunity that could not be ignored. Furthermore, Nasir also offered the Soviet Union his support for what later came to be known as the non-aligned bloc of nations whose creation had its own international political repercussions. All these nations, moreover, were united by the upsurge of nationalism, a political development that was bound to be anti-Western in its political orientation. Though the Soviet Union was non-participatory, it was an active member in this working process, and its major ally, China, served as its spokesman. It was through China that Egypt was able to receive armaments from Czechoslovakia and this, the first practical recognition of the autonomy of an Arab state, both changed the existing balance of power in the region hitherto dominated by the West and opened the way for the Soviet Union's sustained thrust into the Arab world.

Notes

Chapter 1

1 The following analysis is based on Soviet writers Y. S. Yavesyou and L. Vostokou, *al-Sahuiniah fi Russya al-Qaysaria* (Zionism in Czarist Russia), Damascus, 1976.
2 *Ibid.*, p. 25.
3 *Ibid.*, p. 43.
4 *Ibid.*, p. 70.
5 *Ibid.*, p. 75.
6 *Ibid.*, p. 82.
7 Houssam El-Dawla Khalil, *The Soviet Foreign Policy toward Egypt, 1955–1964*, Howard University, Washington, D.C., 1970, pp. 5–6.
8 Branko Lezith and Milorad M. Drachkovitch, *Lenin and the Comintern*, Stanford, Cal., 1972, ch. 9, pp. 365–416.
9 Kermit McKenzie, 'The Soviet Union and World Revolution: the Comintern Patterns', thesis, Columbia University, New York, 1960, p. 2.
10 *Ibid.*, p. 29.
11 *Ibid.*, p. 38.
12 *Ibid.*, p. 44.
13 *Ibid.*, p. 99.
14 *Ibid.*, p. 99.
15 John Joseph Dziak, 'The Soviet Union and National Liberation Movements: an Examination of the Development of a Revolutionary Strategy', thesis, Georgetown University, Washington, D.C., 1971, p. 39.
16 *Ibid.*, p. 54.
17 *Ibid.*, p. 70.
18 *Ibid.*, p. 75.
19 Ran Maron, 'Soviet Russia and the Jewish Communists of Palestine', thesis, Georgetown University, Washington, D.C., 1975, pp. 39–40.
20 *Ibid.*, p. 58.
21 *Ibid.*, p. 64.
22 *Ibid.*, p. 73.

23 Tony Cliff, *Lenin: the Bolsheviks and World Revolution*, vol. 4, pp. 43–5, London, 1979.
24 Alan Adler (ed.), *Theses, Resolutions and Manifestos of the First Four Congresses of the Third International*, London, 1980, p. 328.
25 Maron, 'Soviet Russia and Jewish Communists of Palestine', p. 80.
26 *Ibid.*, p. 84.
27 *Ibid.*, p. 93.
28 *Ibid.*, p. 106.
29 *Ibid.*, p. 117.
30 *Ibid.*, p. 130.
31 *Ibid.*, p. 140.
32 *Ibid.*, pp. 154–5.
33 *Ibid.*, p. 158.
34 *Ibid.*, p. 159.
35 *Ibid.*, p. 168.
36 *Ibid.*, p. 215.

Chapter 2

1 On Communism in Palestine, see Musa Budeiri, *The Palestine Communist Party, 1919–1948; Arab and Jews in the Struggle for Internationalism*, London, 1979.
2 See Jean Pennar, *The USSR and the Arabs: the Ideological Dimension, 1917–1974*, London, 1973.
3 Ivan Kovalenko, *Soviet Policy for Asian Peace and Security*, Moscow, 1979.
4 *Ibid.*, pp. 11–18.
5 Anon., *Lenin and National Liberation in the East*, Moscow, 1978.
6 *Ibid.*, p. 111.
7 *Ibid.*, p. 441.
8 *Ibid.*, p. 465.
9 Tarabulsi, Fawaz (trans.), *al-umaya al-shu'iya wa tahrer al-sharg: al-mu'tamar al-'wal l'shu'b-al-sharg, Baku, 1–8 'Llyal, 1921* (The Communist International and the Liberation of the East: the First Conference of the Peoples of the East, Baku, 1–8 September, 1921), Beirut, 1972, p. 18.
10 *Ibid.*, p. 47.
11 *Ibid.*, p. 64.
12 *Ibid.*, p. 66.
13 *Ibid.*, p. 141.
14 *Ibid.*, p. 168.
15 *Ibid.*, pp. 175–6.
16 *Ibid.*, pp. 199–204.
17 *Ibid.*, p. 203.
18 *Ibid.*, pp. 240–1.
19 Xenia Joukoff Eudin and Robert C. North, *Soviet Russia and the East, 1920–1927*, Stanford, Cal., 1957, p. 79.
20 *Ibid.*, p. 82.
21 *Ibid.*, pp. 85–6.
22 *Ibid.*, p. 91.

Chapter 3

1 Mackenzie E. Kermit, *The Soviet Union and World Revolution: the Comintern Patterns, 1928–1943*, Columbia University, New York, 1960, p. 164.
2 *Ibid.*, pp. 176–7.
3 *Ibid.*, p. 207.
4 *Ibid.*, p. 211.

Chapter 4

1 It was reported at the time that 'Russia had proposed to the United States, Britain, France and China that the Arab–Jewish problem of Palestine be submitted to a conference of the Big Five . . . that the Russians viewed consideration of the problem in the light of the entire Middle East situation, thereby raising the possibility of its extension into a general conference on the Middle East', *New York Times*, 27 Nov. 1945.
2 *Scotsman*, 11 Aug. 1946.
3 *Manchester Guardian*, 22 July 1946.
4 *Christian Science Monitor*, 3 Feb. 1946, and *New York Times*, 3 Feb. 1946.
5 *New York Times*, 30 Dec. 1947.
6 *Observer*, 18 April 1948.
7 *Ibid.*
8 'A Seat of Unrest in the Middle East', no. 11, 1946, pp. 14–17.
9 'Contemporary Palestine', *New Times*, no. 14, 1946, pp. 18–22.
10 *New Times*, no. 47, 1947, pp. 3–5.
11 *Ibid.*
12 *New Times*, no. 11, 1948, pp. 8–12.
13 See *Moscow News*, 15 Nov. 1947. Gromyko declared *inter alia* at the UN that: 'It is essential to bear in mind the undisputable fact that the population of Palestine consists of two peoples, the Arabs and the Jews. Both have historical roots in Palestine.' See also Yaacov Ro'i, *From Encroachment to Involvement*, pp. 39–40.
14 In Israel, appreciation of the Soviet stand at the UN was carefully calculated: 'Dr Moshe Sheh, former Haganeh Commander and likely choice as Defense Minister of the new Jewish State, said in Jerusalem press conference tonight: "The basic tenet of our foreign policy must be friendship with Russia whose stand in the United Nations will never be forgotten".' *Daily Mail*, 2 Dec. 1947.
15 *New Times*, no. 11, 1948, pp. 8–12.
16 *New Times*, no. 19, 1948, pp. 7–11.
17 Oles M. Smolansky, 'The Soviet Union and the Arab East, 1947–1957: a Study in Diplomatic Relations', thesis, Columbia University, New York, 1959, p. 42.
18 *New Times*, no. 19, 1948, pp. 7–11.
19 *Ibid.*, p. 11.

20 'Palestine and the United Nations', *New Times*, no. 48, 9 June 1948.
21 *Ibid.*, p. 2.

Chapter 5

1 Author's interview with members of the Soviet Academy of Social Science, Middle East Section, June 1982.
2 See George Antonius, *The Arab Awakening*, Beirut 1955.
3 'Aziz al-'Azmeh, *al-Yassar al-sahuni min bedaiteh i'alan d'walth Israel* (Left-wing Zionism: from Its Inception to the Declaration of the State of Israel), Beirut, 1969, p. 27.
4 *Ibid.*, p. 34.
5 *Ibid.*, p. 54.
6 *Ibid.*, pp. 69–70.
7 Peretz Merhav, *The Israeli Left: History, Problems, Documents*, San Diego, Cal., 1980, p. 18.
8 *Ibid.*, pp. 28–9.
9 *Ibid.*, p. 22.
10 *Ibid.*, pp. 33–4.
11 *Ibid.*, p. 40.
12 *Ibid.*, p. 63.
13 'Abd al-Rahim Ahmad Hussian, *al-nashat al-sayuni hild al-harb al-'alimiah al-thaniah (1939–1945)* (The Zionist Activity during World War II, 1939–1945), Beirut, 1984, p. 243.
14 *Ibid.*, pp. 245–6.
15 *Ibid.*, p. 247.

Chapter 6

1 John Joseph Dziak, 'The Soviet Union and National Liberation Movements: an examination of the Development of a Revolutionary Strategy', thesis, Georgetown University, Washington, D.C., 1971, pp. 153–5.
2 Michael Pierpont Gehlen, 'Ideological Determinants of Soviet Foreign Policy under Khrushchev', thesis, University of Texas, 1963, p. 67.
3 Edward Mathew Collins, *The Evolution of Soviet Strategy under Khrushchev*, Georgetown University, Washington, D.C., 1966, p. 141.
4 *Ibid.*, pp. 147–9.
5 *New York Times*, 26 June 1948.
6 *Daily Worker*, 10 Aug. 1948.
7 *New York Times*, 26 June 1948.
8 *Soviet News*, 25 May 1948.
9 *Pravda*, in *Current Digest of Soviet Press* (cited as CDSP), vol. II, no. 2, p. 26.
10 *CDSP*, vol. II, no. 27, p. 24.
11 *Izvestia* in *CDSP*, vol. II, no. 44, p. 27.

12 *CDSP*, vol. III, no. 14, pp. 11–13.
13 *CDSP*, vol. III, no. 16, p. 14; see also *Pravda* and *Izvestia*.
14 *CDSP*, vol. II, no. 37, p. 11.
15 *CDSP*, vol. III, no. 38, pp. 4–5.
16 See B. Leontyev's article in *Pravda*, *CDSP*, vol. III, no. 48, 2 Nov. 1951, p. 5.
17 *Ibid.*
18 Berezhbov, 'Imperialist Plan in the Near and Middle East', *New Times*, no. 48, 1951, pp. 11–13.
19 *CDSP*, vol. IV, no. 12, 23 March 1952, p. 15.
20 *BBC-SWB Summaries of World Broadcasts*, 21 Oct. 1952.
21 *BBC-SWB*, 14 Nov. 1952.
22 *CDSP*, vol. IV, no. 8, 25 July 1952, p. 13.
23 *CDSP*, vol. IV, no. 31, Aug. 1952, pp. 23–4.
24 *CDSP*, vol. V, no. 16, pp. 10–11.
25 *Ibid.*, p. 5.
26 *Ibid.*, p. 6.
27 *Ibid.*, p. 7.
28 *Izvestia*, in *CDSP*, vol. II, no. 20, pp. 25–6.
29 *Ibid.*
30 The analysis here relies on the Soviet publication *Tarikh al-agator al-'Arabia al-mu'asor* (Recent History of the Arab Countries), Moscow, vol. 2.
31 *BBC-SWB*, 1 Aug. 1952.

Chapter 7

1 *BBC-SWB*, 17 Feb. 1953.
2 *Ibid.*
3 See, for example, N. Sergev's article in *Trud*, 13 Feb. 1953, in *CDSP*, vol. V, no. 5, p. 10, and M. Klim Potyuk, *Pravda*, 13 Feb. 1953, *ibid.*, pp. 10–11.
4 *al-Nahar*, 26 Feb. 1954.
5 Jamal Abdal-Nasir, *Falasafa al-thawra* (The philosophy of the Revolution), Cairo, 1954.
6 *Ibid.*, pp. 12–13.
7 *Ibid.*, p. 26.
8 *Ibid.*, pp. 60–1.
9 *BBC-SWB*, 30 Nov. 1954.
10 *Ibid.*, 12 Dec. 1954.
11 *Ibid.*, 21 April 1954.
12 *Ibid.*, 22 June 1954.
13 *Ibid.*
14 *Ibid.*, 18 Aug. 1954.
15 *Ibid.*, 4 Sept. 1954.
16 *Ibid.*, 11 March 1955.
17 *Ibid.*, 4 Jan. 1955.
18 *Ibid.*, 21 Jan. 1955.

19 *Ibid.*, 29 March 1955.
20 *Ibid.*, 13 May 1955.
21 Edward Mathew Collins, *The Evolution of Soviet Strategy under Khrushchev*, Georgetown University, Washington, D.C., 1966, pp. 48–50.
22 *Ibid.*, p. 67.
23 Houssam El-Dawla Khalil, 'The Soviet Foreign Policy toward Egypt, 1955–1964', thesis, Howard University, Washington, D.C., 1970, p. 148.
24 E. Maximov, 'Egypt's Legitimate Right', *New Times*, no. 43, 1955, pp. 18–19.
25 *BBC-SWB*, 22 July 1955.
26 *Ibid.*
27 *Ibid.*, 21 Oct. 1955.
28 *Ibid.*
29 *Ibid.*
30 *New York Herald Tribune*, 6 Feb. 1956.
31 *New York Times*, 7 Feb. 1956.
32 *BBC-SWB*, 15 Nov. 1955.
33 *Ibid.*, 22 Nov. 1955.
34 See, for example, *BBC-SWB*, 23 Dec. 1955.
35 Philip Jelab, *Qusat al-Soviet ma'Nasir* (The Story of the Soviets with Nasir), Cairo, 1983, pp. 65–81.
36 See e.g., K. Kozarov, *Pravda*, 11 June 1953, in *CDSP*, vol. V, no. 23, p. 19.
37 *CDSP*, vol. V, no. 34, p. 6.
38 *CDSP*, vol. VI, no. 4, p. 4.
39 *Izvestia*, no. 16, 1954, in *CDSP*, vol. VII, no. 14, p. 31.
40 *Ibid.*, p. 29.
41 See K. Petrov, *Izvestia*, 7 April 1955, in *CDSP*, vol. VII, no. 14, p. 31.
42 *Pravda* and *Izvestia*, 7 April 1955, in *CDSP*, vol. VII, no. 16, p. 18.
43 *Izvestia*, 11 June 1955, in *CDSP*, vol. VII, no. 23, p. 12.
44 Participants were Afghanistan, Burma, Cambodia, Ceylon, Egypt, Ethiopia, Gold Coast, India, Indonesia, Iran, Iraq, Japan, Laos, Lebanon, Libya, Nepal, Pakistan, the People's Republic of China, the Philippines, Saudi Arabia, Sudan, Syria, Thailand, Turkey, the Democratic Republic of Vietnam, the State of Vietnam, and Yemen. The Central African Federation declined to attend.
45 See George M. Kahin, *Asian-African Conference, Bandung, Indonesia, April 1955*, Washington, 1956, p. 3.

Chapter 8

1 *New York Times*, 14 Feb. 1956.
2 *The Times*, 15 Feb. 1956, and *New York Times*, 15 Feb. 1956.
3 *New York Times* and *The Times*, 24 March 1956, respectively.
4 *New York Times* and *Daily Telegraph*, 8 April 1956, respectively.
5 *New York Times*, 17 June 1956.

6   *New York Herald Tribune*, 17 June 1956.
7   *New Times*, no. 5, 1956, pp. 30–1.
8   'The Middle East', *New Times*, no. 2, 10 May 1956, pp. 1–2.
9   'Good-Will Mission', *New Times*, no. 28, 5 July 1956, pp. 1–2.
10 *BBC-SWB*, 24 July 1956.
11 *Ibid.*, 25 July 1956.
12 'Egypt's Legitimate Right', *New Times*, no. 32, 1956, pp. 10–12.
13 'Suez and the "Free World"', *New Times*, no. 34, 1956, pp. 8–10.
14 *Ibid.*
15 'Realistic Approach', *New Times*, no. 35, 23 Aug. 1956, pp. 1–3.
16 'The Suez Conference and its Outcome', *New Times*, no. 36, 1956, pp. 4–7.
17 *New Times*, no. 36, 30 Aug. 1956, pp. 34–40.
18 *Pravda*, 16 Sept. 1956.
19 *Soviet News*, 30 July 1956.
20 *Manchester Guardian*, 30 July 1956.
21 *Scotsman*, 2 Aug. 1956.
22 *Christian Science Monitor*, 3 Aug. 1956.
23 *New York Herald Tribune*, 15 Aug. 1956.
24 *Ibid.*
25 *Ibid.*, 20 Aug. 1956.
26 *New York Times*, 16 Sept. 1956; *Daily Telegraph*, 17 Sept. 1956.
27 See also the Polish government statement, *New China News Agency*, 29 Sept. 1956, and support by Czechoslavakian Central Trade Union Council in *New China News Agency*, 20 Sept. 1956.
28 *New York Herald Tribune*, 31 Oct. 1956.
29 *Soviet News*, 1 Nov. 1956.
30 *New York Times*, 11 Nov. 1956.
31 *Soviet News*, 11 Dec. 1956.
32 *New York Herald Tribune*, 29 Dec. 1956.
33 *Ibid.*, 21 Dec. 1956.
34 *Soviet News*, 6 Nov. 1956.
35 *Ibid.*
36 *New York Times*, 6 Nov. 1956.
37 See, for example, the collection of interviews in 'Suez: Ten Years After', *BBC-SWB*, 5, 7, 14, and 18 July 1966, respectively.
38 *BBC-SWB*, 26 Nov. 1956.
39 *New York Times*, 2 Jan. 1957.
40 *Ibid.*, 13 Jan. 1957.
41 Alastair Buchan, 'Seen from Whitehall: Soviet Overtures', *Observer Foreign News Service*, no. 11, 960, p. 1.
42 *Christian Science Monitor*, 14 Feb. 1957.
43 *Hsinhua News Agency*, 18 Feb. 1957.
44 *Soviet News*, 26 Feb. 1957.
45 *Ibid.*, 29 March 1957.
46 *New York Times*, 26 April 1957.
47 *Ibid.*, 13 June 1956.
48 *The Times*, 13 June 1957.
49 *New York Times*, 9 Aug. 1957.

50 *New York Herald Tribune*, 29 Aug. 1957.
51 *Soviet News*, 5 Sept. 1957.
52 *Ibid.*
53 *Scotsman*, 3 Sept. 1957.
54 *Financial Times*, 5 Sept. 1957.
55 See, for example, *New York Times*, 25 Sept. 1957.
56 *Daily Worker*, 26 Sept. 1957.
57 See, for example, *New York Herald Tribune* and *Manchester Guardian*, 16 Oct. 1957.
58 *The Times*, 16 Oct. 1957.
59 See, for example, *New York Herald Tribune*, 17 Oct. 1957.
60 See, for example, *Norwegian Press Summary* and *Swedish Press Summary*, 17 Oct. 1957.
61 See, for example, *Dawn*, 1 Nov. 1957.
62 See, for example, *Christian Science Monitor*, 25 Nov. 1957.
63 *Soviet News*, 28 Nov. 1957.
64 'The Blockade that Failed', *New Times*, 25 Nov. 1957, pp. 4–6.
65 'The Soviet Union and the Arab East', *New Times*, 1 Nov. 1958, pp. 12–14.
66 *The Egyptian Gazette*, 27 April 1958.
67 *Ibid.*
68 *New York Times*, 4 May 1958.
69 *New York Times* and Soviet News, 16 May 1958.
70 *Pravda*, 16 May 1958, in *CDSP*, vol. X, no. 20, p. 3.
71 *New York Times*, 18 May 1958.
72 *Ibid.*; see also Khrushchev's speech *Soviet News*, 19 May 1958.

Chapter 9

1   *Pravda*, 30 July 1958, in *CDSP*, vol. X, no. 30, p. 14.
2   *Ibid.*, 31 July 1958, in *CDSP*, vol. X, no. 31, p. 9.
3   See, for example, *Izvestia*, 26 March 1959.
4   *Pravda*, 22 Oct. 1958, in *CDSP*, vol. X, no. 42, pp. 14–15.
5   *Izvestia*, 29 Oct. 1958, in *CDSP*, vol. X, no. 43, pp. 16–17.
6   *Pravda*, 30 March 1959, in *CDSP*, vol. XI, no. 13, pp. 21–3.
7   *Ibid.*, p. 22.
8   *Pravda*, 20 April 1959, in *CDSP*, vol. XI, no. 16, p. 16.
9   *Ibid.*, 19 July 1959, in *CDSP*, vol. XI, no. 24, pp. 19–20.
10 *Trud*, 26 May 1959, in *CDSP*, vol. XI, no. 24, pp. 24–6.
11 *BBC-SWB*, 19 Dec. 1958.
12 *Ibid.*, 22 Dec. 1958.

Chapter 10

1   *BBC-SWB*, 12 June 1961.
2   *Egyptian Gazette*, 1 Jan. 1965.

3   See Hashim S. H. Behbehani, *China's Foreign Policy in the Arab World, 1955–75: Three Case Studies*, ch. 2, London, 1981.
4   *Egyptian Gazette*, 11 Jan. 1965.
5   *Dawn*, 22 Jan. 1965.
6   See, for example, *Egyptian Gazette*, 7 March 1965, for the Czechoslovakian loan agreement to Iraq.
7   See, for example, M. Heikal's article in *Egyptian Mail*, 1 May 1945.
8   *Soviet News*, 7 Aug. 1965.
9   *CDSP*, vol. XVII, no. 2, 10 Jan. 1965, p. 27.
10 *Pravda*, 30 May 1965, in *CDSP*, vol. XVII, no. 22, p. 18.
11 See *Pravda*'s commentary of 21 July 1965, in *CDSP*, vol. XVII, no. 29, p. 29.
12 *Pravda*, 7 Aug. 1965, in *CDSP*, vol. XVII, no. 32, p. 18.
13 Anon., *Sources of Conflict in the Middle East*, Adelphi Papers, no. 26, March 1966, p. 28.
14 *Egyptian Gazette*, 7 July 1965.
15 *Soviet News*, 10 Nov. 1965.
16 *Hsinhua*, 6 Dec. 1965.
17 *Egyptian Mail*, 8 Jan. 1966.
18 *Egyptian Gazette*, 2 Feb. 1966.
19 See, for example, *The Guardian*, 21 Feb. 1966, and also *The Times* and *New York Herald Tribune*, respectively, 21 Feb. 1966, and *The Guardian*, 6 April 1966.
20 *Egyptian Gazette*, 8 Feb. 1966.
21 See, for example, *New York Times*, 5 April 1966.
22 See, for example, *New York Times*, 11 May 1966.
23 *Egyptian Gazette*, May 1966.
24 *Ibid.*, 19 May 1966.
25 *al-Yumiyat al-filistinia*, 20 May 1966, p. 181.
26 *Ibid.*, p. 184.
27 See *New York Times*, 5 April 1966.
28 See, for example, *New York Herald Tribune*, 21 Jan. 1966.
29 See *Daily Telegraph*, 23 Feb. 1966.
30 *Financial Times*, 30 June 1966.
31 *Egyptian Gazette*, 30 June 1966.
32 See, for example, Y. Konstatinov, 'International Notes: Anti Popular Budget', *Izvestia*, 6 March 1966, in *CDSP*, vol. XVIII, no. 10, p. 19.
33 *Pravda*, April 1966, in *CDSP*, vol. XVIII, no. 17, pp. 23–4.
34 See, for example, 'Tass Statement', *Pravda*, 28 May 1966, in *CDSP*, vol. XVIII, no. 21, p. 38; and I. Belyayev, 'Provacateurs', *Pravda*, 20 July 1966.
35 'Joint Soviet–Iraqi Communiqué', *Izvestia*, 5 Aug. 1966, in *CDSP*, vol. XVIII, no. 31, p. 24.
36 See, for example, R. Petrov, 'Gen. Rabin Rattles His Saber', *Pravda*, 3 Oct. 1966, in *CDSP*, vol. XVIII, no. 40, p. 25; and K. I., 'Notes to the Point: Is It Not Time to Think Better of It?', *Izvestia*, 7 Nov. 1966, in *CDSP*, vol. XVIII, no. 45, p. 17.

Bibliography

Articles

'Palestine and the United Nations', *New Times*, 9 June 1948.
'Plans for a New Deal on Palestine', *New Times*, 14 July 1948.
'Good-will mission', *New Times*, no. 28, 5 July 1956.
'International Notes', *New Times*, no. 8, 1957.
'International Notes', *New Times*, no. 14, 1957.
'Science in Egypt', *New Times*, no. 39, 1957.
'First year of the U.A.R.', *New Times*, no. 9, 1959, pp. 2–3.
'Whose Solution?', *New Times*, no. 9, 1959.
'Israel Letter', *New Times*, no. 12, 1959, pp. 14–16.
'Aswan: the First Year', *New Times*, no. 4, 1961, pp. 14–15.
Editorial comment, *New Times*, no. 1, 1 Jan. 1962, pp. 3–4.
'The Johnson Mission – Middle East', *New Times*, no. 21, 1962, p. 27.
'Cairo–Baghdad–Damascus', *New Times*, no. 21, 1962.
Editorial comment, *New Times*, no. 2, 1964.
'Arab–Soviet Friendship', *New Times*, no. 13, 1964.
'New Times Interviews: Storming the Nile', *New Times*, no. 17, 1964.
'U.A.R. Letter: Ahlan Wasahlan, Nikita Khrushchev!', *New Times*, no. 17, 1964.
'The Soviet Union and the Arab World', *New Times*, no. 20, 19 May 1964.
'World Press on Khrushchev's U.A.R. Visit', *New Times*, no. 21, 1964.
'Roots of Soviet–Arab Friendship', *New Times*, no. 22, 3 June 1964.
'From N. S. Khrushchev's speeches in the U.A.R.', *New Times*, no. 22, 1964.
Editorial comment, *New Times*, no. 30, 1964.
'Documents: Exchange of Messages between the U.S.S.R. Supreme Soviet and the U.A.R. National Assembly', *New Times*, no, 31, 1964.
'The Trade Union Movement in the Countries of the Middle East: Interview with Mustafa el-Ariss', *New Times*, no. 13, 1 July 1946, pp. 12–14.
'New Times Interview: Soviet Cooperation with the United Arab Republic', *New Times*, no. 37, 1965.
'New Times Interviews: U.S.S.R. Minister of Culture N. Mikhalov on Cultural Relations with the United Arab Republic', *New Times*, no. 17, April 1958, p. 13.
'President Nasser's Visit', *New Times*, no. 18, May 1958, p. 28.

'Sources of Conflict in the Middle East', *Adelphi Papers*, no. 26, London, 1966.

Abu-Jaber, Faiz, 'The Soviets and the Arabs, 1917–1955', *Middle East Forum*, vol. 45, no. 1, 1969, pp. 13–44.

————, 'Soviet attitude toward Arab Revolutions: Egypt, Algeria, Iraq and Palestine', *Middle East Forum*, vol. 46, no. 4, 1970, pp. 41–65.

Aksanov, Oleg, 'Current Comment: the Arab Summit', *New Times*, no. 14, 6 April 1966, pp. 20–1.

Baba, Khalid, 'Arab Positive Neutrality', *Middle East Forum*, vol. 43, no. 4, spring 1965, pp. 9–16.

Badeau, John S., 'The Middle East: Conflict in Priorities', *Foreign Affairs*, vol. 36, no. 2, 1958, pp. 232–40.

Baldwin, Hanson W., 'Strategy of the Middle East', *Foreign Affairs*, vol. 35, no. 4, July 1957, pp. 654–65.

Belyaev, Igor, 'Changes on the Nile', *New Times*, no. 18, 1 May 1964, pp. 9–12.

————, and Primakov, E., 'Cairo', *New Times*, no. 21, 25 May 1966, pp. 3–4.

Ben Tzur, Avraham, 'Soviet–Egyptian Relations', *New Outlook*, vol. 7, no. 4, May 1964, pp. 26–37.

Berezhkov, V., 'Imperialist plans in the Near and Middle East' (Foreign press review), *New Times*, no. 48, 28 Nov. 1951, pp. 11ff.

Bochkaryov, Y., 'Political Developments in Lebanon', *New Times*, no. 28, 8 July 1953, pp. 8–11.

————, 'False Friends of the Arabs', *New Times*, no. 2, 9 Jan. 1954, pp. 11–15.

————, 'The Middle East Situation', *New Times*, no. 19, 5 May 1956, pp. 17–19.

————, 'The Middle East', *New Times*, no. 20, 10 May 1956, pp. 1–2.

————, 'Egypt's Legitimate Right', *New Times*, no. 32, 2 Aug. 1956, pp. 10–12.

————, 'Suez and the "Free World"', *New Times*, no. 34, 16 Aug. 1956, pp. 8–10.

————, 'Realistic Approach', *New Times*, no. 35, 23 Aug. 1956, pp. 1–3.

————, 'Egypt – New Spirit', *New Times*, no. 3, 17 Jan. 1957, pp. 6–8.

————, 'Jordan Impressions', *New Times*, no. 10, 7 March 1957, pp. 24–6.

————, 'U.S. Double Game', *New Times*, no. 11, 14 March 1957, pp. 14–15.

————, 'The first fruits', *New Times*, no. 44, 1 Nov. 1957, pp. 37–9.

————, 'The Soviet Union and the Arab East', *New Times*, no. 1, 1 Jan. 1958, pp. 12–14.

————, 'Report from Cairo', *New Times*, no. 7, Feb. 1960, pp. 25–8.

————, 'Cairo Prepares to Welcome Khrushchev', *New Times*, no. 19, 10 May 1964, pp. 15–16.

————, 'The Soviet Union and the Arab World', *New Times*, no. 20, 19 May 1964, pp. 1–3.

————, 'Unforgettable Days in Cairo', *New Times*, no. 20, 19 May 1964, pp. 4–5.

————, 'The Harnessing of the Nile', *New Times*, no. 21, 27 May 1964, pp. 4–7.

————, 'Battle for Progress', *New Times*, no. 19, 9 May 1966, pp. 3–5.

Campbell, John C., 'From "Doctrine" to Policy in the Middle East', *Foreign Affairs*, vol. 35, no. 3, April 1957, pp. 441–53.

Dawisha, Karen, 'Soviet Cultural Relations with Iraq, Syria and Egypt, 1955–70', *Soviet Studies*, vol. XXVII, no. 3, pp. 418–41.

Devejian, G., 'Beyrouth–Damascus Travel Notes', *New Times*, vol. 51, 17 Dec. 1947, pp. 16–21.

Dimeshkie, Nadim, 'The Impact of the Cold War on the Arab World', *Middle East Forum*, Dec. 1963, vol. 39, no. 10, pp. 15–20.

Erikson, John, 'The "Military Factor" in Soviet Foreign Policy', *International Affairs* (RIIA), vol. 39, no. 2.

Kalishyan, G., 'Cairo: Travel Notes', *New Times*, no. 50, 8 Dec. 1955, pp. 27–9.

Kanunnikov, A., 'The Partition Plan for Palestine: Questions and Answers', *New Times*, vol. 10, 3 March 1948, pp. 30–1.

———, 'The Palestine Question', *New Times*, vol. 9, 5 May 1948, pp. 8–11.

———, 'Hostilities in Palestine', *New Times*, vol. 22, 26 May 1948, pp. 8–11.

———, 'Palestine and the United Nations', *New Times*, vol. 24, 9 June 1948, pp. 1–2.

———, 'Who is Guilty of the Palestine Tragedy?', *New Times*, vol. 37, 8 Sept. 1948, pp. 29–31.

Kanzov, P., 'Trip to Israel: Travel Notes', *New Times*, no. 35, 29 Aug. 1951, pp. 22–5.

———, 'Trip to Israel: Travel Notes', *New Times*, no. 36, 5 Sept. 1951, pp. 25–9.

Katz, Ze'ev, 'Ways of Improving Israel–Soviet Relations', *New Outlook*, vol. 6, no. 9, Nov.–Dec. 1963, pp. 7–12.

———, 'A Change in Soviet–Israel Relations', *New Outlook*, vol. 7, no. 3, March–April 1964, pp. 6–10.

Kemp, Geoffrey, 'Arms and Security: the Egypt–Israel Case', *Adelphi Papers*, no. 52, London, 1968.

Khmelyov, N., Kazakov, B., and Balashov, A., 'A Mission to Egypt', *New Times*, no. 5, 31 Jan. 1957, pp. 22–4.

Khrushchev, N. and Nasser, Gamal A., 'Joint Statement on Conversation between Chairman of the U.S.S.R., Council of Ministers N. S. Khrushchev and U.A.R. President Gamal Abdel Nasser', *New Times*, no. 23, 10 June 1964, pp. 34–40.

Krammer, Arnold, 'Soviet Motives in the Partition of Palestine, 1947–48', *Journal of Palestine Studies*, vol. 2, no. 2, 1972, pp. 102–19.

Laqueur, Walter Z., 'The Appeal of Communism in the Middle East', *Middle East Journal*, vol. IX, no. 1, Winter, 1955, pp. 17–27.

———, 'The "National Bourgeoisie": a Soviet Dilemma in the Middle East', *International Affairs*, vol. 35, no. 3, July 1959, pp. 324–31.

———, 'Towards National Democracy: Soviet Doctrine and the New Countries', *Survey*, no. 37, July–Sept. 1961, pp. 3–11.

Lewis, Bernard, 'The Middle Eastern Reaction to Soviet Pressure', *The Middle East Journal*, vol. 10, no. 2, Spring 1956, pp. 125–37.

Lowenthal, Richard, 'Russia, the One-Party System and the Third World', *Survey*, no. 58, 1966, pp. 43–58.

Malik, Charles, 'Call to Action in the Near East', *Foreign Affairs*, vol. 34, no. 4, July 1956, pp. 637–54.

Maximov, E., 'Egypt's Legitimate Right: Foreign Press Review', *New Times*, no. 43, 20 Oct. 1955, pp. 18–19.

———, 'Evil Theory', *New Times*, no. 42, Oct. 1959, pp. 9–11.

———, 'The Jordanian Scene', *New Times*, no. 36, Sept. 1958, pp. 5–7.

Mirsky, G., 'The Blockade that Failed', *New Times*, no. 35, 20 June 1957, pp. 4–6.

———, 'The Changing Arab East', *New Times*, no. 2, 15 Jan. 1964, pp. 3–4.

———, 'Basic Trends in the Arab World', *New Times*, no. 6, 10 Feb. 1965, pp. 3–7.

———, 'Suez in Retrospect', *New Times*, no. 43, 26 Oct. 1966, pp. 9–11.

Morad, Khaled Mohamed, 'Miracle on the Nile', *New Times*, no. 2, 15 Jan. 1964, pp. 13–14.

Morison, David L., 'Arab Affairs through Soviet Eyes', *Middle East Forum*, vol. 37, no. 1, Jan. 1961, pp. 11–36.

Moseley, Philip E., 'Soviet Foreign Policy: New Goals or New Manners?', *Foreign Affairs*, vol. 34, no. 4, July 1956, pp. 541–53.

———, 'Soviet Policy in the Developing Countries', *Foreign Affairs*, vol. 43, no. 1, Oct. 1964, pp. 87–98.

Mohie El Din, Khaled, 'The October Revolution and the Arab World', *New Times*, no. 43, 24 Oct. 1957, pp. 9–10.

Murwa, Karim, 'Al-Jathur al-tarkhya l'il al-'alaqat al-'arbiya al-sovietya' (The deep historical roots of Arab–Soviet relations), *Shu'un filistiniya* (Palestine Affairs), no. 43, March 1975, pp. 16–25.

Nalbandyan, A., and Pogosyan, E., 'From Alexandria to the Soviet Homeland', *New Times*, vol. 44, 29 Oct. 1947, pp. 18–21.

'Observer', 'The Suez Conference and its Outcome', *New Times*, no. 36, 30 Aug. 1956, pp. 4–7.

———, 'Free Egypt', *New Times*, no. 25, 14 June 1956, pp. 3–5.

———, 'Common Sense Must Triumph', *New Times*, no. 40, 27 Sept. 1956, pp. 7–9.

———, 'The Suez and the Security Council', *New Times*, no. 42, 11 Oct. 1956, pp. 1–2.

———, 'New Stage in the Suez Issue', *New Times*, no. 44, 25 Oct. 1956, pp. 11–13.

———, 'Good-will Mission', *New Times*, no. 28, 5 July 1956, pp. 1–2.

———, 'Hands Off Egypt', *New Times*, no. 46, 7 Nov. 1957, pp. 4–8.

———, 'Defeat for the Colonialists', *New Times*, no. 49, 29 Nov. 1956, pp. 1–2.

———, Suez Crisis Retrospect', *New Times*, no. 17, 25 April 1957, pp. 14–15.

Orunajiv, E., 'A Legitimate Urge', *New Times*, no. 38, 15 Sept. 1955, pp. 6–9.

Osipov, G. 'The Palestine Doings of Charles Clayton', *New Times*, vol. 52, 22 Dec. 1948, pp. 8–12.

P.K., 'Covering Up the Tracks: Spotlight on Slander', *New Times*, no. 16, 16 April 1952, p. 28.

Pravda, 'Statement of the Soviet Government on the Necessity of a Peaceful Settlement of the Suez Issue', *New Times*, no. 39, Sept. 1956, pp. 9–13.

———, 'Statement of the Soviet Government on the Armed Aggression against Egypt', *New Times*, no. 45, 1 Nov. 1956, p. 34.

_____, 'Progress at Aswan', *New Times*, no. 4, 27 Jan. 1965, pp. 23–5.

Primakov, E., 'The Situation in Jordan', *New Times*, no. 47, 21 Nov. 1957, pp. 12–14.

_____, 'U.A.R.: Economic Ties', *New Times*, no. 21, May 1959, pp. 9–11.

Ra'anan, Uri, 'Tactics in the Third World: Contradictions and Dangers', *Survey*, no. 57, Oct. 1965, pp. 26–37.

Rustow, Dankwert, 'Defense of the Near East', *Foreign Affairs*, vol. 34, no. 2, Jan. 1956, pp. 271–86.

Savchenks, L., 'Beyrouth Encounters', *New Times*, no. 42, Oct. 1952, pp. 26–9.

Scott, N. B., 'Soviet Economic Relations with the Under-developed Countries', *Soviet Studies*, vol. 10, 1958–59, pp. 36–53.

Sedin, E., 'The Arab East and the Palestine Problem', *New Times*, vol. 47, 19 Nov. 1947, pp. 3–5.

_____, 'The Arab League', *New Times*, vol. 11, 10 March 1948, pp. 8–12.

Seifulmulyukov, E., 'The Arab–Israeli conflicts: Answers to Readers' Questions', *New Times*, no. 5, 26 Jan. 1956, pp. 30–2.

Serezhin, K., 'The Problems of the Arab East', *New Times*, vol. 3, 1 Feb. 1946.

_____, 'A seat of Unrest in the Middle East', *New Times*, vol. 11, 1 June 1946, pp. 14–17.

_____, 'Contemporary Palestine: Geographical Sketch', *New Times*, vol. 15, 1 Aug. 1946, pp. 18–22.

Sergeyev, V. A., 'Soviet Economic Co-operation with the United Arab Republic', (interview), *New Times*, no. 19, 10 March 1964, pp. 8–9.

Shepilov, D. T., 'Results of the London Conference on the Suez Canal Issue', *New Times*, no. 36, 30 Aug. 1965, pp. 35–40.

Sobeih, Mohamed, 'Sixteen Days in the U.S.S.R.', *New Times*, no. 21, May 1958, pp. 5–6.

Tishin, I., 'Peoples of the Middle East Fight for Peace', *New Times*, vol. 8, 22 Feb. 1950, pp. 6–9.

Tuganova, O., 'The Arab Movement for Unity', *International Affairs* (Moscow), Jan. 1965, no. 1, pp. 32–6.

_____, 'Political Trends in the Arab East', *International Affairs* (Moscow), March 1966, no. 3, pp. 31–7.

Ushakov, Georgi, 'Dulles "Aswan Gambit": the Story of a Cold War Fiasco', *New Times*, no. 20, 19 May 1964, pp. 26–9.

Vasilyen, D., 'Science in Egypt', *New Times*, no. 39, 16 Sept. 1957, p. 16.

Vatolina, M., 'The New Phase in Egypt', *New Times*, no. 37, Sept. 1955, pp. 6–8.

Viktorov, Y., 'Three Lies, and Forty Fables in Every Lie: Spotlight on Slander', *New Times*, vol. 36, 1 Sept. 1948, pp. 26–7.

Vilner, Meir, 'The Political Situation in Israel', *New Times*, no. 47, 23 Nov. 1966, pp. 10–11.

Volsky, D., 'Moscow and Cairo', *New Times*, no. 22, 31 May 1966, pp. 7–8.

Vorobyov, E., 'Men of Aswan', *New Times*, no. 34, 26 Aug. 1964, pp. 22–6.

Yermashov, I., 'Reptiles', *New Times*, vol. 17, 26 April 1950, pp. 29–30.

Zaslavsky, D., 'A British Officer in Palestine', *New Times*, vol. 25, 16 June 1948, pp. 13–14.

———, 'Plans for a New Deal on Palestine', *New Times*, vol. 29, 14 July 1948, pp. 1–2.

———, 'Equal Co-operation', *New Times*, no. 6, Feb. 1958, pp. 1–2.

———, 'The United Arab Republic', *New Times*, no. 7, Feb. 1958, p. 4.

———, 'Good Intentions and Bad', *New Times*, no. 17, April 1958, p. 2.

Zvyagin, Y., 'Total Diplomacy in the Near East', *New Times*, vol. 27, 5 July 1950, pp. 11–15.

———, 'The Anti-imperialist Movement in the Arab Countries: Foreign Press Review', *New Times*, no. 49, 5 Dec. 1951, pp. 19–20.

———, 'Aswan's Second Stage: Spotlight on Slander', *New Times*, no. 5, Jan. 1960, pp. 9–11.

Books

Abdal-Nasir, Jamal, *Al-democratia: Min'iqual al-ra'is Jamal 'Abd al-Nasir* (Democracy: From the Sayings of President Jamal Abd al Nasir), Cairo, n.d.

———, *Falasafa al-thawra* (The Philosophy of the Revolution), Cairo, 1954.

Agwani, M. S., *Communism in the Arab East*, London, 1969.

Al-Azmeh, 'Aziz, *al-Yassar al-sahuni min bedaiteh hata 'i'alan do'walth Israel* (Left-wing Zionism: From its Inception to the Declaration of the State of Israel), Beirut, 1969.

Al-Ghadri, Nihad, *Al-tarih al-siri li-'l al'alaqat al-shu'iah-al-sahuniah* (The Secret Historical Relations of Communism–Zionism), Beirut, 1969.

Al-Hussain, Talah (trans.), *Bayanat wa mudtha't wa muqerarat al-amuwayh al-shu'iay'a al-mu'tamar al-'awal wa thani, 1919–1920: al nusus al kamalah* (The Declarations and Topics of the First and Second International, 1919–1920: The Complete Texts), Beirut, 1972.

al-Hut, Byan Nuwahth, *al-qyadat wa al-mu'sasat al-syasiah fi Filistin, 1917–1948* (The Leadership and the Political Institutions in Palestine, 1917–1948), Beirut, 1981.

Alush, Noji, *Al-Marxiah wa al-mas'lah al-yahudieh, 1844–1968* (Marxism and the Jewish Question: 1844–1968), Beirut, 1969.

Antonius, George, *The Arab Awakening*, New York, 1946.

Anon., *Political and diplomatic documents, December 1947 – May 1948*, 2 vols., Jerusalem, 1979.

———, *Lenin and National Liberation in the East*, Moscow, 1978.

———, *Correspondence between the Chairman of the Council of Ministers of the USSR and the Presidents of the USA and the Prime Ministers of Great Britain during the Great Patriotic War of 1944–1945*, vol. 1, Moscow, 1957.

———, *Recent History of Arab Countries*, 2 vols., Moscow, 1975.

———, *Anti-Semitism in the Soviet Union: Its Roots and Consequences*, 2 vols., Jerusalem, 1979.

———, (trans. by Alex and Barbara Holland; intro. by Bertil Hessel), *Theses, Resolutions and Manifestos of the First Four Congresses of the Third International*, London, 1980.

———, *The Hague Congress of the First International, September 2–7, 1872; Minutes and Documents*, Moscow, 1976.

_____, *Yearbook on International Communist Affairs, 1966*, Stanford, Cal., 1967.

Araslian, Bugush, *et al.*, *Siyasiah al-Ithad al-Sovieyati al-harijiah* (The Foreign Policy of the Soviet Union), Moscow, n.d.

Bardin, Shlomo, *Pioneer Youth in Palestine*, New York, 1932.

Behbehani, Hashim S. H., *China's Foreign Policy in the Arab World, 1955–75: Three Case Studies*, London, 1981.

Braunthal, Julius, *History of the International: World Socialism, 1943–1968*, London, 1980.

Breacher, Michael, *Decisions in Israel's Foreign Policy*, Oxford, 1974.

Breaner Lenni, *The Iron Wall: Zionist Revisionism from Jabotinsky to Shamir*, London 1948.

Budeiri, Musa, *The Palestine Communist Party, 1919–1949: Arab and Jew in the Struggle for Internationalism*, London, 1979.

Caplan, Neil, *Palestine Jewry and the Arab Question, 1917–1925*, London, 1978.

Cliff, Tony, *Lenin*, 3 vols., London, 1976.

Cohen, Hayyim J., *The Jews of the Middle East, 1860–1972*, Jerusalem, 1973.

Coshen, Lionel (ed.), *The Jews in Soviet Russia*, Oxford, 1972.

Confino, M. and S. Shamir (eds.), *The U.S.S.R. and the Middle East*, Tel-Aviv, 1973.

Conolly, Violet, *Soviet Trade from the Pacific to the Levant: with an Economic Study of the Soviet Far Eastern Region*, Connecticut, 1935.

Dankus, Helen Carier (trans. Abdullah Iskander), *al-syasah al-sovietieh fi al-sharq al-'awast, 1955–1975* (Soviet Policy in the Middle East, 1955–1975), Beirut, 1983.

Diky, Andrei, *Jews in Russia and the USSR*, New York, 1967.

Dimont, Max I., *The Jews in America*, New York, 1978.

Donovan, John (ed.), *U.S. and Soviet Policy in the Middle East, 1957–1966*, New York, 1974.

Dubnow, S. W., *History of the Jews in Russia and Poland*, 2 vols., New York, 1975.

Eckman, Lester Samuel, *Soviet Policy towards Jews and Israel*, New York, 1974.

Eisenhower, Dwight D., *Waging Peace: 1956–61*, New York, 1965.

Eudin, Xenia Joukoff and North, Robert C., *Soviet Russia and the East, 1920–1927: Documentary Survey*, Stanford, Cal., 1957.

Fletcher, William C., *Religion and Soviet Foreign Policy, 1945–1970*, Oxford, 1973.

Frank, Pierre, *The Fourth International: the Long March of the Trotskyists*, London, 1972.

Fublykuv, D. R., Kytiyv, S. B., *et al.* (eds.), *Tarikh al-iqatar al'arabia al-m'aser, 1917–1970* (The Recent History of Arab Countries, 1917–1970), 2 vols., Moscow, 1976.

Gorny, Joseph, *The British Labour Movement and Zionism, 1917–1948*, London, 1983.

Hakim, Sami, *Isra'il wa al-dawal al-shu'ay'a* (Israel and Communist States), Beirut, n.d.

Hamid, Rashed (Comp.), *Muqararat al-majlis al-watni al-Falistini, 1964–1974* (The Decisions of the Palestinian National Congress, 1964–1974), Beirut, 1975.

Husain, Abd al-Rahim Ahmad, *Al-nashat al-sahuni hilal al-harb al-a'alimiah al-thaniah (1939–1945)* (Zionist activity during WWII (1939–1945)), Beirut, 1984.

Israel, Gerard, *The Jews in Russia*, New York, 1975.

Kahin, George M., *Asian–African Conference, Bandung, Indonesia, April 1955*, Washington, 1956.

Khalidi, Walid (ed.), *From Heaven to Conquest: Readings in Zionism and the Palestine Problem until 1948*, Beirut, 1971.

Khrushchev, N. (Introduction, commentary and notes by Edward Granshow; trans. by Strobe Talbott), *Khrushchev Remembers*, London, 1971.

Kimball, Warren, F. (ed.), *Churchill and Roosevelt: the Correspondence*, 3 vols., Princeton, N.J., 1985.

Klieman, Aaron S., *Soviet Russia and the Middle East*, Baltimore, Md., 1970.

Krammer, Arnold, *The Forgotten Friendship: Israel and the Soviet Bloc, 1947–53*, Illinois, 1974.

Laqueur, Walter, *The Struggle for the Middle East: the Soviet Union in the Mediterranean, 1958–1968*, London, 1969.

Lazitch, Branck, and Drachkovitch, Milorad, M., *Lenin and the Comintern*, vol. 1, Stanford, Cal., 1972.

Lederer, Ivo, Vucinich, J., and Wayne, S., *The Soviet Union and the Middle East: the Post World War II Era*, Stanford, Cal., 1974.

Lenczowski, George, *Soviet Advance in the Middle East*, Washington, D.C., 1971.

———, *The Middle East in World Affairs*, New York, 1980.

Lenin, V. I., *Selected Works*, 3 vols., New York, 1967.

Lloyd, Selwyn, *Suez 1956: a Personal View*, London, 1978.

Levering, Ralph B., *American Opinion and the Russian Alliance, 1939–1945*, North Carolina, 1976.

Lilienthal, Alfred M., *The Zionist Connection: What Price Peace?*, Pennsylvania, 1978.

London, Kurt (ed.), *The Soviet Union in World Politics*, London, 1967.

Love, Kennett, *Suez: the Twice Fought War*, New York, 1969.

Lutskii, V., *Tarikh al-aqatar al-'arabya al-hadith* (Contemporary History of Arab Countries, Moscow), n.d.

Macmillan, Harold, *Riding the Storm: 1956–1959*, London, 1971.

Marqus, 'Ilyas, *al-marksia wa al-sharq, 1850–1918* (Marxism and the East, 1850–1918), Beirut, 1968.

———, *al-marksya al-sovietya wa-qiathaya al- 'arbya* (Soviet Marxism and Arab Issues), Beirut, 1973.

McLane, Charles B., *Soviet–Middle East Relations*, London, 1973.

Merhav, Peretz, *The Israeli Left: History, Problems, Documents*, London, 1980.

Mendes–Flohr, Paul R., and Reinharz, Jehuda, *The Jew in the Modern World: a documentary History*, Oxford, 1980.

Mursi, Fouad, *al-ilaqat al-ma'srya al-sovietya: 1943–1956* (Egyptian–Soviet Relations: 1943–1956), Cairo, n.d.

Naser, Marlyn, *al-taswar al-qaumy al-arabii fi fikr Jamal 'abd al-Nasir, (1952–1970)* (Arab nationalism in Jamal 'abd al-Nasir's Thought (1952–1970)), Beirut, 1984.

Nedava, Joseph, *Trotsky and the Jews*, Philadelphia, 1971.

Ponomaryov, B., Gromyko, A., and Khvostov, V. (eds.), *History of Soviet Foreign Policy: 1945–1970*, Moscow, 1973.

Ponomaryov, B., Shirokov, G., *et al.*, *Developing Countries in the Contemporary World*, Moscow, 1981.

Primakov, Y. M., *The East after the Collapse of the Colonial System*, Moscow, 1982.

Ra'anan, Uri, *The USSR Arms the Third World: Case Studies in Soviet Foreign Policy*, Massachusetts, 1969.

Ro'i, Yaacov, *From Encroachment to Involvement: a Documentary Study of Soviet Policy in the Middle East, 1945–1973*, Tel-Aviv, 1974.

———, *Soviet decision-making in Practice: the USSR and Israel, 1947–1954*, New York, 1980.

Rubin, Barry, *The Great Powers in the Middle East, 1941–1947: the Road to the Cold War*, London, 1980.

Rubinow, Issac, *Economic conditions of the Jews in Russia* (A study written in 1907), New York, 1975.

Salim, Muhamad 'abd al-Ra'uf, *Nashat al-wakalah al-yahudia l'il Falistin menth insha'ha wa hata qiyam dawalh Israel, 1922–1948* (The development of the Jewish Agency for Palestine from its Inception until the Establishment of the State of Israel, 1922–1948), Beirut, 1982.

Salim, Muhamad al-sayed, *al-tahlil al-siyasi al-Nasri: Dirasah fi al-iq'ta'd wa al-siyasah al-harijiah* (The Nasirist Political Analysis: a Study in Beliefs and Foreign Policy), Beirut, 1983.

Sayeg, 'Inis (Comp.), and Helda Sha'ban Syeg (trans.), *Umiyat Hertzel*, (Diary of Hertzel), Beirut, 1973.

Schechtman, Joseph B., *Zionism in Soviet Russia: Greatness and Drama*, New York, 1969.

Shapira, Anita, *The Biography of a Socialist Zionist: Berl Katznelson, 1887–1944*, Cambridge, 1984.

Sharif, Maher, *al-shu'iah wa al-mas'alh al-quawamyah al-'arabia fi Falestine, 1919–1948* (Communism and the Arab National Question in Palestine, 1919–1948), Beirut, 1981.

Smolansky, Oles M., *The Soviet Union and the Arab East under Khrushchev*, New Jersey, 1974.

Spector, Ivar, *The Soviet Union and the Muslim World, 1917–1958*, London, 1959.

Stevens, Richard, *American Zionism and US Foreign Policy, 1942–47*, New York, 1970.

Tansky, Leo., *U.S. and U.S.S.R. aid to Developing Countries: a Comparative Study of India, Turkey and the U.A.R.*, New York, 1967.

Tarabulsi, Fouad (trans.), *al-mu'itamar al-'awal l'shu'b al-Sharq: Baku, 8 September, 1921* (The First Conference of the Peoples of the East, Baku, 8 September 1921), Beirut, 1972.

Tarbin, Ahmad, *Falistin fi hatat al Sahunia wa al-ist'amar: al intdaf al-Biratani fi halfia al-dawalah al-yahudia, 1922–1939* (Palestine in Zionist and Colonialists' Plans: the Background of the Jewish State during British Mandate, 1922–1939), Damascus, 1971.

Teller, Juddh L., *The Kremlin, the Jews and the Middle East*, New York, 1957.

Teveth, Shabtai, *Ben-Gurion and the Palestinian Arabs: from Peace to War*, Oxford, 1985.

Thomas, Hugh, *The Suez Affair*, London, 1967.

Ulam, Adam B., *Expansion and Co-existence: Soviet Foreign Policy 1917–1973*, New York, 1974.

Ulyanovasky, R., Pavlov, V., *et al.*, *Newly Free Countries: Specifics of Development*, Moscow, 1981.

Ulyanovsky, R. A. (ed.), *The Comintern and the East*, Moscow, 1978.

———, *The Comintern and the East: a Critique of the Critique*, Moscow, 1981.

Viteles, Harry, *A History of the Co-operative Movement in Israel: the Evolution of the Kibbutz Movement*, vol. 2, London, 1967.

Voth, Alden H., *Moscow Abandons Israel for the Arabs: Ten Crucial Years in the Middle East*, Washington, D.C., 1980.

Vucinich, Wayne, S. (ed.), *Russia and Asia: Essays on the Influence of Russia on the Asian Peoples*, Stanford, Cal., 1972.

Weelock, Keith, *Nasser's Egypt: a Critical Analysis*, New York, 1960.

Weizmann, Naim, *Letters and Papers*, London, 1971.

Wilson, Harold, *The Chariot of Israel: Britain, America and the State of Israel*, London, 1981.

Woolfson, Marion, *Prophets in Babylon: Jews in the Arab World*, London, 1980.

Yavesyav, Y., Vostokuhuv, A. (trans., Hashim Hamady), *al-Sahuiniah fi Russiya al-qaysaria* (Zionism in Czarist Russia), Damascus, 1976.

Yasin, 'abd al-qader, *Tarih al-tabah al-'amalah al-filistania*, 1918–1938 (The History of the Palestinian Working Class, 1918–1938), Beirut, 1980.

Theses

Akhavi, Shahrough, 'The Egyptian Image of the Soviet Union, 1954–1968: a Study in Press Communication', Columbia University, New York, 1969.

Burnett, Jr., John Howard, 'Soviet-Egyptian Relations during the Khrushchev Era: a Study in Soviet Foreign Policy', Emory University, Atlanta, Ga., 1966.

Dziak, John Joseph, 'The Soviet Union and National Liberation Movements: an Examination of the Development of a Revolutionary Strategy', Georgetown University, Washington, D.C.

Eran-Feinberg, Oded, 'Soviet Thought on the Role of the Communist Party in the Third World, with Special Reference to the Arab-radical Regimes: a Study of Opinion Groups within the Soviet Union', Indiana University, 1971.

Gehlen, Michael Pierpont, 'Ideological determinants of Soviet Foreign Policy under Khrushchev', University of Texas, 1963.

Hackley, Lloyd Vincent, 'Soviet Behavior in the Middle East as a Function of Change in the Interactive environment, 1950–1970', University of North Carolina, 1976.

Irwin, Zachary Tracy, 'Soviet Policy towards Israel, 1953–1967', Pennsylvania State University, 1978.

Kabbara, Mahmoud Farouk, ''Abd al Nasir's Egypt and the Soviet Union: an Egyptian View, 1952–1970: the Impact of Differences between Arab Socialist and Marxist-Leninist Ideologies', University of Arizona, 1981.

Khalil, Houssam El-Dawla H., 'The Soviet Foreign Policy toward Egypt, 1955–1964', Howard University, Washington, D.C., 1970.

Marom, Ran, 'Soviet Russia and the Jewish Communists of Palestine, 1917–1921', Georgetown University, Washington, D.C., 1975.

McKenzie, Kermit E., 'The Soviet Union and World Revolution: the Comintern Patterns', 1928–1943', Columbia University, New York, 1960.

Nelson, Gail Harwood, 'Ideological Constraints on Soviet Decision making for Defense', University of Colorado, 1979.

Roberts, James Weston, 'The Soviet Use of Lenin's Theory of Imperialism', University of North Carolina, 1973.

Smolansky, Oles M., 'The Soviet Union and the Arab East, 1947–1957: a Study in Diplomatic Relations', Columbia University, New York, 1959.

Slessinger, Seymour, 'The Idea of Nationalism in Soviet Foreign Policy', Boston University, 1961.

Periodicals and Newspapers

Al-Nahar
Al-Yumiyat al-filistinia
Christian Science Monitor
Daily Express
Daily Herald
Daily Telegraph
Daily Worker
Dawn
Egyptian Gazette
Egyptian Mail
Financial Times
The Guardian
The Hindu
Hsinhua News Agency
Izvestia
Manchester Guardian
New Times
New York Herald Tribune
New York Times
News Chronicle
Norwegian Press Summary
Observer
Observer Foreign News Service
Pravda
Scotsman
Soviet News
The Sunday Telegraph
Swedish Press Summary
The Times
Trud

Index

For Product Safety Concerns and Information please contact our EU
representative GPSR@taylorandfrancis.com
Taylor & Francis Verlag GmbH, Kaufingerstraße 24, 80331 München, Germany

www.ingramcontent.com/pod-product-compliance
Lightning Source LLC
Chambersburg PA
CBHW070356270326
41926CB00014B/2580